ROUTLEDGE LIBRARY EDITIONS:
THE ECONOMY OF THE MIDDLE EAST

Volume 13

THE ECONOMIC DEVELOPMENT OF THE UNITED ARAB EMIRATES

THE ECONOMIC DEVELOPMENT OF THE UNITED ARAB EMIRATES

RAGAEI EL MALLAKH

LONDON AND NEW YORK

First published in 1981

This edition first published in 2015
by Routledge
2 Park Square, Milton Park, Abingdon, Oxon, OX14 4RN

and by Routledge
711 Third Avenue, New York, NY 10017

Routledge is an imprint of the Taylor & Francis Group, an informa business

© 1981 Ragaei El Mallakh

All rights reserved. No part of this book may be reprinted or reproduced or utilised in any form or by any electronic, mechanical, or other means, now known or hereafter invented, including photocopying and recording, or in any information storage or retrieval system, without permission in writing from the publishers.

Trademark notice: Product or corporate names may be trademarks or registered trademarks, and are used only for identification and explanation without intent to infringe.

British Library Cataloguing in Publication Data
A catalogue record for this book is available from the British Library

ISBN: 978-1-138-78710-0 (Set)
eISBN: 978-1-315-74408-7 (Set)
ISBN: 978-1-138-81012-9 (Volume 13)
eISBN: 978-1-315-74639-5 (Volume 13)
Pb ISBN: 978-1-138-82015-9 (Volume 13)

Publisher's Note
The publisher has gone to great lengths to ensure the quality of this reprint but points out that some imperfections in the original copies may be apparent.

Disclaimer
The publisher has made every effort to trace copyright holders and would welcome correspondence from those they have been unable to trace.

The Economic Development of the United Arab Emirates

Ragaei El Mallakh

CROOM HELM LONDON

© 1981 Ragaei El Mallakh
Croom Helm Ltd, 2–10 St John's Road, London SW11

British Library Cataloguing in Publication Data

El Mallakh, Ragaei
   The economic development of the United
   Arab Emirates.
   1. United Arab Emirates – Economic conditions
   I. Title
   338.9'53'57   HC497.U/
   ISBN 0-7099-0209-3

Typeset by Leaper & Gard Ltd, Bristol
Reproduced from copy supplied
Printed and bound in Great Britain
by Billing and Sons Limited
Guildford, London, Oxford, Worcester

CONTENTS

List of Tables/Map
Abbreviations and Acronyms
Foreword

1. Background and Current Perspectives	1
Profiling the UAE: Its Regional and International Roles	1
Introducing the Sheikhdoms	5
Tracing the Past	10
Forging the UAE: Government Structure and Direction	12
2. Economic Development Policies	20
The UAE: A Brief Economic History	20
UAE Strategy for Development	31
Agriculture	36
Fishing	41
Leading Sectors	43
Industry	45
Impediments to Industrial Development	59
3. Social Infrastructure	64
Education	64
Health	68
Housing	70
4. Economic Infrastructure	74
Airports	75
Roads	76
Port Facilities	77
Public Utilities	82
Telecommunications	83
Industrial Zones	84

Construction	86

5. Fuelling UAE Development: Oil — 88
The Development of the Oil Industry — 88
Utilization of Natural Gas Resources — 107

6. The Foreign Trade Sector — 115
Composition of Imports — 116
Direction of Import Trade — 126
Composition and Direction of Exports — 126
The Tourist Trade — 127

7. The Financial Sector — 132
Structure of the Banking System — 132
Development as a Financial Centre and an Aid Source — 145

8. Business and Investment: Patterns and Opportunities — 160
The Indigenous Market — 160
Legal Environment for Business in the UAE — 165

Appendix I: Government of the UAE — 171
Appendix II: Special Education Programmes in the UAE — 173
Appendix III: Oil Companies and Affiliates Operating in the UAE — 177
Appendix IV: Text of Law Concerning Abu Dhabi Ownership of Gas Resources — 185
Appendix V: Abu Dhabi Fund for Arab Economic Development — 188
Appendix VI: Establishing Business in the UAE — 198
Bibliography — 203
Index — 206

LIST OF TABLES/MAP

Map 1.1: United Arab Emirates   6

Tables

1.1:	United Arab Emirates, Area and Population	10
2.1:	UAE Federal Budget: Revenues, 1980	27
2.2:	UAE Federal Budget: Expenditures, 1980	28
2.3:	Government of Abu Dhabi Development Expenditure, 1976–8	30
2.4:	UAE Balance of Payments, 1978–80	32
2.5:	*Per Capita* GNP of Selected Countries, 1977–8	33
2.6:	UAE Consolidated Accounts Showing Surpluses, 1972–9	34
2.7:	Distribution of Workers (10 years and over) by Economic Activity	40
2.8:	Planned Industrial Projects for Ruwais Complex (Abu Dhabi)	49
2.9:	Planned Industrial Projects in Abu Dhabi	50–1
2.10:	Planned Industrial Projects in Other Emirates	52
2.11:	Dubai Development Expenditure for Planned Projects and Projects Under Construction	57
3.1:	Estimated Population by Age-Group and Sex, Beginning of 1979	65
5.1:	UAE Oil Prices by Fields and Gravity, 1978–80	101
5.2:	Production of Crude Oil, 1962–80	103
5.3:	Details of UAE Crude Oil Production	104
5.4:	Well Completions	105
5.5:	Summary Statistics of Oil and Gas in the UAE	106
5.6:	Abu Dhabi Production and Utilization of Natural Gas, 1975–9	108

5.7:	Abu Dhabi Exports of Liquefied Natural Gas (LNG) and Liquefied Petroleum Gas (LPG), 1977–80	109
6.1:	Commodity Classification of Imports (Abu Dhabi and Dubai)	117
6.2:	Commodity Classification of Imports, Major Groups (Abu Dhabi and Dubai)	118
6.3:	Imports by Major Country of Origin: Value and Per Cent (Abu Dhabi and Dubai)	120–1
6.4:	Destination of Crude Oil Exports	122–3
6.5:	Non-oil Exports and Re-exports by Major Country of Destination: Value and in Per Cent	124–5
7.1:	UAE Monetary Survey, 1974–9	138
7.2:	Bank Credit to Residents by Economic Activity	139
7.3:	Basic Data on Investment Companies in the UAE	140
7.4:	Regulation Project Lending by UAE Development Bank	142
7.5:	Geographical Distribution of ADFAED Loans, 1974–9	147
7.6:	Regional Allocation of Abu Dhabi Fund, 1976–9	148
7.7:	ADFAED Allocation to Projects, 1974–9	148
7.8:	Shareholders of the Arab Fund for Economic and Social Development (AFESD)	149
7.9:	Abu Dhabi Capital Payments, 1970–8	151
7.10:	UAE Participation in Regional and International Organizations, 1978–80	152–3
7.11:	Regional Bodies with Initial UAE Participation	154
7.12:	UAE Contributions to the OPEC Fund as of 31 December 1979	155
7.13:	Flow of Official Assistance from Development Assistance Committee (DAC) Members of OECD to Developing Countries and Multilateral Institutions, 1965, 1970, 1975–80	157
A.1:	Fund Financial Status, 1974–9	189
A.2:	Classification of Fund Loans According to Sectors, 1974–9	191 192
A.3:	Fund Technical Assistance and Financing of Studies, 1975–9	
A.4:	Fund Loans by Geographical Distribution, Countries, Terms and Purpose, 1974–9	194–7

ABBREVIATIONS AND ACRONYMS

ADFAED	Abu Dhabi Fund for Arab Economic Development
ADGLC	Abu Dhabi Gas Liquefaction Company Limited
ADIA	Abu Dhabi Investment Authority
ADMA	Abu Dhabi Marine Areas, since 1978 known as ADMA-OPCO or Abu Dhabi Marine Operating Company
ADNOC	Abu Dhabi National Oil Company
ADOC	Abu Dhabi Oil Company
ADPC	Abu Dhabi Petroleum Company, since 1978 known as ADCO or Abu Dhabi Company for Onshore Oil Operations
AFESD	Arab Fund for Economic and Social Development
b/d	barrels per day
BP	British Petroleum
cfd	cubic feet per day
CFP	Compagnie Française des Pétroles
Dh	Dirham; 1 Dirham is composed of 100 Fils; par value of 1 Dh (end of November 1978) was 0.186621 g of fine gold, equivalent to the International Monetary Fund's SDR (Special Drawing Right) or 0.200797. The mid-exchange rates of Dh to 1 US $ during 1978 were: to 27 January, Dh 3.893 = $1; to 14 September, Dh 3.858 = $1; to 26 October, Dh 3.838 = $1. The 1979 and 1980 mid-rate exchange rates of dirham to dollars were: March 1979, Dh 3.838 = $1; December 1979, Dh 3.766 = $1; January 1980, Dh 4.92544 = $1; March 1980, Dh 4.6913 = $1. Another method of comparison is the dirham against the SDR in 1978–80: January 1978, Dh 4.71224 = 1 SDR; April 1978, Dh 4.75478 = SDR; July 1978, Dh 4.88574 = 1 SDR; October 1978, Dh 5.17666 = 1 SDR; December 1978, Dh 5.00011 = 1 SDR; March 1979, Dh 4.9388 = 1 SDR; December 1979, Dh 4.96106 = 1 SDR; January 1980, Dh 4.92544 = 1 SDR; March 1980, Dh 4.6913 = 1 SDR.
DPC	Dubai Petroleum Company

IMF	International Monetary Fund
JODCO	Japan Oil Development Company
LNG	liquefied natural gas
LPG	liquefied petroleum gas
NGL	natural gas liquids
PDTC	Petroleum Development (Trucial States) Ltd
UDECO	Umm Al-Dalkh Development Company, jointly owned by ADNOC and JODCO

To my sisters and brothers, sisters-in-law and brother-in-law, who have given me such encouragement, support, and affection over so many years: Albert and Faiza, Betty, Nellie, Yousef and Jo, Fayek and Hilda, Naima, and Kamal.

FOREWORD

This volume is the result of almost two decades of first-hand observation and research on the area now comprising the United Arab Emirates. In a span of less than 20 years, these sheikhdoms have undergone astonishing change, accompanied by myriad pressures, in the transformation from among the world's poorest to among the world's richest nations.

The reasons for this study are many. Although the United Arab Emirates (UAE) has a population of around 1 million, its oil reserves are greater than those of the United States. Given its high economic growth rate, the United Arab Emirates is an excellent laboratory in which to test and evaluate policies and programmes to effect rapid economic development. Moreover, there have been no recent economic studies on the UAE aside from that published several years ago by Dr Mana Saeed al-Otaibi, a leading economist and Minister of Petroleum and Mineral Resources of the UAE. This book seeks to trace the process of economic integration as fostered by the political federation of the seven Trucial coast emirates in 1971.

The international stature of the United Arab Emirates is far greater than its physical size, population, and breadth of resources would seem to indicate. As a member of the Organization of the Petroleum Exporting Countries (OPEC), the UAE has played a vital role within the moderate oil-pricing bloc of that body. Its petroleum policy is concerned with not only moderation in price increases but with the stability resulting from smooth, spaced and planned price hikes. Following the outbreak of hostilities between Iran and Iraq in 1980, the UAE raised its crude-oil production to help avert panic over possible supply shortfalls. Moreover, along with crude oil, the federation can boast of vast potential in natural gas.

Preparing a study on the economy of the United Arab Emirates suffers from certain difficulties and obstacles. First, because the federation is relatively young and still evolving, statistical data are often dispersed among the individual emirates rather than fully centralized

Foreword

in a federal statistics bureau. Abu Dhabi and Dubai have the most established documentation departments. The UAE Currency Board, replaced in December 1980 by the Central Bank, led the way in attempting to gather federation-wide economic data. The expanded power of the Central Bank in holding a specified level of revenues from the oil-producing emirates (Abu Dhabi and Dubai) should further solidify and strengthen the statistical and research arms of that institution. It should be noted that Sharjah and Ras Al-Khaimah are now upgrading their statistical collection capabilities.

Secondly, while the UAE does have a federal budget, ministries, and projects, there is a high degree of emirate autonomy in administration; this administrative unevenness is compounded by the varying degrees of development achieved by each of the seven Emirates. Abu Dhabi, Dubai, Sharjah, and Ras Al-Khaimah are more economically advanced than the three remaining emirates of Ajman, Fujairah, and Umm Al-Quwain. The differing levels of development reflect, in addition to the presence or absence of oil-generated revenues, historical biases in economic activity. For example, both Abu Dhabi and Ras Al-Khaimah have long had modest yet viable agricultural bases; Dubai's major economic activity has been in its bustling trade sector with ties well beyond the nearby Gulf states.

The following study has several objectives: to present basic economic data on the UAE; to delineate the conceptual problems in the economy and to analyze these problems; and to offer practical information on the developmental process in the emirates. The readership to whom this volume is addressed includes economists, those interested in this undeniably strategic region of the world and the global energy scene, businessmen, and those involved in trade, investment and finance.

Over the years, many have graciously assisted me in my research through interviews and the provision of documents and relevant information. Those to whom my appreciation is due are: from the Ministry of Petroleum and Mineral Resources and the Abu Dhabi Department of Petroleum, His Excellency Dr Mana Saeed al-Otaiba (Minister), Mohammed al-Qassemi (Director of Economic Affairs of the Ministry), Zaki Abbas, Lutfi M. Tayeb (both of the Ministry), and Sheba Sa'id al-Hamili and Saleh Akasha (Under Secretary and Director of Petroleum, respectively, Abu Dhabi Department); from the Abu Dhabi National Oil Company, Sheikh Tahnoun Ibn-Mohammad al-Nahayyan (Chairman

Foreword

of the Board); from the Abu Dhabi Marine Operating Company, A.J. Horan (General Manager); from the Ministry of Planning, His Excellency Said Ghubash (Minister) and Ahmad Abdullah Mansour (Under Secretary); from the Ministry of Foreign Affairs, Abdul Rahman al-Jarwan (Under Secretary), Ya'cub al-Kindi (Director, Political Affairs), Mohammed Khalifa al-Yusuf (Director, Economic Affairs), Najmuddin Hammudi (Energy Adviser), Fawaz Qudsi (Head of Protocol), and Abdullah Abdul Rahman Hussain (Gulf/Peninsula Affairs); from the Ministry of Information and Culture, Abdullah Nuwais (Under Secretary) and Ibrahim al-Abid (Director, Press Department); from the Ministry of Health, His Excellency Hamad Abdel-Rahman al-Madfa (Minister and former UAE Ambassador to the United States); from the Presidential Court, Zaki Nuseibeh (Press Adviser to the President); from the Mission of the UAE to the United Nations in New York, Mohammed Tajir; from the Embassy of the United Arab Emirates to the United States, Saeed al-Shamsi (Counsellor and Chargé d'Affaires *ad interim*) and Dr Edward Ghareeb; from the UAE Currency Board, Dr Faika El-Rifai; from the Abu Dhabi Documentation Department, Dr Mohammed Kamel Morsy, Ali Tajir, and Abdullah Abu Ezzah; from the Diwan Emiri of Abu Dhabi, Ali al-Sharafah (Head), Dr Ezzadin Ibrahim (Adviser for Cultural Affairs), Dr Hassan Abbas Zaki (Adviser), Hamdi Tamam (Adviser to the Crown Prince); from the Abu Dhabi Fund for Arab Economic Development, Nasser al-Nowais (Director) and Dr Hassan Selim (Adviser); from the Abu Dhabi Investment Authority, His Excellency Mohammed Habroush al-Suweidi (Director of the Board) and Hareb al-Darmaki (Director, Bonds and Equities); from the National Bank of Abu Dhabi, A.S. Assad, Abdullah Ismail and Hussein Nuwais; and United States Ambassador to the UAE, William D. Wolle. Special acknowledgement also must go to Sheikh Ahmed Khalifa al-Suweidi, former Minister of Foreign Affairs of the United Arab Emirates, who has been a guiding force for and instrumental in the federation and integration of the emirates.

A number of research associates, assistants, and staff at the International Research Centre for Energy and Economic Development have aided me in compliation, tabulation, preparation of the manuscript, and the tasks of proof reading and indexing: Dr Jacob Atta, Glenda Bolin, Dennis Miller, Nancy Nachman-Hunt and Kathleen O'Brien. My debt to them is extensive. Finally, thanks must also go to my

Foreword

wife, Dorothea, for her help and encouragement throughout. Any omissions or errors, however, are my own.

1 BACKGROUND AND CURRENT PERSPECTIVES

The emergence of the so-called oil crises in the 1970s has stimulated considerable discussion and studies on oil-rich Middle East countries, aimed principally at examining the potential of individual countries to absorb the oil revenues which have been accruing to them. Middle East members of the Organization of the Petroleum Exporting Countries (OPEC) especially have come under an unprecedented international focus since 1973, a focus which has been predicated upon the economic and political importance of oil in international trade. Despite a proliferation of country studies undertaken within regional-wide discussions by the news media, political analysts, economists, and other scholars, the distribution of the attention attracted by the Middle East has not been all that equitable. One country which has received a share of the focus well below its roles in both the regional and international scenes is the United Arab Emirates (UAE).

The principal reasons for the relatively low profile accorded the Emirates in research and writing are the recency of the federation's creation and the diversion which excessive attention given to petroleum 'giants,' such as Saudi Arabia and Iran, has created. Yet the UAE has been quick to assume a significant place in regional and international affairs. In particular, its status in the oil industry, in both the Organization of the Arab Petroleum Exporting Countries (OAPEC) and OPEC, and in multinational aid/assistance organizations, by far surpasses the attention given to it. In addition, the UAE is one of the fastest growing markets for goods and technology from Europe, North America, and Japan.

Profiling the UAE: Its Regional and International Roles

Clearly, the importance of the UAE lies in its role as an oil producer and exporter and the potential it holds for the future in the form of reserves, the vital position it possesses among aid donors and within the regional institutions to which it belongs, and finally, its contribution to international capital movements. These are put in a better perspective by reference to some statistical features of both the economy of the UAE and its international contributions.

The average UAE citizen is widely considered to be the richest in the world, next only to a Kuwaiti. Thus, although the population of the Emirates is small (estimated by the government at 1,061,000 in mid-1978), effective demand is considerable. The prosperity of this nation has been buttressed by increased oil output, which at a level of about 1.83 million barrels per day (b/d) in 1979, ranks eighth among the 13 OPEC members and fifth among OAPEC members. More significant from the point of view of consuming countries is the contribution which the Emirates make to the world oil trade. In this connection, two examples will suffice. In 1977, the UAE was the fourth major exporter of crude oil to Japan among OPEC members after Saudi Arabia, Iran and Indonesia. Similarly, the dependence of the United States on UAE oil, despite the former's relatively greater diversified sources of oil supply, is quite significant. The Emirates ranked eighth among OPEC exporters of oil to the United States in 1977 and 1978, while attaining the fourth position among OAPEC exporters. In the latter year, about 12 per cent of total UAE crude exports was destined for the United States.

Although the North Sea oil has reduced the imports of the United Kingdom from virtually all Middle East oil-producing countries, the direction of export trade has shifted slightly towards the UAE. From a low percentage of 4.2 in 1972, the UAE's share of United Kingdom exports to the Middle East rose consistently over the years to 11 per cent in 1977. In the late 1970s the United Kingdom was the second largest source of Emirates' imports. Japan has not only been increasing its imports from the UAE, but also its exports to this nation; it is the UAE's largest single supplier (19 per cent of the UAE's total imports in 1978/79). Finally although the proportion of United States Middle East exports which go to the UAE has declined somewhat, its slowdown has been only slight and may be regarded as temporary, given that the volume in actual fact has risen; the United States share of the UAE market in 1978/79 was between 10 and 11 per cent.

The role which the UAE has played in OPEC and OAPEC has been instrumental within the 'moderate' grouping on oil-price increases. For example, the Emirates joined Saudi Arabia in opting for a 5 per cent oil-price increase at the Doha OPEC meeting in 1976, in the face of pressures from other members for a larger price hike. The contribution of this nation to regional organization has been notable; as 1977 opened, the UAE had contributed to no fewer than 23 regional organizations.

Even after the Iranian crisis of 1979 and the reduction in Iranian oil output which tightened supply in the world petroleum market, the UAE followed a relatively moderate course in pricing policy.

Perhaps the most glaring consequence for producing nations of the oil-price boom is the emergence of OPEC capital fund surpluses, and the increasing role which they have come to play in international capital movements and monetary arrangements. The UAE, being one of the low absorbers among the OPEC nations, has had to face the problem of recycling the foreign exchange which exceeds its domestic spending requirements. It is believed that, apart from Kuwait, there is no other capital-surplus nation which has more effectively created institutions to efficiently invest these surpluses abroad. As with all surplus-funds countries, however, the UAE has only three choices: extend bilateral aid to less-developed nations both within and without the Arab world; contribute to multinational organizations, such as the International Monetary Fund (IMF) and the World Bank; and/or invest in both advanced Western and developing nations. In 1976 alone, aid allocations totalled $1.2 billion (US) or 25 per cent of the country's gross national product (GNP). Comparable averages for the industrialized Western nations (as a group) and for OPEC *per se* were 1 per cent and 6 per cent, respectively.

Although the United Arab Emirates is a so-called low absorber of funds, it has greater potential for a diversified economy than many Gulf states. Its potential for agricultural development, despite the harsh climate with which all desert states must contend, has been expanded by well-planned, controlled experimental farms, the establishment and operation of which has involved foreign technology and experts.

The importance of the UAE to the Western world is also derived from non-economic factors. The geography of this nation confers upon it both political and military strategic positions in a region full of political uncertainties. It appears, therefore, that in spite of its recent creation, the potential for conflicts which are inherent in a federal system, and its small population size, the United Arab Emirates can be considered none the less as having attained a significant international status on a par with other Middle East countries about which so much has been written. This holds from both regional and worldwide frames of reference. With proven crude oil reserves in 1980 of approximately 29.5 billion barrels, somewhat larger than those of the United States (including Alaska), the UAE must be expected to continue its role in international political, and especially economic, arenas in the future.

Prior to 2 December 1971, when the independence of the United Arab Emirates was recognized, the Emirates were collectively known as the 'Trucial States', a designation derived from the maritime truce forced upon the sheikhdoms of the Gulf by Great Britain in the nineteenth century. In the few years since this Portugal-sized country gained its independence, it has left its colonial past well behind (indeed, the former Trucial States appellation has been all but forgotten) and now must be reckoned a major independent economic power — a status which is directly attributable to the new nation's reserves of oil and natural gas.

Those revenues have been utilized to great effect domestically. The UAE of 1976 could boast of 269 schools with 73,372 enrolled students as well as one of the most advanced national health programmes in the world offering complete and free medical care for every citizen. In contrast, the Trucial States of 1953 possessed not a single school, except for the *kuttabs* (classes held in the mosques where a few of the boys learned only to recite the Koran). Medical care, too, was available to a relatively fortunate few. Oil and the utilization of revenues have made it possible for the UAE to overcome the twin legacies of poverty and illiteracy with astonishing and unprecedented alacrity and to transform the old differences between the ruling families of the area into a positive commercial rivalry. While not all of the past has been easily subsumed, much of it has been rendered irrelevant by the burgeoning youth of the population which, as of 1976, had tripled in 8 years to 690,000 and was still increasing at an annual rate in excess of 10 per cent. The increasingly educated citizenry and its leaders are understandably concerned with the coming decades. The future of the

UAE's economic development is bright, given its abundance of natural resource wealth and its sizable potential for the structuring of a viable, diversified economy; it has been blessed with a relative abundance of arable land (by Arabian peninsula standards), a scenic coastline and strategic position as well as an ambitious and versatile populace.

Introducing the Sheikhdoms

The United Arab Emirates is situated on the southern coast of the Arabian/Persian Gulf. The emirates of Abu Dhabi, Dubai, Sharjah, Ajman, Ras Al-Khaimah, and Umm Al-Quwain extend south on the coast from Qatar (see Map 1.1) to the Musandam Peninsula on the Gulf of Oman — a distance of nearly 400 miles — while the seventh entity, Fujairah, is located on the Batinah coast of the Gulf of Oman. Excepting Ajman, which holds inland territorial enclaves, and Sharjah, which has dependencies on the Batinah coast, all the emirates are coastal settlements which take their names from the capital or principal city of each sheikhdom.

Although the *subkhah* or salty coastal sands (overpoweringly hot deserts), the two major oases and numerous smaller ones, and an eastern mountain range with 7,000 to 8,000-foot elevations provide some contrasts, the terrain is almost uniformly sandy, flat, and featureless. The 30,000-square-mile area is arid, with wells, oases, and underground springs and canals furnishing a limited supply of fresh water to the agricultural settlements and urban areas.

The climate is in keeping with the terrain and is typical of the subtropical arid zone of the Middle East marked by frequent dust storms and high humidity despite sporadic rains. The climate is particularly harsh in summer when temperatures are routinely in excess of 100°F.

Abu Dhabi is both the largest sheikhdom (26,000 square miles or 85 per cent of the federation's total area) and the westernmost, stretching from the Qatar peninsula along the Arabian Gulf shoreline to a point roughly 40 miles from the city of Dubai. Since the first oil concessions were granted by its government in 1939, oil has been the foundation and mainstay of its economy which currently boasts the highest *per capita* income in the world. In 1976, Abu Dhabi's oil exports reached a high of 1.582 million barrels per day which provided

Map 1.1: United Arab Emirates

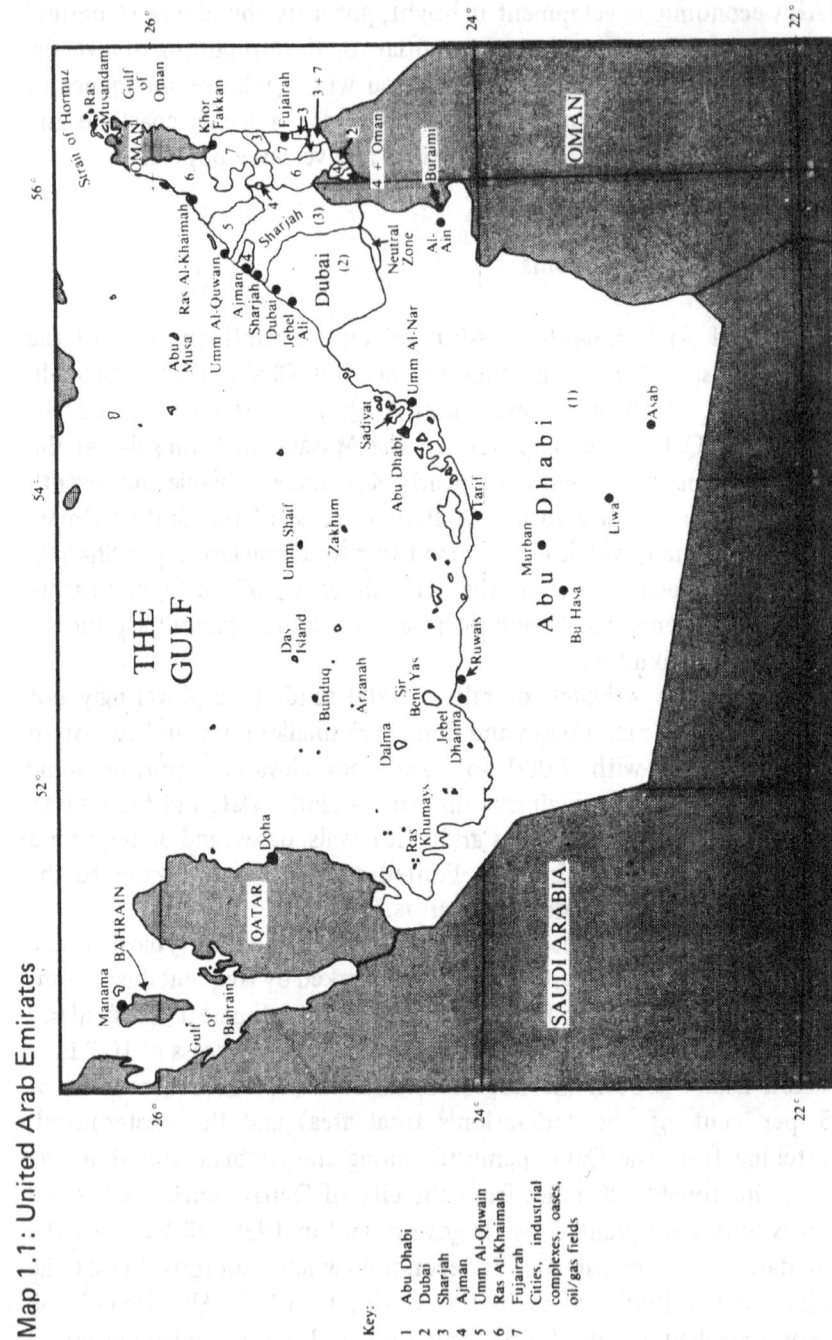

Key:
1 Abu Dhabi
2 Dubai
3 Sharjah
4 Ajman
5 Umm Al-Quwain
6 Ras Al-Khaimah
7 Fujairah
● Cities, industrial complexes, oases, oil/gas fields

its government with oil revenues totalling Dh 19,663.3 million (approximately US $5 billion at a 1978 exchange rate of Dh 3.88 = $1.00) for the year. Total production for the UAE as a whole in 1977 and 1978 was 1.999 and 1.831 million b/d, respectively; however, Abu Dhabi accounted for 82.5 per cent of the UAE's 1977 output (16 per cent by Dubai and 1.4 per cent by Sharjah) and about 79 per cent of the federation's 1978 and 1979 production (about 20 per cent for Dubai and approximately 1 per cent for Sharjah).[1] Clearly the emirate of Abu Dhabi is the premier economic power of the federation as well as the source of financing for the vast majority of its sovereign territories' recent development programmes. Its ruler Sheikh Zayed Ibn-Sultan al-Nahayyan, who assumed control of the emirate in 1966, is the President/Head of State of the UAE.

Dubai ranks second in importance in the federation, with 32 per cent of the UAE's population and accounting for 20 per cent of its oil output. It has an area of 1,500 square miles which is largely desert and a 45-mile coastline. A relatively large population lives in the city of Dubai due to Dubai's traditional position as the main port of entry for the Trucial States and to the interior of Oman. This excellent harbour at Dubai Creek permitted the emirate of Dubai to reach a modest level of economic prosperity without oil-generated revenues. Although oil production may provide Dubai's economy with greater impetus, the emirate's largest revenue source in the near term will likely remain its productive port facility which handled Dh 11,975 million (US $3 billion) in imports in 1977.[2] Of course the share of predominance of petroleum in Dubai's national income will reflect the level of oil prices. The sole ruler of Dubai since 1958, Sheikh Rashid Ibn-Said al-Maktoum is Vice President of the Supreme Council of Rulers as well as Prime Minister of the UAE.

Fujairah is the only emirate which lies wholly on the Gulf of Oman. It was once an integral part of Sharjah, from which it obtained independence in 1952, and has been ruled by Sheikh Hammad Ibn-Mohammad al-Sharqi since 1974. The emirate controls an uninterrupted belt of palm trees, gardens and villages along the Batinah coast. The capital city of Fujairah lies in this fertile plain and is connected by road to Sharjah via the Wadi-al-Quar and Kalba. Fujairah is not as flat and sandy as the other United Arab Emirate sheikhdoms and possesses water resources more abundant than those of most of its fellow states.

Much of its territory is mountainous where cooler temperatures prevail and fosters the cultivation of tobacco, vegetables, dates, and citrus fruit. In this emirate, taxes on agricultural produce and payments on oil concessions generate most government revenues.[3]

Ras Al-Khaimah, literally meaning 'the tip of the tent,' is situated on the northeastern point of the Arabian peninsula. It is bounded on the south by Sharjah, on the southwest by Umm Al-Quwain and on the west by the Gulf. Ras Al-Khaimah governs inland enclaves bordered by Sharjah, Ajman, Dubai and Oman, as well as a small number of islands. The present ruler is Sheikh Saqr Ibn-Mohammad al-Qasimi who has held the leadership position since 1948. The terrain is varied and mountainous inland, with the land between the mountains and the shoreline suitable for agriculture – this region boasts the most abundant water reserves of the Emirates. Ras Al-Khaimah's economy is as varied as its topography, with fishing, livestock breeding, and agriculture complementing the revenues garnered from rents on oil concessions. Gulf Oil Corporation has recently undertaken some seismic activities in an offshore concession with the possibility of an agreement between the emirate and Gulf Oil in 1980.

Sharjah's 10-mile coastline faces the Gulf and accommodates the vast majority of the 1,000-square-mile emirate's population within the confines of several small coastal towns. The largest of these, the capital Sharjah, is relatively prosperous with a number of buildings, shops and housing units, and claims 60 per cent of the Emirate's total population of 40,000. Sharjah was once the major port of the Trucial Coast until heavy silting in the 1940s and 1950s forced it into rapid decline. Only recently has its government, headed by Sheikh Sultan Ibn-Mohammad al-Qasimi (ruler since 1972), been able to undertake investments to upgrade the port's facilities and place both it and the state on the road to recovery.

With the discovery of the Mubarak field, Sharjah became the third oil sheikhdom among the seven which would later form the United Arab Emirates. Optimistic forecasts first projected production of 200,000 barrels per day (b/d); however, actual output had risen until 1975 only to 38,200 b/d and thereafter declined to 22,100 b/d in 1978.[4] Sharjah possesses exploitable red oxide mineral resources from which it also derives revenue.

Umm Al-Quwain, like Abu Dhabi, is consolidated in one land mass,

95 per cent of which is desert. Its one major coastal town is also its capital, Umm Al-Quwain. Until recently the emirate lacked such amenities as adequate water, housing and roads. Despite advances in the past few years under the rule of Sheikh Ahmad Ibn-Rashid al-Mualla (who came to power in 1939) and his son Sheikh Rashid Ibn-Ahmad, the export of dried fish remains the main economic activity in this underdeveloped and economically depressed emirate whose only major link with the rest of the UAE is a coastal road which passes through the capital and threads its way inland.

The smallest and poorest of the UAE sheikhdoms is the coastal state of Ajman. With an area of only 100 square miles and a short coastline of 5 miles, it is nearly surrounded by the neighbouring emirate of Sharjah. Ajman possesses two landlocked enclaves near the Oman border as well as the aforementioned coastal area which is largely occupied by the capital city of Ajman, home to 88 per cent of the sheikhdom's population. Within the past few years efforts have been made to provide the emirate with modern roads, electricity, and piped water systems as well as an industrial and financial base. Despite these efforts at modernization by the state government of Ajman under Sheikh Rashid Ibn-Humaid al-Nuaimi (who became ruler in 1928) and his son Sheikh Humaid Ibn-Rashid, the emirate continues to derive most of its income from fishing, postage stamps, rents on some oil concessions, and both foreign and domestic aid.

Table 1.1 provides a brief statistical comparison of the seven emirates with regard to area and population. The population estimates of the UAE and its component emirates vary because no census has been carried out since 1968 and each publication or report bases its figure on its own sources. The coming and going of expatriate labour complicates the task of estimation. Abu Dhabi, the richest in oil, is not surprisingly the largest. Dubai, the most active entrepôt and a recent exporter of crude, proves to be the most densely populated. Sharjah, which ranks third in the Emirates' petroleum resources, occupies a similar position with regard to its population and area. Ras Al-Khaimah, the most fertile of the seven emirates, ranks fourth in size and population, while Ajman, Umm Al-Quwain, and Fujairah make do with their smaller indigenous populations and resources.

Table 1.1: United Arab Emirates, Area and Population

	Area (sq. miles)	Population[a] 1968 census Males	1968 census Females	Total	1975 census Total
Abu Dhabi	26,000	34,863	11,512	46,375	236,000
Dubai	1,500	35,620	23,351	58,971	207,000
Sharjah	1,000	17,660	14,008	31,668	88,000
Ras Al-Khaimah	650	13,249	11,138	24,387	57,000
Ajman	100	2,212	2,034	4,246	22,000
Umm Al-Quwain	300	1,982	1,762	3,744	17,000
Fujairah	450	5,220	4,515	9,735	26,000
Trucial Oman Scouts[b]	–	1,100	–	1,100	–
Totals	30,000	111,906	68,320	180,226	656,000

Source: K.G. Fenelon, *The United Arab Emirates: An Economic and Social Survey* (London: Longman Group Ltd, 1973), p. 126; Organization of the Petroleum Exporting Countries (OPEC), *Annual Statistical Bulletin 1978* (Vienna: OPEC, September 1979), p. 1.
a. The population of the federation has increased considerably since 1975, especially in Abu Dhabi, and was estimated officially by mid-1978 at about 1,061,000.
b. Composed of military contingents for defence purposes during the period of the British protectorate.

Tracing the Past

The history of the area is a long one. The earliest known inhabitants of what is now the UAE settled the area in approximately 3000 BC, probably to exploit its proximity to one of the earliest maritime trading routes. Ships from Ur and Babylon are believed to have sailed to Bahrain and along the coasts in search of gold, precious stones, ivory, frankincense, teak wood, and copper from India, the Far East, and the mines of Oman. Archaeological excavation is presently being undertaken by a Danish expedition from the historic Museum of Aarhus in Ras Al-Khaimah and at the Al-Ain oases (located in the interior of Abu

Dhabi) to further clarify the ancient history of the United Arab Emirates.[5] As an aside, the cylinder seal for ancient Dilmun utilized the figure of a gazelle; 'Abu Dhabi' translates as 'father of the gazelle.' Could this possibly indicate an ongoing oral tradition in the area over centuries?

The emirates were first exposed to more modern European influence in the sixteenth century when the Portuguese established settlements and forts in the area to protect their trading posts. These were manifestations of the Portuguese attempts to monopolize the spice and other markets. The dominance of Portugal within the Gulf was first challenged in the seventeenth century when traders from Holland, France, and Britain began to attack the monopoly. An intermittent struggle for command of the Gulf then ensued among the four European powers whose interest in the region waxed and waned with their fortunes in Europe.

Throughout the course of the European power struggles in the Gulf, the sheikhdoms which would later coalesce and become the UAE were of little concern to any of the Westerners who were more intent upon controlling the major trade markets of Bahrain and the Indian subcontinent or the profits from the prized pearls of the Gulf itself. Eventually Britain sought to consolidate its newly won dominance of the Gulf and in doing so entered into a formal arrangement with the sheikhs of the Trucial Coast, which effectually precluded the latter from allying themselves with any foreign power other than Great Britain.

The first agreement between the British and the sheikhs was the Perpetual Maritime Truce of 1853. The document, among other things, proved to be the first written agreement denouncing the slave trade (in Article 9 of the treaty) as well as the first in a series of agreements between the rulers of the Trucial Coast and the rulers of much of the rest of the world.

During the 1870s and 1880s other powers threatened British hegemony in the Gulf. However, the British were able to thwart first Turkish and the subsequent French and Russian encroachments upon their monopoly. An exclusive agreement was imposed on the Gulf rulers by the British, prohibiting them from entering into any agreements or correspondence with powers other than Great Britain. Furthermore, the rulers were not to consent to the residence within their territories of any agent of another government and on no account to cede, sell, mortgage, or otherwise give occupation of any part of their territory to any but the British government.[6]

A half-century later the British confronted an adversary more formidable than any of the great powers of the nineteenth century – oil. The discovery of petroleum in the neighbouring Gulf states and the likelihood of similar discoveries in the Trucial Emirates began to undermine the British imperial pre-eminence as the indigenous leaders began to seek a more prominent role in both internal and external affairs. Eventually the individual sheikhdoms would begin to grant oil concessions which were clearly in violation of the 'exclusive agreement' and force Great Britain to react, which it did in 1952. In an attempt to arrest its declining influence, Britain created the Trucial Oman Council. Under the British imprimatur this council established an organization which provided a meeting place for a group of Gulf state rulers who ordinarily had no reason for assembling. Initially the British strategy was successful, allowing it a leading role in the council. Within a few years, however, the organization broke from the British agency and established its own meetings. Subsequently the sheikhs gradually and largely assumed many of the functions formerly performed by the British government.

By 1968 the British position in the area had eroded to such an extent that the costs of maintaining a military presence there (and elsewhere east of Suez) could not be justified. In that year Great Britain announced that it would withdraw all its forces from the Trucial States by the end of 1971. The evacuation was effected on schedule and brought to a close over a century and a half of direct British influence.

Forging the UAE: Government Structure and Direction

After Great Britain announced its intention to withdraw, the nine Gulf States of Abu Dhabi, Dubai, Sharjah, Fujairah, Ras Al-Khaimah, Umm Al-Quwain, Ajman, Bahrain, and Qatar sent representatives to a conclave which sought to forge an economic and political union to ensure the security and stability of the area. Several years of frustrating negotiations then ensued. On 18 July 1971, after Abu Dhabi and Dubai – the two most affluent and advanced Trucial sheikhdoms – had previously established a common citizenship, flag, defence force, and foreign policy (and thus provided the necessary impetus and example), a qualified success was announced. Six of the nine states reached an agreement which would eventually culminate in the establishment of a federation to be known as the 'State of the United Arab Emirates.' At that time, three states — Ras Al-Khaimah, Bahrain, and Qatar — chose to remain independent.[7] Bahrain and Qatar have since established themselves as sovereign, independent nations and joined the United Nations. It is also true that their absence might have worked to ensure a greater degree of internal stability and cohesion than might otherwise have been possible in the new federation. Had Bahrain and Qatar joined the nascent UAE, the division of power would have been less clear-cut than it is at present between Abu Dhabi, Dubai, and the lesser states. Ras Al-Khaimah, the third dissenter, later joined the federation on 10 February 1972, after first rejecting union with Oman.[8] The original six — Abu Dhabi, Dubai, Sharjah, Fujairah, Umm Al-Quwain and Ajman — proclaimed the establishment of the union on 2 December 1971, two months before Ras Al-Khaimah's belated acquiescence. This was seen as a collectively bold and progressive step, heralded throughout the Arab world.

On that same day, the rulers of the six states met in Dubai to officially ratify the Provisional Constitution of the federation and thereby establish the United Arab Emirates as a member of the community of nations. At the same meeting the ruler of Abu Dhabi, Sheikh Zayed Ibn Sultan al-Nuhayyan, was elected President and head of the newly formed Supreme Council which was composed of Sheikh Rashid Ibn-Said al-Maktoum, ruler of Dubai (as its Vice-President), and the rulers of the other four states. Sheikh Maktoum Ibn-Rashid al-Maktoum, the Crown Prince of Dubai, was appointed President of the Federal Council of Ministers at this time as well.[9]

Using the following words the Supreme Council announced

> to the people of the State of the United Arab Emirates (its establishment) as an independent and sovereign state forming part of the Arab homeland. Its aim is to preserve its independence, sovereignty, security, and stability, to ward off any aggression against itself or any of its member emirates, to safeguard the rights and freedoms of its people, and to establish close cooperation between its member emirates for their common benefit. For these objectives and in order

to promote its prosperity and advancement in all fields, to ensure a better life for all its citizens, to support Arab and Islamic causes and interest, and to cement ties of friendship and cooperation with all states and peoples on the basis of the principles of the Arab League Charter, the U.N. Charter and international morality, the State of the United Arab Emirates was created.[10]

The Provisional Constitution of the UAE, originally drafted by the Trucial States Council, currently provides the legal framework upon which the enunciated goals are to be effected. Approximately 12 articles in the document stress education 'as a fundamental factor in the progress of the society' and mandate a free and compulsory educational system. Another article provides for general welfare assistance and other social programmes; '... society shall guarantee to all citizens health care, protective facilities and treatment for illnesses and epidemics.' Two other articles deal with economic matters. The first, Article 23, is clearly concerned with the use and disposition of oil wealth:

> the natural wealth and resources in every emirate shall be considered as public property of that emirate. Society shall regulate the protection and beneficial exploitation of such resources to the good of the national economy.[11]

The second, Article 24, delineates 'the Union's Basic and Economic Principles' in the following words:

> National economy shall be based on social justice and on sound cooperation between the public and private sectors. Its aim shall be to realize economic development, increase production, raise the standard of living and provide prosperity for the citizens within the framework of the law. It shall also encourage cooperation and savings.[12]

Both articles implicitly promise an expansive governmental role in the economy of the new federation. The drafters of the Provisional Constitution reserved a few paragraphs within it to provide for the establishment of a new capital as well as a new state and society. The new capital, Al-Karameh, was to have been situated on the Abu Dhabi-Dubai border, scheduled for completion no more than seven years from its date of commission. In the interim, Abu Dhabi continues to serve as the seat of government. The Provisional Constitution which mandated such a solution will remain in force until the permanent constitution is completed and ratified.

Later, in December 1971, the United Arab Emirates was admitted to membership of the United Nations and thereby formally entered the international arena as a sovereign state. Diplomatic relations have since been established with most regional states, India, Pakistan, and most Western nations. To staff the new diplomatic service, the Abu Dhabi Ministry of State for Premiership Affairs has organized and administered a diplomatic training programme from which has graduated the first group of men who will represent the new nation to the world at large, both in the recently established embassies as well as in the international bodies which have conferred membership upon the UAE. The United Arab Emirates now is a member of the Arab League, the International Monetary Fund, and the World Bank. The UAE has also sought membership in the various service organizations of the United Nations — the World Health Organization, the United Nations Educational, Scientific and Cultural Organization, and the Children's Fund, in particular — as it is desirous both of expanding its contacts and influence and of assuming its perceived proper place as an active, involved and responsible nation in the global community.

To maintain this newly won independence, a 1,700-man Union Defence Force (UDF) was created upon the foundation provided by the now-superseded Trucial Oman Scouts.[13] The UDF is buttressed by the defence forces maintained by each individual state to deal with internal affairs. These forces are available for the defence of the entire federation should their services be requested. The Union Defence Force is ultimately responsible to the Federal Minister of Defence and the Higher Defence Council, the chairman of which is the President of the Federation. The Federation President in turn presides over a federal government composed of the Supreme Council of the Union (consisting of the rulers of the participating states), the Union's Council of Ministers (Cabinet), the Federal National Council (a consultative assembly), the Federal Judicature, and the President of the Union and his Deputy.

The Federal National Council (FNC) is similar to that of Abu

Dhabi's which was established in July 1971. It holds an open session of not less than six months each year beginning in November, during which time it reviews and debates all draft legislation submitted to it by the government. The FNC may approve, reject or amend the draft laws and must be informed by the government of all treaties and agreements entered into with other states and international organizations. Additionally, the Council has the right to debate any general topic relating to affairs of state that is not detrimental to the Union, and to refer its recommendations to the Ruler of the Council of Ministers for action. The Federal National Council consists of 40 members with seats distributed among the member emirates as follows: Abu Dhabi and Dubai eight seats each; Sharjah and Ras Al-Khaimah six seats apiece; and Ajman, Umm Al-Quwain, and Fujairah four seats each.[14]

The Cabinet, or Federal Council of Ministers, presently consists of the following members: (1) the prime minister, who is also the vice president of the Supreme Council of Rulers (presently the ruler of Dubai), (2) two deputy prime ministers (in the cabinet formed 1 July 1979, one from Abu Dhabi and the other from Dubai), the ministers of (3) foreign affairs, (4) interior, (5) defence, (6) finance and industry, (7) justice, Islamic Affairs, and Awqaf, (8) education, youth and sports, (9) health, (10) public works and housing, (11) communications, (12) labour and social affairs, (13) economy and trade, (14) information, (15) planning, (16) petroleum and mineral resources, (17) electricity and water resources, (18) agriculture and fisheries, and (19) five ministers of state (see Appendix I).

Desirous of augmenting the powers of these federal branches of government and setting an example to the other states in the union, the state of Abu Dhabi passed a law on 14 January 1974, which simultaneously reorganized the state's governmental structure and delegated many powers, previously reserved to the state, to the federal government. The law abolishes Abu Dhabi's ministerial system and replaces it with an executive council which includes eleven administrations: defence; finance; public works; municipalities and agriculture, water and electricity; purchases; organization and management; petroleum; social services; planning; and Abu Dhabi's municipality and city planning. It is apparent from this listing that the reorganization laid the foundation for an Abu Dhabi state government only marginally dissimilar to the national government it has chosen to promote.

Background and Current Perspectives 17

If the absolute rise in federal revenues and expenditures in the years following 1974 are any indication of the effect of Abu Dhabi's example, the latter must be deemed a success. The transfer of several ministries from the government of Abu Dhabi to the federal government was accompanied by a large revenue increase in the national government's budget — from Dh 419.8 million in 1973 to Dh 800.5 million in 1974. By the 1977 budget, revenues had swelled to Dh 13,150 million, 98 per cent of which represent individual emirate governments' contributions.[15] (The negligible remaining revenues are those from customs, interest, and the like.) The expenditures of the federal government have increased just as dramatically. In 1977, the Federal National Assembly approved a budget of Dh 13,150 million, a fourfold increase over the 1976 budget of Dh 2,522.3 million.[16] Current expenditures accounted for 75 per cent of the budgeted expenditures for 1977 and 58 per cent of those for 1976. The UAE draft budget for 1980 allocated expenditures of Dh 11,256 million ($2.988 billion (US)), nearly a 16 per cent increase over the 1979 level of Dh 9,715.7 million ($2.572 billion (US)). For 1980, current expenditures account for just under 80 per cent of total allocations, development for about 14 per cent, and foreign investment slightly over 6 per cent.[17]

The vast majority of current expenditures are funnelled through the main federal ministries — state, finance and industry, economy and commerce, communications, information, interior, justice, defence, housing and public works, health, labour and social affairs, education and youth, fisheries, foreign affairs, petroleum, electricity and water, and planning. In contrast, total development projects received 29.6 per cent of the total federal expenditure for 1976, 10.7 per cent for 1977, 11.9 per cent for 1978, and 14.1 per cent for 1980. (Development expenditures include capital contributions and net lendings to public corporations.) State budgets and revenues have exhibited a similar trend over the course of the last decade. Abu Dhabi's, for example, quadrupled from 1967 to 1975 and nearly doubled again in 1976, despite the reorganization of 1974 which diverted several thousands more to the federal government. The 1976 budget allocated a total expenditure of Dh 19,896.6 million by the state government of Abu Dhabi, 47.7 per cent of which was earmarked for current expenditure.[18] The remainder was divided among various development programmes, the federal government, and assistance to foreign governments and international organizations. Clearly, the state and federal governmental units of the UAE have evidenced a willingness to utilize the new-found and even more recently and profitably exploited wealth of the country to augment both their revenues and thus their powers. The following chapters will describe primarily the economic aspects of the United Arab Emirates' rapid development, the functions of the private sector, and the role of its government in co-ordinating the allocation of national wealth in the interests of economic efficiency.

Notes

1. United Arab Emirates (UAE), Currency Board, *Bulletin*, November 1977, pp. 111-15; Organization of the Petroleum Exporting Countries (OPEC), *Annual Statistical Bulletin 1978* (Vienna: OPEC, September 1979), pp. 14, 36, 75. The 1979 UAE production has been estimated at 1.825 million b/d, *Oil and Gas Journal*, 31 December 1979, p. 70.

2. UAE, Currency Board, *Bulletin*, November 1977, p. 125. (Estimated from import statistics through the third quarter of 1977.)

3. Donald Hawley, *The Trucial States* (London: George Allen and Unwin Ltd, 1971), pp. 126-7.

4. Keith McLachlan and Narsi Ghorban, *Oil Production, Revenues, and Economic Development* (London: The Economist Intelligence Unit Ltd, 1974), p. 52; *Oil and Gas Journal*, 27 December 1976, p. 104; OPEC, *Annual Statistical Bulletin 1978*, p. 36.

5. K.G. Fenelon, *The Trucial States* (London: Longman Publishers, 1973), p. 13. Archaeological linking of Bahrain to the capital of ancient Dilmun and to a large area within the Gulf region which was once part of the Dilmun empire is described in Geoffrey Bibby, *Looking for Dilmun* (New York: Alfred A. Knopf, 1969).

6. Fenelon, *Trucial States*, pp. 128, 137. A remarkably similar stipulation was also agreed to by the Emir of Kuwait in the British-Kuwaiti protectorate agreement.

7. *Middle East Economic Survey*, 3 December 1971, pp. 8-9. (Hereafter *Middle East Economic Survey* will be cited as *MEES*.)

8. Fenelon, *Trucial States*, p. 183. Ras Al-Khaimah also made specific demands of UAE. These were: (1) that the UAE break off relations with Iran over the latter's seizure of two islands in the Strait of Hormuz which were claimed by Ras Al-Khaimah, (2) representation equal to that of Abu Dhabi was requested with both sheikhdoms possessing a veto power in the Supreme Council, and (3) that payment of aid from the oil-producing members of the federation be made directly to the rulers of the non-producing states rather than through some form of federal agency.

9. *Arab Economic Review*, January-February 1972, p. 1.

10. *MEES*, 3 December 1971, p. 9.

11. Provisional Constitution of the United Arab Emirates, *Middle East*

Journal, summer 1972, p. 309.
  12. Ibid.
  13. The negotiations and decision to turn the Trucial Oman Scouts into the nucleus of the federation defence forces are described by John Duke Anthony in 'The Union of Arab Emirates,' *Middle East Journal*, summer 1972, p. 274. British advisers organized the Union Defence Forces (UDF) into five armoured-car companies led by about 24 British officers and 100 British non-commissioned officers. In his article Anthony concluded that:

> with additional forces on call from the individual emirates, and particularly from the relatively powerful Abu Dhabi Defence Force, the activities of the UDF will probably be confined to performing police and paramilitary roles in the course of patrolling village and desert regions and preventing incidents of tribal dissidence from escalating into intersheikhdom warfare.

Part 9 of the Provisional Constituion of the United Arab Emirates consists of seven articles – 137 to 143 concerning the armed forces and the security forces. The Provisional Constitution is quoted in full English translation as a document in the *Middle East Journal*, summer 1972, pp. 307-25. It should be noted that Ras Al-Khaimah did not sign this Provisional Constitution as did the other six sheikhdoms on 18 July 1971.
  14. *MEES*, 3 September 1972, p. 6. Chapter 4, the Federal National Council (Articles 68 to 93), Provisional Constitution of the United Arab Emirates, *Middle East Journal*, summer 1972, pp. 314-17.
  15. *Middle East Economic Digest*, July 1977, p. 50.
  16. State of Abu Dhabi, *Official Gazette*, 3rd year, no. 2, 31 January 1974, pp. 1811-16 (in Arabic), and the *Quarterly Economic Review*, vol. 4, no. 1, 1974, pp. 17 and 18.
  17. *MEES*, 17 December 1979, p. IV.
  18. Computed from statistical tables in UAE, Currency Board, *Bulletin*, November 1977, p. 112.

2 ECONOMIC DEVELOPMENT POLICIES

The UAE: A Brief Economic History

Prior to the late 1940s the vast majority of the population of the Trucial States lived at a subsistence level, virtually indistinguishable from that which they had reached centuries before. During the nineteenth and early twentieth centuries, pearling was vitally important to the economies of the Trucial States and before oil made the difference between a meagre subsistence level of living and a lifestyle with a few luxury items for some.[1] Only the inhabitants of those states directly bordering the Gulf were allowed to indulge in pearling, with this stipulation enforced by the British maritime peace effort.

The pearling industry fell on hard times during the early 1900s and, as a result, the Trucial States slid backwards in their drive toward progress. The reasons for the decline of the pearling industry were primarily four: (1) the Japanese had introduced a new 'cultured pearl.' Japanese pearl farming was much cheaper, making it possible to sell pearls on the world market at a price below that of the natural pearls harvested in the Trucial States. (2) The worldwide depression during the 1930s resulted in the loss of luxury markets, such as in France and Italy. (3) World War II caused a reduced demand for Trucial Coast pearls, as their large American and European markets were lost. (4) The fatal blow came in 1946, when India, a large market for pearls, forbade the importation of pearls from the Trucial Coast. The Indian Law was later repealed and replaced with an import levy on pearls so heavy that the pearling industry was still unable to export to India.[2]

As a result of the declining demand for pearls, the number of pearling boats gradually decreased. The Trucial States' contact with the rest of the world began to shrink at an ever increasing rate as the industry faltered and World War II accelerated the backsliding.[3]

Abu Dhabi was extremely hard hit by the pearling depression, and only Dubai was able to sustain an economy, albeit small, which was built on the traffic in gold. In India the price of gold was almost double that of the world market's level, giving rise to unrecorded or clandestine movements of gold which offered an opportunity to buy at lower prices. Thus Dubai's economy survived the pearling depression.

With its harbour facilities lying only five days or 1,200 miles from India via the Gulf of Oman, Dubai possessed an entrepôt position for Middle East transit trade. The importance of the Dubai harbour to the economy of the sheikhdom is evident when the financial statistics involved are examined. In 1966, more gold went to Dubai from London than to any other country except France and Switzerland. Four million ounces valued at the equivalent of 10 per cent of the total gold mined by the free world in that year were channelled through Dubai.[4]

British commitment prior to the war was limited to the enforcement of the maritime truce, thus avoiding any internal direct involvement in social or economic development. The United Kingdom first began to push for some improvement in living conditions when in 1939 Great Britain opened a dispensary in Dubai and provided an Indian doctor. This was followed in 1941 by plans to establish a hospital in Dubai, with construction beginning in 1949. The new hospital was one of the first signs of the new British policy oriented toward internal socio-economic development.

From this frugal beginning, the rate of development in the Trucial States has grown progressively. In 1952 money was allocated for preliminary water resource studies which included a survey of Dubai and Sharjah Creeks, both affected by heavy silting. In 1954/5, British allocations included a water resource study in Ras Al-Khaimah, restoration of the *falaj* (underground canals) at Buraimi oasis, improvements to the Dubai hospital, and the building of a modern school in Sharjah. Total allocations for 1954/5 totalled £50,300.

The implementation of the initial projects was deemed such a success that the British political agent submitted a five-year plan for initiating development in the Trucial States which would entail expenditures of £450,000. The plan was met with enthusiasm by the British government and was eventually approved. Under its auspices the first police force was established in Dubai in 1957, agricultural trial stations were set up in Ras Al-Khaimah, and a small agricultural loan programme was instituted.

In health and education, four elementary schools, a vocational centre in Sharjah, and teacher-training for men at Bahrain were created, as well as the expansion of Dubai's hospital, establishment of a number of dispensaries, and an anti-malaria campaign.

The first British 5-year plan, like the initial development schemes, was deemed a success. The political agent again requested funds, this time on a more generous scale, but because of the British economic crisis at that time only £550,000 was obtained for the years 1961/6. These funds underwrote such projects as the establishment and running of a trade school in Dubai (in conjunction with the ruler of that sheikhdom) and storm erosion repair in Ras Al-Khaimah.

Other aid to the Trucial States during the 1960s came from such sources as Kuwait, Qatar, Bahrain, and Saudi Arabia. Of these, Kuwait instituted a sizable financial and technical assistance programme for the Trucial region beginning with a mission in 1962 to investigate the future potential of the Trucial States as an aid recipient. This resulted in the establishment of a state office in Dubai with a director and subordinate staff designed to co-ordinate educational and health projects.

Both Qatar and Bahrain entered into a joint venture to provide teachers to promote educational development. Qatar also supplied aid which helped create a fresh water supply for the capital city, Dubai, as well as the first bridge linking both sides of Dubai Creek. Saudi Arabia developed the truck road from Sharjah to Ras Al-Khaimah at a cost of £1 million. The Arab League also took a great interest in providing aid for the Trucial States. This intra-aid experience is unique in the emphasis placed on education and health to rapidly improve the standard of living and potential of the population. Along with Qatar and Bahrain, Egypt was a source for teachers, indicating the transfer of skills from relatively more advanced countries to the lesser developed.

British contributions were usually made in the form of grants-in-aid and were channelled through the Trucial States Council Development Fund. This newly formed fund was an offshoot of the Trucial State Council which was established in 1952, with the initial purpose of bringing the rulers together and promoting co-operation. Over the years, the Council gained strength and independence from the British government. To further separate the Trucial States Council from British control, the political agents withdrew from the chairmanship of the Council, creating an autonomous Council run by the Trucial States themselves, and through which all aid was channelled. British advisers

Economic Development Policies

did, however, remain attached to the Council.

Initial contributors to the Trucial States Development Office and Fund were Britain, £1 million; Qatar, £250,000; Abu Dhabi, £200,000; and Bahrain, £40,000.[5] Abu Dhabi's growing stature as an oil producer is evident in that sheikhdom's contribution which increased when Sheikh Zayed Ibn-Sultan came to power in 1966. Abu Dhabi's share rose rapidly from £0.5 million in 1966 upon Sheikh Zayed's accession to £1 million in September 1967.

In July 1965, the Conference of Rulers decided to fund 15 development projects. The project with the greatest impact on the region was the provision of the modern, paved road which was built between Dubai and Sharjah. This was later extended from Sharjah to Ras Al-Khaimah with direct aid from the neighbouring country of Saudi Arabia. The road construction affected favourably the integration of the union as a step towards a unified infrastructure. The other projects covered a wide range of activities, such as a hydrological survey of all states, a well-boring and testing programme, and water supply schemes for Ras Al-Khaimah, Ajman, Sharjah, and Umm Al-Quwain, among others. Total estimated costs of these projects were put at $7.225 million, of which about $3.563 million was allocated in 1968.[6]

For the year 1969, capital expenditures were in the neighbourhood of $4.608 million, an increase of 29 per cent over the previous year. The allocation of those funds between the individual states was roughly 37 per cent for inter-state projects, 17.5 per cent to Sharjah, 4 per cent for Ajman, 7 per cent to Umm Al-Quwain, about 16 per cent for Ras Al-Khaimah, 18 per cent allocated to Fujairah, and only 0.5 per cent to Dubai.[7]

As a result of their rising oil revenues, both Dubai and Abu Dhabi received little, if any, aid from the Trucial States Council Development Fund. Both Abu Dhabi and Dubai have since become donors instead of recipients. In addition to the Trucial States Council Fund, Abu Dhabi has established the Abu Dhabi Fund for Arab Economic Development (ADFAED) which will be discussed later in some detail.

Abu Dhabi remains the only emirate to initiate a development plan on its own. In 1968 the first 5-Year Plan covering 1968-72 was initiated, with total appropriations equalling $612.3 million.

Economic infrastructure, including the communications and municipalities division in the plan, received the lion's share of financing, 41 per cent of the total. Some $95.5 million was set aside for a road system throughout the country (684 miles in length), badly needed because of the relatively large size of Abu Dhabi. Of special note is that $63 million of the plan's allocations to loans and investment was designated regionally for development projects in the other Trucial States. To remedy the congested port conditions, a programme to deepen the shallow harbour of Abu Dhabi City and provide needed jetties was planned and a temporary harbour was completed in 1969. Among other communication projects were the expansion and modernization of the postal and telephone systems and airports at Abu Dhabi City and Al-Ain. The second largest municipality of the state, located in Buraimi, Al-Ain is an oasis and the headquarters for the eastern province.

The municipalities programme included town planning for the major cities, street improvements in towns throughout the country (413 miles), a potable water supply and distribution system, sewerage, refrigeration facilities and public parks.

The plan's sectoral emphasis was on economic and social infrastructure, industry, and agriculture, in that order. Funds allocated to agriculture were modest, reflecting the limited agricultural base of the country. Some 42 per cent of total plan allocations supported a general industrial survey, electrical power and distribution (including a desalination plant for Abu Dhabi City), and petrochemicals. The latter industry was heavily capital-intensive, envisaging a gas liquefication plant, refinery, and chemical production such as insecticides. Important for meeting construction demand was the completion of the building materials industries. Moreover, such plants as those for cement manufacture are economically more feasible as economies of scale are reached with relatively small units. Finally, the plan recognized certain of the older industrial pursuits in its allocations to fishing and pearling.

Certain characteristics appear when evaluating the plan. One is its dual function of both an income-distributive and economy-diversifying nature. Systematization of growth via planning at a very early stage in Abu Dhabi's development can be favourably compared with countries which share the impact of rapid exploitation of a non-renewable natural resource, such as Kuwait. Abu Dhabi's plan was actually a 5-year budget, and because of the low developmental base, priorities were both comprehensive and apparent, stressing requirements of economic and social infrastructure. With succeeding plans, however, a plateau in the overall level of economic infrastructure will be reached, and it will be possible to discern through forthcoming priority decisions what directions will be taken and what the base and rate of economic growth can be.

Recent development indicates, however, that inflation seriously undercut the plan's allocations, leaving many projects under-budgeted. In 1969 Abu Dhabi incurred an overall budget deficit of approximately $31.8 million, partly due to lower realized oil revenues for 1968 than anticipated.[8] In an effort to counter this condition, the government instituted some deflationary measures such as reducing staff, deferring certain payments, and concentrating more on ongoing development projects rather than beginning new ones. Although there had been a curbing of redundant bureaucratic staff, a second major problem remained, i.e. the shortage of specialized labour.

Two positive elements in the plan should be elucidated. One was the relative modesty of and low priority given to public buildings (only 3.8 per cent of total allocations). Many developing countries stumble into the trap of excessive spending on prestige and spectacular public edifices; to date Abu Dhabi has largely avoided this pitfall. Secondly, in developing countries with a capital surplus, there is a temptation to utilize rather immediate and direct wealth distributive measures, such as a land purchase programme similar to Kuwait's, where the government buys land from private citizens at highly inflated prices, often reselling to individuals at a very low rate. This can easily lead to a dimming of the relationship between economic effort and reward. In Abu Dhabi only $8.4 million (under the municipalities division) was set aside for property acquisition, a small proportion considering the totality of plan allocations.

In attempting a greater sectoral balance through diversification, it is encouraging that agriculture was given serious attention. There is a deep interest in this sector, especially in the eastern province. This has been reinforced by the personal concern of Abu Dhabi's ruler who earlier was in charge of the eastern region. It had been estimated that expansion of the agricultural potential could not only meet the basic food needs of Abu Dhabi but those of the neighbouring emirates as well.[9] Industrial projects selected for the plan indicated that import-substitution industries are of limited potential because of the narrowness of the domestic market. However, certain industries such as cement and building materials can reach efficiency with a small facility; additionally, the other emirates offer a market for these specific products. Industrial specialization in petrochemicals and refining of course is anchored in and related to oil and oil receipts.

Another characteristic of the first plan and subsequent economic activity has been the rapidly increasing oil receipts, rising from $422.1 million in 1970 to $8,705.0 million in 1978. Recent estimates for 1979 were in the area of $12.5 billion (US).[10] Moreover, the ratio of current to development expenditures was close to 1 until 1970. Thereafter, when oil revenues began to soar dramatically, this ratio started to rise consistently. It reached about 3.1 in 1976 and declined to 2.3 in 1978. This shows that current expenditures are more responsive to increases in oil receipts. Such is to be expected, however, since the adjustment of the economy to substantially higher levels of capital investment is generally a slow process, especially if the resources base is limited and factors of production are in flagrant imbalance. Nevertheless, Abu Dhabi was able to increase its development expenditures in the 12-year span from Dh 168.0 million in 1967 to Dh 7,432.9 million in 1978. The ratio of current to development expenditures should decline, however, as the economy further develops and the absorptive capacity for investible funds increases.

Another characteristic evident in the period under study is that while 4 of the 10 years reported realized small deficits, the other 6 showed surpluses which in 1971, 1972, 1974 and 1975 were considerable. In fact, the 1973 deficit is exceptional since it was due mainly to Abu Dhabi's large contribution to Egypt and Syria during and after the October 1973 Middle East war. If oil revenues continue at their recent levels (and the 1979 and 1980 oil-price picture would support this possibility), Abu Dhabi's budget is likely to show consistent surpluses in the future. The budget of the federation displays similar trends.

Total federal revenue, which consists mainly of the emirate government's contributions, is rapidly rising. Except for 1972, 1977 and 1978, total revenues were in line with total expenditures and the budget was balanced. Again, the ratio of current expenditures to development expenditures was always higher than 1, but this ratio registers a slow if consistent decline up to 1976. The reversal of this trend in 1977, 1978 and 1979 indicates a recent lower capital absorption of the

Table 2.1: UAE Federal Budget: Revenues, 1980 (in millions of Dh)[a]

	1980	1979
Emirates' contributions	15,767.030	9,515.407
Income from the Ministries:	205.286	200.286
Deputy Prime Minister's Office	0.005	0.015
State for Council of Minister's Affairs	0.005	0.015
State	0.001	0.006
Comptroller's Office	0.020	0.020
Interior	27.065	15.000
Justice, Islamic Affairs and Awqaf	27.000	27.000
Finance and Industry	50.000	55.000
Planning	0.050	0.050
Petroleum and Mineral Resources	0.030	0.030
Economy and Trade	0.010	0.010
Foreign Affairs	4.000	4.000
Information and Culture	5.000	5.000
Education and Youth	3.000	3.000
Health	3.000	3.000
Public Works and Housing	11.000	11.001
Communications	50.000	50.000
Water and Electricity	11.000	12.000
Agriculture and Fisheries	10.000	11.000
Labour and Social Affairs	4.000	4.000
Others	0.100	0.150
Total	15,972.316	9,715.694

Source: Ministry of Finance and Industry, Abu Dhabi, as reported in *Middle East Economic Digest*, Special report, October 1980, p. 27.
a. Exchange rates applicable: 1980, $1=Dh 3.6900, and in 1979, $1=Dh 3.7920.

federal economy despite the fact that greater attention to development by the federal government has been planned.

For example, expenditure allocations in the 1980 federal budget were up some 64 per cent over the preceding year. In this budget (see Tables 2.1 and 2.2), development allocations increased about 40 per cent over 1979, current expenditures up more than 14.5 per cent, and allocations for foreign investments down more than 6.5 per cent. Allocations of Dh 9,715.7 million ($2,579.2 million) in 1979 were 80.5 per cent for current expenditures, 11.9 per cent for development expenditures, and 7.7 per cent earmarked for foreign investment; out of the Dh 15,972 million ($4,328 million) expenditures in 1980,

Table 2.2: UAE Federal Budget: Expenditures, 1980 (in millions of Dh)[a]

	Current	Development	Total
President's Office and Council of Ministers	78.386	6.000	84.386
Federal National Council	13.800	1.600	15.400
Comptroller's Office	27.480	0.500	27.980
Ministry of Defence	4,500.000	–	4,500.000
Ministry of Interior	1,224.921	157.156	1,382.077
Ministry of Justice, Islamic Affairs and Awqaf	160.336	39.430	199.766
Ministry of Finance and Industry	53.660	3.000	56.660
Ministry of Planning	32.425	1.600	34.025
Ministry of Petroleum and Mineral Resources	18.017	0.800	18.817
Ministry of Economy and Trade	11.789	–	11.789
Ministry of Foreign Affairs	177.092	75.500	252.592
Ministry of Information and Culture	209.945	61.650	271.595
Ministry of Education and Youth	1,081.393	306.625	1,388.018
Ministry of Health	1,071.628	243.050	1,314.678
Ministry of Public Works and Housing	53.855	352.600	406.455
Ministry of Communications	73.217	234.423	307.640
Ministry of Electricity and Water	291.322	244.547	535.869
Ministry of Agriculture and Fisheries	79.981	170.563	250.544
Ministry of Labour and Social Affairs	307.659	3.950	311.609
General expenditure	2,833.450	–	2,833.450
Foreign investments	1,768.966	–	1,768.966
Total	14,069.322	1,902.994	15,972.316

Source: Ministry of Finance and Industry, Abu Dhabi, as reported in *Middle East Economic Digest*, Special report, October 1980, p. 27.
a. Exchange rate in 1980, $1=Dh 3.6900.

77 per cent went to current requirements, some 12 per cent to development allocations, and 11 per cent for foreign investment.[11] Given the substantial increase in oil prices during 1979, beginning with the posted

price of the OPEC 'marker' crude (Arabian Light 34°) at $13.335 per barrel and ending with the UAE price hike of 13 December to $27.56 for its most expensive crude (Murban 39°),[12] it is likely the 1980 federal budget as well as those of Abu Dhabi and Dubai will reflect greater surpluses and a larger allocation to foreign investment under the existing absorptive capacity constraints.

Planning officials in Abu Dhabi have called for the creation of an overall federal development plan to help individual emirates establish economic objectives.

Following the first 5-year plan, Abu Dhabi was involved in drawing up a 3-year socio-economic plan for the period 1977-9, based on a detailed sector-by-sector study covering the years 1970-4 with particular reference to investment, public finance and public services. The second planning exercise offers an insight into the planning processes used, the spending and development priorities, and the expectations of the economic decision-makers in Abu Dhabi. The groundwork studies for the 3-year plan showed Abu Dhabi's gross domestic product (GDP) rising by an annual average of 65 per cent between 1970 and 1974. At current prices, GDP increased from Dh 1,200 million ($303 million) to Dh 19,700 million ($4,975 million) between 1970 and 1974. The 3-year plan was to have been worked out by a series of committees, supervised by a steering committee, and sectoral committees were to submit basic reports containing provisional targets.[13] The 1977-9 plan proposal projected a GDP increase of 13.5 per cent annually from a base of $4,256 million in 1976. Sectoral growth was anticipated to average 126 per cent during the 3-year period for the petrochemicals industry and 55 per cent in the building materials industry. The contribution of the oil sector was still projected at 96 per cent of the emirate's income by 1979, and no important investment was foreseen by the private sector, except in light industry. The labour requirement of the plan was estimated by the planning department of Abu Dhabi at some 183,000 additional workers. The allocations for development in the plan were to have risen by 10 per cent in 1977 to a total of $1,371 million with most of the funds devoted to three sectors: industry (25.5 per cent), public services (25.4 per cent), and construction and public buildings (20.7 per cent.)[14] Interestingly, the actuals in expenditures in the 3-year period (1977-9) showed a consistent expansion of development allocations in total budgeted expenditures. For example, in 1977

Table 2.3: Government of Abu Dhabi Development Expenditure, 1976-8 (in millions of Dh)

	1976 Actuals			1977 Actuals				1978 Actuals			
	Amount	Share (%)	IR[a]	Amount	Share (%)	Rate of Increase (%)	IR[a]	Amount	Share (%)	Rate of Increase (%)	IR[a]
Agriculture	39.3	1.0	20.9	55.5	1.5	41.2	46.7	87.9	1.7	58.4	73.6
Industry & Electricity	1,103.9	37.0	99.2	1,286.9	34.4	16.6	120.7	1,356.6	25.5	5.4	89.2
Housing	111.1	3.7	64.6	212.8	5.7	91.5	47.2	357.7	6.7	68.1	79.2
Communication	412.6	13.9	80.1	618.8	16.5	50.0	99.5	720.9	13.6	16.5	97.9
Municipality[b]	954.0	32.0	66.6	976.3	26.1	2.3	75.8	1,766.1	33.2	80.9	130.9
Health	32.0	1.1	13.6	50.9	1.4	59.1	59.3	98.8	1.9	94.1	122.3
Education	92.6	3.1	40.9	99.0	2.6	6.1	119.1	12.4	0.2	−698.4	37.8
Others[c]	245.2	8.2	39.4	440.3	11.8	79.6	41.5	913.7	17.2	107.5	123.9
Total	2,981.7	100.0	66.8	3,740.5	100.0	25.4	78.3	5,314.1	100.0	42.1	100.0

Source: UAE, Currency Board, *Bulletin*, December 1978, p. 49.
a. Implementation ratio.
b. Includes drainage.
c. Includes Social Affairs, Information and Tourism, Public Buildings, and Islamic Affairs Departments.

development expenditures in Abu Dhabi (defined to include equity participation, foreign aid, and transferable funds to the Abu Dhabi Investment Authority) were Dh 5,182.9 million or about one-third of total expenditures of Dh 16,595 million.[15] A breakdown of development expenditures from 1976 to 1978 is offered in Table 2.3.

Although Abu Dhabi's planners have advocated a federal development plan, the idea apparently did not receive immediate heavy backing on the grounds that such a plan could reduce the government's freedom to act according to circumstances.[16] However, as the 1980s opened, the federal Ministry of Planning had undertaken preparatory work on an economic year plan to commence in 1981. This first federal plan is envisaged as providing the framework for co-ordinated development throughout the emirates.

UAE Strategy for Development

The United Arab Emirates, like many other developing nations, must rely largely on a single-commodity export sector for capital to further its economic development programmes. In 1978, oil accounted for over 95 per cent of total exports. However, unlike other developing nations, the UAE is a capital-surplus economy. This position of capital surplus has not always been the case in the United Arab Emirates. Prior to oil discoveries, the emirates were among the poorest states in the world, yet the relatively young federation in the decade of the seventies has achieved a level of wealth unparalleled in its traditional history. By 1974, largely sparked by its increasing oil revenues, the UAE attained one of the highest *per capita* incomes in the world, boasted a surplus balance of payments (see Table 2.4), provided funding through several aid organizations to its poorer neighbours, and implemented numerous projects to expand and integrate the various sectors of the economy. Today, as seen in Table 2.5, its *per capita* GNP surpasses that of many industrialized nations.

Oil revenues, expenditures, and surpluses in recent years are displayed in Table 2.6. The rapid surge of oil output from established fields, coupled with the quadrupling of oil prices as well as the development of new fields are responsible for the leap in oil revenues. Indicators are that output from existing fields could grow further from current rates

Economic Development Policies

Table 2.4: UAE Balance of Payments, 1978-80 (in billions of Dh)

	1978	1979	1980[a]
Merchandise Trade	17.29	32.93	48.41[b]
Oil exports	33.33	52.06	72.91
Abu Dhabi	26.52	42.26	57.50
Dubai	6.60	9.60	15.01
Sharjah	0.21	0.20	0.40
Gas exports	0.51	0.63	1.30
Other exports and re-exports	4.22	6.76	9.70
Total exports and re-exports (fob)	38.06	59.45	83.91
Imports (cif)	−20.77	−26.53	−35.50
Abu Dhabi	−6.28	−7.70	−9.50
Dubai	−12.66	−16.68	−23.00
Sharjah	−1.83	−2.15	−3.00
Other current transactions and private capital	−11.54	−15.71	−23.71
Current account balance	5.75	17.22	24.70
Capital account balance (Official)	−1.44	−7.66	−10.20
Official grants and loans	−4.05	−6.41	−8.50
Official borrowing (net)	3.50	−0.70	−0.80
Official equity participation	−0.89	−0.55	−0.90
Overall balance	+4.31	+9.56	+14.50
Monetary movements	−4.31	−9.56	−14.50
Monetary institutions	−0.10	−0.90	
Governmental	4.31	−8.72	
IMF position	+0.10	+0.06	

Source: UAE, Currency Board, *Bulletin*, June 1980, p. 40.
a. Preliminary.
b. Oil exports estimated on daily average production of 1.712 million b/d (1.35 million b/d for Abu Dhabi, 350,000 b/d for Dubai, and 12,000 b/d for Sharjah); average price assumed of $33.47/barrel.

as the proven reserves in all of Abu Dhabi's fields are substantial. The only factors which may limit the rate of petroleum production are logistic bottlenecks, world demand, and production conservation policies. In fact, Abu Dhabi instituted a production ceiling of 1.45 million b/d which held in 1977 and 1978; that ceiling was further reduced to 1.375 million b/d for 1980.[17] For Dubai, oil revenues are comparatively not large and the oil industry will require greater utilization of expensive, secondary methods of recovery if it is to maintain

Table 2.5: *Per Capita* GNP of Selected Countries, 1977-8 (in Dh)[a]

	1977	1978
UAE	50,696	50,608
US	34,158	37,538
Japan	24,117	33,413
UK	17,078	18,307[b]
(West) Germany	32,420	39,900
France	27,843	29,460[b]
Italy	14,840	17,661

Source: UAE, Currency Board, *Bulletin*, June 1979; *MEED*, Special report, December 1979, p. 4.
a. Conversion from national currencies with UAE dirham made on the basis of cross-rates in relation to the dollar. The average 12-month market mid-rate was used.
b. Supplied by *MEED* on the basis of cross-rates of exchange for June 1978.

the present levels of production and revenues. Oil production has risen in Sharjah but now appears to have levelled off. In the mid-1970s the UAE's oil revenues were projected for 1980 at $10,400 million and forecast to reach $14,350 million by 1985.[18] These figures did not include the possibility of production starts in Ajman, Fujairah, Ras Al-Khaimah or Umm Al-Quwain. The projections to 1980 have proven quite close to the actual mark as of 1979; however, the 1979 and January 1980 price increases of more than 90 per cent in 12 months must necessarily make the 1980-5 forecasts fall far below actuals.

Whether or not the oil surpluses peak in the next five years or so, they will continue to provide additional funds for investment in the region and in international financial markets. At the same time the pronounced deficit in the non-oil trade activity exemplifies the Emirates' overwhelming dependence on imports for domestic consumption and investment. Imports have risen at an extremely rapid rate in the 1970s, mirroring again the UAE's growing affluence. The rate of import growth is expected eventually to slacken due to the accumulated stocks, sheer market size, and a move toward stricter controls over re-exports, which are at present a significant part of recorded imports. Budget constraints in conjunction with growing domestic production

Table 2.6: UAE Consolidated Accounts Showing Surpluses, 1972-9a (in millions of Dh)

	1972	1973	1974	1975	1976	1977	1978	1979b
Revenues	2,180.8	3,221.8	14,131.1	15,015.3	19,663.3	27,857.3	27,504.4	37,346.1
of which:								
Oil receiptsc	2,075.2	3,043.3	13,702.5	14,390.4	18,953.9	26,116.2	24,018.1	36,700.0
Expenditures	1,735.6	3,390.7	6,023.5	11,456.9	19,896.6	23,550.1	26,195.4	31,561.6
Current	1,274.4	2,512.8	4,667.3	6,505.8	9,497.2	12,598.1	13,387.3	18,078.7
Development	371.3	524.4	1,009.9	2,249.9	3,037.7	9,273.9	10,954.5	11,417.1
of which:								
Industry and Electricity	40.3	101.5	327.1	760.2	1,103.9	2,010.9	2,410.8	3,664.3
Communications	79.1	95.4	137.5	339.3	412.6	3,653.4	3,908.4	3,232.3
Housing and Public Buildings	35.9	50.8	96.2	217.1	352.0	1,815.7	2,018.3	1,349.5
Health and Education	25.4	60.0	152.2	165.6	124.6	429.7	293.8	387.3
Equity participation and capital paymentsd	90.0	353.5	1,236.3	2,701.2	7,361.7	1,678.1	1,853.6	2,065.8
Surplus (+) or deficit (—)	+445.2	−168.9	+7,207.6	+3,558.4	−233.2	+4,307.2	+1,309.0	+5,784.5

Sources: UAE, Currency Board, *Bulletin*, December 1978, p. 128, June 1979, p. 149, and June 1980, p. 145.
a. For the years 1972 to 1976, the statistics refer only to Abu Dhabi; for the years 1977 to 1979, the statistics include the federal government, Abu Dhabi, Dubai, Ras Al-Khaimah, and Sharjah accounts.
b. Estimates.
c. Royalties and tax (net income) to Abu Dhabi, Dubai, and Sharjah as application to 1972-6 and 1977-9.
d. Includes capital contributions in the form of participation, loans to foreign governments and other lending (net).

Economic Development Policies

of import substitutes are the primary forces which will signal smaller import increases in subsequent years. Imports in the mid-1980s were foreseen to grow at 10 per cent per year reaching $6 billion to $8 billion in 1985 as basic infrastructure requirements reach saturation and the implementation of industrial diversification projects begin to run smoothly. Table 2.6 indicates that imports were approaching the lower figure by 1979. These projections are most characteristic of the larger, developed emirates, while the smaller emirates would continue to pursue independent development efforts. As an overview then, imports to the UAE will most likely continue to rise, with the actual rate of growth hinging on many underlying factors, such as the timing of implementation of budgeted projects, expansion of port facilities to alleviate import bottlenecks, and the pace of surpluses and oil revenue increases. However, it is questionable if the massive annual growth rate in imports which characterized the middle of the 1970s will be repeated on the same scale.

Since almost all developing countries face stringent capital limitations, the trend in much economic literature has been to conclude that many problems could be simplified with sufficient capital. The experience of the UAE, Kuwait, Saudi Arabia, and Libya – all capital-surplus countries – has shown that capital can bridge the gaps in other production factors, but only temporarily and to a certain degree. A nation can purchase technological skills, labour, and entrepreneurial ability through expatriates until indigenous human resources can be developed, but this method evidently has its limitations. The vulnerability of a capital-surplus economy overwhelmingly dependent on the exploitation of a primary and wasting asset is inherent in (1) the eventual depletion of the physical resource and (2) the possibility of a drastic reduction in demand for the product. Since the oil-based capital-surplus countries are also basically single-product economies, the long-term objective of planning is to diversify the economy to reduce the reliance on one source of income or revenue.

The remaining economic life of oil reserves in the Middle East cannot be predicted with precision as it is dependent upon the level of production, prices, and competition from other sources of energy. Regardless of whether the reserves are sufficient for 15 or 100 years, there is an unquestionable end to the resource and hence, some definable limit to the present source of revenue. This not only reinforces the need for planning and development but for parameters to delineate the horizon of future revenues with which to finance the development. This is the dilemma the UAE must face today. If government revenues continue to mount and go unaccompanied over the years by investment in other self-generating and non-oil sectors, the final outcome could be a return to a much lower standard of living and severely restricted economic opportunities.

Agriculture

Development theory usually emphasizes the importance of agriculture as a sector in the process of economic growth. Agriculture, however, has always been of relatively minor importance to the emirates. Located in the subtropical arid zone, the sheikhdoms are characterized by great heat and high humidity. During the summer months rainfall is limited to sudden flash floods, and the majority of the UAE's soil is of a sandy desert nature. The inland oases, which have fertile soil as well as water suitable for irrigation, and the coastal areas are the major areas of agricultural importance. Agriculture in the federation is entirely dependent on underground water and desalinated water as there are no rivers or lakes in the UAE. Underground water is transported by a system of underground canals, known locally as *falaj*. These canals tap a water source in the hills or mountains, bringing water through gradually sloping tunnels to the farms, a distance of 20 miles or more. Many of the falaj systems are of considerable antiquity, and their constructors displayed great ingenuity and a high degree of technical expertise both in locating sources of underground water and in constructing the tunnels. Falaj are to be found in many parts of the federation, in the Al-Ain oasis, in Fujairah, Dubai, Sharjah, and Ajman.[19]

The UAE aims at developing its agricultural sector to provide its population with as many home-grown staples as possible. Crops most commonly cultivated include: dates, bananas, apricots, mangoes, pomegranates, guavas, Indian almonds, limes, bitter limes, sweet lemons, and other citrus fruits. Most of these crops are consumed locally with only small amounts being exported. Although the combined output of all fertile lands can only partially satisfy the needs of its people, numerous organizations are helping to provide the materials for intense concentration on mechanization and specialization. The application of modern technology to all stages of production is fostered by the

Economic Development Policies

Emirates' government, and technological assistance is being obtained from universities and agricultural centres in developed countries which are eager to meet the agricultural challenge.[20] In its effort to expand food output, the government faces two serious obstacles: the farmer's reluctance to abandon embedded traditional methods, and the need to settle the nomadic tribes in the agricultural regions so as to increase the manpower to work the land at maximum efficiency.

Ras Al-Khaimah has emerged as the leader in utilizing intensive agrarian research. This emirate is blessed with more suitable land and greater rainfall (6-8 inches per annum) than the other sheikhdoms. Topography allows for accumulation of large underground fresh-water deposits, and the amount of cultivated land is estimated to be 90 square miles or 15 per cent of the 600-square-mile sheikhdom.[21] Ras Al-Khaimah produces sufficient quantities of fruits and vegetables to feed not only itself, but also to contribute to the food requirements of its neighbours.

The potential of agricultural production in Ras Al-Khaimah was recognized in the mid-1950s with the initiation of the Agricultural Trials Station at Digdagga. The station, containing 400 acres of land under intense experimental cultivation, is an early example of the diversity of the contributions each emirate can make to welding the country together. An agricultural school, with day and boarding facilities, acts as a training centre for students from all over the UAE and other Arab countries. It follows a three-year course on theoretical and practical studies, providing the students with the necessary skills to stimulate local development. The trial station must be deemed a success as it has helped Ras Al-Khaimah to introduce a wide variety of truck-garden products which are of an intensive cultivation nature and destined for short-term consumption. The experiments proved that vegetables and fruits could be grown with remarkable success and could be highly profitable. These crops included: alfalfa, wheat, various grasses, tobacco, and such truck-garden products as melons, tomatoes, onions, cabbage, cauliflower, lettuce, beets, turnips, carrots, radishes, peppers, okra, pumpkins and gourds, beans, cantaloupe, eggplant, cucumber and sweet pepper. Experimental fruits receiving tests to upgrade yields or for suitability for cultivation were mango, Indian almonds, guava, figs, grapes, bananas, limes, oranges, lemons and grapefruit.[22] By 1980 fresh milk was being produced at Digdagga on a commercial basis along with a poultry farm, scheduled for early completion in that year, with a production capacity of 15 million to 16 million eggs annually, some earmarked for export to Oman.[23]

Ras Al-Khaimah, yet to find oil in commercial quantities, has become increasingly agriculturally oriented. The importance of this sector to the government is evidenced by its land-use policies. First, graduates of the experimental trial station's institute are offered land free of charge to start their own farms; secondly, anyone not holding land, but wishing to become a farmer, will be given four acres for development provided he undertakes improvements within five years. Free seed and farm equipment (such as pumps) are available, plus cash support for the first two years of the new farm's life. A 300-acre development unit at Mileiha, eventually designed for distribution to local farmers, has been developed to demonstrate modern irrigation methods.

An agricultural centre, similar to that in Ras Al-Khaimah, recently began operating in Abu Dhabi. Established in 1967 and using fertile land as a fulcrum, over 200 acres are devoted to intensively empirical farming.[24] The main purpose of the centre is to find the vegetable species best suited to the area's climate and soil conditions and the development of new farming techniques. Practical research is available to emirate farmers as well as suitable plant strains, free two-acre arable plots, and regular monetary grants. The Al-Ain scheme thus far has turned 1,200 acres into productive land.

At Sadiyat, not far from the capital city of Abu Dhabi, horticultural experiments are taking place aimed at providing an economic means of agricultural production in the desert environment. Plants are grown indoors with necessary water derived from the desalination plant.[25] The Arid Land Research Centre at Sadiyat is testing over 170 types of vegetables for possible commercial use. Designed and operated by the Environmental Research Laboratory experts from the University of Arizona, and now financed by the Abu Dhabi government, the centre parallels the highly successful operation at Puerto Penasco in Mexico. The year-round growing season combined with warm temperatures provides an atmosphere of high crop yields in comparison with conventional farming. At Sadiyat, one acre can produce 71 tons annually versus a conventionally farmed acre which could produce 31 tons. Half the acreage is covered by 48 air-supported semicircle cylinders of plastic devoted to low-growing crops such as cabbage, spinach, and beans. The remaining acres utilize steel-framed polythene-covered houses, for growing cucumbers and tomatoes. Power is supplied by three diesel engines with waste-heat recovery mufflers fitted to each engine and the excess energy supplying power to a 70,000-gallon a day seawater distillation plant. The government is considering other soilless culture schemes elsewhere in the sheikhdoms as a result of the success of the Arid Land Research Centre.

The agricultural products from the Centre were high priced at first and during the winter months could compete with crops from Europe rather than those of Ras Al-Khaimah and the inland oases. The project involved large initial capital outlays as well as high variable costs for water. None the less, the Arid Land Research Centre moved to bring costs and returns closer into line before the mid-1970s, increasing competitiveness with more traditional means of agricultural production.

On 16 April 1977, Abu Dhabi inaugurated its new Desert Development Station in the Sulaymat area in Al-Ain. The station, built by the Japanese Institute for Desert Development, will mainly produce vegetables and will be supervised in the first three years by the constructing company itself. The project consists of laying an asphalt coating at a depth of 18-18.5 ins below the land surface to counteract the extreme porosity of the sandy soil. Table 2.1 indicates levels of development-spending in this sector by Abu Dhabi. Agriculture's actual allocation and share in total development-budget expenditures have been rising.

In 1972 an experimental farm was open at Rowaya, Dubai. The farm is an area of 0.8 square miles designed primarily to attract the Bedouin away from pastoral pursuits to settled farming. Properly managed the 478 square yard plots are adequate for the average family and help to provide an excess over the settled farmer's requirements when marketed.

The UAE is one of 11 Arab states represented in the newly formed Arab Institute for Investment in Agricultural Development (AIIAD). The decision to establish the Institute was made at the annual meeting of the Governors of the Arab Fund for Economic and Social Development (AFESD) held in Rabat in April 1976. The Institute hopes to assist member states in achieving self-sufficiency in food production, with the immediate goal to create an Arab 'bread basket' which would reduce shortages and lessen dependence on the costlier food imports.[26]

Table 2.7: Distribution of Workers (10 years and over) by Economic Activity

Economic Activity	1975 Number	Per cent	1977 Number	Per cent
Agriculture and related activities	13,229	4.5	14,580	3.0
Construction and buildings	93,411	31.5	157,150	32.4
Mining, quarrying, and oil exploration	6,791	2.3	10,200	2.1
Wholesale and retail trade	37,524	12.7	74,690	15.4
Transport, storage and communications	23,383	7.9	52,350	10.8
Other activities	122,178	41.2	176,180	36.3
Total	296,516	100.1[a]	485,150	100.0

Source: UAE, Currency Board, *Bulletin*, December 1978, p. 160.
a. Total not 100 per cent due to rounding.

Goats predominate as a meat and milk source to the Emirates' populace and the experimental farm at Ras Al-Khaimah is moving with much success toward the development of cattle breeds able to survive local conditions. A veterinary clinic is available to the cattle farmers for advice on preventive medicine, disease treatment, and the need to keep herds in carefully controlled, penned compounds to minimize the risk of infection.[27]

In the area of forestation, over 1,700 acres have been planted along the Abu Dhabi-Al-Ain highway with similar plans foreseen for the Abu Dhabi-Dubai highway and other selected areas. Acacia and eucalyptus are two of the three types that seem to thrive best in the soil and available water conditions of the area; the Ministry of Agriculture is concentrating on a total of 14 varieties as the basis for the distribution of many hundreds of thousands of seedlings, suitable for planned local planting.

In summary then, agriculture provides profitable if limited employment and satisfies in part the need for various foodstuffs. The UAE, however, has never had an agricultural sector of great magnitude, and much work is being undertaken to increase the agricultural potential,

Economic Development Policies

particularly in areas such as the Liwa and Buraimi oases. With greater increases in population, agriculture, with its limited physical growth potential, will most likely only be able to develop as a local market activity and not as an economic base activity.[28] It is the base activities, moreover, which are mainly responsible for a rise in the real total income of the country. Nor will agriculture and its related activities, for example, fishing, become major employers of the labour force (Table 2.7).

Fishing

The sea has been a traditional source of wealth and employment for the sheikhdoms, via trade in plying its water, in pearling, in fishing, and even an element of piracy. At the opening of the nineteenth century the sheikhs of Sharjah and Ras Al-Khaimah had a navy of 163 large vessels, in more than 800 smaller craft, and some 19,000 sailors. The symbol or seal of the UAE exhibits a dhow, the unique and ancient Gulf-style boat, in the centre, indicating the importance of maritime activities throughout the years. Fishing is a source of income common to all of the Trucial Coast sheikhdoms. It has been estimated that nearly 17 per cent of the total population of the Emirates relies on the sea for livelihood.[29] From September until March fish are usually abundant in the Straits of Hormuz and the first 100 miles into the Gulf.

The Federal Ministry of Agriculture and Fisheries has put forth ambitious plans to develop a modern industry in the area. Fujairah and the enclaves belonging to Sharjah could possibly be established as a major fishing industry as they lie on the Gulf of Oman, which has much better fishing facilities than the Gulf proper. The possibilities of developing a well-based fishing industry are good for the area and should be considered in greater detail. At present, the fishing fleets existing throughout the federation include many types of craft, ranging from diesel ships of varying power up to 150 h.p. to very simple boats known as *shasha*, constructed from the stems of palm trees. The total capital value of the fishing fleets of Trucial Oman early in the 1970s has been estimated at only about $1.2 million.[30]

The United Nations Food and Agriculture Organization has conducted a basic survey of the Emirates. The report presents recommendations on necessary methods, storage facilities, berthing and unloading needs, processing possibilities, and other aspects of developing a modern fishing industry. The stationing of a fisheries research vessel at Khor Fakkan and the appointment of a Fisheries Adviser are other steps on the road to modernization. The completion of the road network linking the Emirates would ensure efficient transport communication, thus integrating the market of the nation for fish and other products. The United States-based consulting firm Arthur D. Little, Inc. submitted a report to the Abu Dhabi government in 1969 recommending the following: (1) The quality of shrimp in the territorial waters of Abu Dhabi (also applicable to other sheikhdoms) does not warrant commercial exploitation. If it were possible to use the Gulf of Oman for shrimp fishing, it might be commercially feasible.[31] (2) The abundance of other fish types in the Arabian Gulf warrants the establishment of a fishing industry. (3) The construction of fish factories to process fish should be encouraged. It could be financed either by direct investment or foreign loans.[32]

Another report by the International Bank for Reconstruction and Development, or World Bank, also points to the possibility of establishing a fishing industry in the United Arab Emirates. It found that in the nine Arabian Gulf principalities (the UAE plus Qatar and Bahrain), the annual catch is approximately 23,000 tons or 6.6 lbs per 2.47 acres. In other parts of the world the yield is much higher, 22-88 lbs per 2.47 acres. This suggests that, with more efficient fishing methods, the yields in the sheikhdoms' fishing industry could increase three to four times.[33]

As a conclusion, agriculture and fishing should be encouraged as they will diversify the economic base and provide profitable employment opportunity. In 1975, some 4.5 per cent (13,229) of the workers over 10 years of age in the UAE were employed in agricultural and related activities (Table 2.7). By 1977, the agriculture and fishing sector's share had fallen to 3 per cent (14,580 of a total of 485,150 workers).[34] The distribution among the Emirates and dates of creation of establishments involved in agriculture, forestry, hunting and fishing activities, are of some interest as they account for less than half of 1 per cent of the total establishments in the UAE. Three of the seven showed no establishments in this sector as of the opening of 1978: Ajman, Fujairah and Sharjah. Umm Al-Quwain's one such establishment came into being only in 1977, whereas Ras Al-Khaimah's 17 were all in existence prior to 1973. Dubai still has only one establishment in this classification of economic activity (created in the period up to 1972) while Abu

Economic Development Policies

Dhabi has shown the greatest expansion, having had three in existence prior to 1973, one added in 1974, three in 1975, and two each in the years 1976 and 1977.[35]

It is significant, however, to note again that agriculture will not be the key to the future development of the UAE as the more traditional growth model might suggest. It is in this light that the quandary of the Emirates is obvious: there is a need to find developing sectors which are not heavily dependent on oil for their livelihood, yet the traditional development model, which would suggest agriculture, will not completely solve the diversification problem.

Before developing any sectors, the UAE must take into consideration comparative advantage. That is to say, it must specialize in the production and export of those commodities requiring large amounts of productive factors in relatively abundant supply in the country, and to import from abroad those commodities requiring in their production large amounts of productive factors which domestically are in relatively scarce supply. From the previous analysis, it is obvious that the factors of production (land, labour, and management) are in relatively scarce supply when compared to capital. The UAE should, therefore, export those commodities which are capital intensive and import those which are land, labour, and perhaps management intensive. It should be noted that the above factoral ranking need not always maintain its present position; the large capital surplus, brought about by oil exportation, could be used to strengthen other sectors, which then may develop a position of comparative advantage.

Leading Sectors

It is clear that leading sectors must be developed in the Emirates, and it is likewise clear that Abu Dhabi and Dubai will continue to be the leading sheikhdoms in development owing to their sizable oil revenues, population bases, and historical roles. It should be noted, however, that Sharjah and Ras Al-Khaimah are beginning to assume a larger place in the UAE's economic life. Before any study of potential sector development can be undertaken, it is necessary to evaluate the resources which are available — physical, locational, and human.

A study by the consultant firm of Arthur D. Little on the economic future of the United Arab Emirates suggested the following points.[36] With respect to physical resources, there are four considerations: soil, water, hydrocarbons and minerals.

Throughout the region the sandy silt soil is high in potassium. Crop production has historically been limited to the Ras Al-Khaimah area and the inland soil has low water-holding capacity. The coastal regions have high concentrations of mineral salts, which limit their agricultural use to specific plants with salt tolerance such as mango and palm.

Because of the small amount of annual rainfall, fresh ground water for irrigation is very limited. To overcome this impairment, desalination plants are a must. As a part of its national development plan, Abu Dhabi's first desalination plant was built for a capacity of 8 million gallons of water per day.

Hydrocarbons, especially crude oil and natural gas, are the most plentiful and valuable natural resources. The development of these resources is providing not only domestic energy sources, but, more importantly, foreign exchange via international trade.

Other mineral resource development likely would be marginal in nature because of the geological setting of the United Arab Emirates. Nonetheless, mineral-resource development in the future may play a role in sustaining general economic growth, but will most likely not act as an economic base activity. This does not imply that mineral exploitation should be neglected, as there exists large and sufficient quantities of limestone, silica-bearing and colitic beach sands, gypsum, iron ore, concrete aggregate and salt. The potential of exploiting these for domestic use appears to be good, particularly as some would form the base for construction material.[37]

In locational resources, the UAE has a trading and mercantilist background of long standing and a geographical site near India, Pakistan, and southeast Asia. The Gulf region, however, is a considerable distance from Europe and the United States, the more advanced and affluent regions. As the Emirates continues its economic growth, protection may be needed for its infant industries. High transportation costs will help keep out many competitors in the domestic market, providing in turn some protection for the infant industries. But as the domestic industries grow in size, this could prove a deterrent. The narrowness of the domestic market, caused by a relatively small population, will make efficient, large-scale industries primarily export oriented. Transport costs could then be a factor mitigating against the Emirates. Development policy does recognize the locational advantage of the UAE as

Economic Development Policies

reflected, for example, in the expansion of Port Rashid in Dubai to permit the handling of the world's largest vessels; this allows the United Arab Emirates to be an originating port as well as a stopover point for large ships in transit.

As for human resources, the indigenous population of the UAE is relatively small with a limited degree of skilled labour. In the short run, importation of labour will have to fill the necessary development requirements. In the longer run, educational facilities will have functioned over a long enough period of time to have trained sufficient numbers of the Emirates' indigenous population. While formal education may have been at a low level in pre-oil years, the traditional commercial ability of people of the sheikhdoms should not be overlooked or under-estimated.

To effectively analyze the growth of the UAE, it is essential to determine the various sectors producing for the domestic market and for export. Since the population of the federation is limited, it will be necessary to promote domestic expansion of industries not requiring a substantial volume of output to attain a profit-maximizing position, such as cement and cinder-block factories. This situation will more than likely continue for a considerable length of time until the population increases substantially. There are four factors which will contribute significantly to the protection of the domestic industries: (1) availability of raw materials; (2) the unique requirements of the domestic market; (3) high transportation costs; and (4) the availability of relatively cheap energy sources.

Export industries must be chosen so as to allow high value and low cost. Because capital is abundant, it is evident that capital-intensive industries should initially be developed. Given the above constraints on economic activity, the UAE government's long-run development plans and priorities will be premised on the most effective utilization of existing resources. By looking at present and future planning and government policies, this development trend can be discerned.

Industry

Industry in the United Arab Emirates is estimated to contribute only 4 per cent to the GNP. Existing industry is generally small, employing manual or limited techniques to supply some needs of the domestic market. The recent upsurge of economic activity connected with the oil sector, however, has created a situation in which industry is given priority over other sectors. Two factors seem important in this regard: (1) Rising incomes and the enlarged market have stimulated entrepreneurial talents and industrial awareness. The prospects of economic and efficient industry have also improved as a result. (2) The lure of oil and prosperity has attracted foreign capital and expertise on a large scale. Businessmen and representatives of international firms in all fields are literally crowding the government and private offices throughout the country. The pace of the industrialization drive will be determined once the results of the extensive surveys that are being undertaken now, are known. The government is sponsoring these surveys in order to assess scientifically the country's potential and hence define the development strategy on a solid basis.

The first industrial survey was undertaken by the Arthur D. Little group in 1968. The results of the survey were submitted in 1970 and were being used by the Ministry of Oil and Industry to draw up industrial plans. In addition, an international consultant firm has recently completed a survey of the nation's minerals.

To back up the effort, the government has recently opened two vocational training centres; one in Abu Dhabi and the other in Sharjah. In addition, the government is presently sponsoring a training abroad programme for its nationals to acquire skills needed for the development programme.

The first 5-Year Plan for Abu Dhabi (1968-1972) allocated 20 per cent of its budget to industry (including water and power projects). In 1972 Dh 115,720 or 15 per cent of the annual allotment was allocated for industry.[38]

The major characteristics of the industrial policy of the UAE can be summarized as follows:[39]

Projects that utilize domestically available raw materials such as oil refineries and cement factories are to be financed by the government and given top priority.

Private-sector participation in industrial development is to be encouraged. For example, Abu Dhabi's Law No. 10 for the year 1971 specifies the many customs and tax exemptions that apply to the imports of needed tools, accessories and raw materials. The Law also provides for free industrial location.

Industrial projects requiring foreign markets for efficient operation

Economic Development Policies

are to be established only with foreign participation to ensure the international marketing outlets necessary.

Industries based on crude petroleum and natural gas are to be encouraged. Mere tax collection is to be reduced as the UAE increases its vertical control of the oil sector.

For example, the oil agreement concluded on 20 December 1972 and other subsequent agreements mandate the establishment of refineries and petrochemical industries in the country by foreign oil companies.

Government participation in the oil industry currently stands at 60 per cent. The Dubai Natural Gas Company (Dugas) is 80 per cent owned by the Dubai government. Abu Dhabi National Oil Company (ADNOC) formed a gas company, Abu Dhabi Gas Industries Company (GASCO) in 1978 in which it held a 68 per cent interest. ADNOC also owns, since 1977, 51 per cent of the Abu Dhabi Gas Liquefication Company. Ras Al-Khaimah holds 50 per cent interest in a consortium that is exploring for offshore gas and oil. (See Appendix II for details on the oil companies and affiliates operating in the UAE.)

The Arthur D. Little report mentioned above recommended two types of industries which occasionally overlap — (1) those of immediate value, and (2) those that depend on future economic policies. Under the first type, the report listed the following: the manufacturing of sulphur and construction material, the setting up of repair and mechanical workshops, and printing and stationery, all of which are considered important in meeting domestic needs and viable on economic grounds.

Abu Dhabi's sulphur and construction-material plant are prominent examples of the first type of immediate value industries. The sulphur project produces 35,000 tons of pure sulphur yearly and 40,000 tons of sulphuric acid daily. It supplies the sulphur needs of the country's desalination plants and reduces the amount of pollution of the air. The construction-material plant at Al-Ain in Abu Dhabi produces 230,000 tons of cement per year. The output of the Al-Ain quarry has been put to immediate use in Abu Dhabi City construction projects.

The second type of industry, which hinges upon future economic policies, is divided into two categories:

(1) Short-run projects — cement manufacturing, oil refining, tyre recapping, dry cleaning units and bakery units.

(2) Long-run projects — ice and refrigeration warehouses, lubricant oils recycling, flour mills and ammonia plants.

48 *Economic Development Policies*

The World Bank has also made a study of Abu Dhabi and recommended the establishment of several industries. The study is less detailed than Arthur D. Little's and divides the proposed projects into small, intermediate and export-oriented industries. The criteria used for categorization are: (1) availability of raw materials, (2) domestic needs and (3) efficiency in the allocation of the national effort.

The UAE is apparently benefiting from these studies. Current and planned construction projects the country has either already contracted for or opened to competitive bidding as tabulated in Tables 2.8, 2.9 and 2.10 are not dissimilar to those suggested by Little and/or the World Bank reports. Both short and long-run projects are listed. Reflected therein as well is a recognition of the availability of native raw materials and the most efficient allocation thereof in light of domestic requirements. Tables 2.8 and 2.9 list planned industrial projects in the emirate of Abu Dhabi, while Table 2.10 does the same for the other six emirates. The three tables reflect both the geographic distribution of the planned industrial projects as well as the current emphasis on the development of Abu Dhabi and Dubai – the most populous of the seven emirates.

The UAE's second plan (the first formal one) will emphasize several changes from the earlier 1968-72 plan. This new plan, encompassing 1981-5, is long term in its scope. Fundamental changes in the nature of the UAE (e.g. population which has increased from 180,000 in 1968 to 840,000 in 1977, and tremendous changes in oil revenues and the level of infrastructure) have necessitated reorientation. The infrastructure is almost in place. Decisions must be made which will determine what areas of the UAE will receive priority development. The increasing unification of the UAE requires a reassessment of the rich Emirates' obligation towards its members less well endowed with petroleum. The establishment of a central bank will enable a degree of unification unprecedented regarding monetary affairs. The rudiments of the long-term 1981-5 plan, as at mid-1980, had not been completed. However, the changes mentioned above were likely to be central concerns of the new plan.[40]

The three tables do not show the entire range of industrial planning in the UAE and merely serve to highlight the most up to date information available – the majority of which deals with Abu Dhabi. However, certain industrial sectors deserve separate mention here in recognition of their future value to the UAE and of the fact that the three tables

Table 2.8: Planned Industrial Projects for Ruwais Complex (Abu Dhabi)

Plant	Completion date	Capacity
Crude oil loading	Existing	1.28 million b/d
Natural gas liquids (NGL) — 1	1980	2.2 million tons/year
Ammonia-urea — 1 (Phase 1)	1981	1,000 tons/day ammonia
Ammonia — 11 (Phase 1)	1981	1,000 tons/day ammonia
NGL — 11	1981	2.8 million tons/year
Refinery — 1	1983	230,000 b/d
Ammonia-urea — 111	1983	1,000 tons/day ammonia
Iron-steel — 1	1983	1.1 million tons/year pellets
Petrochemicals — 1	1985	300,000 tons/year ethylene LDPE (low-density polyethylene)
Ammonia-urea — 1 (Phase 2)	1985	1,000 tons/day ammonia
Ammonia-urea — 11 (Phase 2)	1985	1,000 tons/day ammonia
Liquefied natural gas (LNG) — 1	1985	2.4 million tons/year
Condensate	1985	5.0 million tons/year
Refinery — 11	1986	230,000 b/d
Petrochemicals — 11	1986	665,000 tons/year LDPE/PVC (polyvinyl chloride)/caustic soda
LNG — 11	1990	2.4 million tons/year
Crude oil loading expansion[a]	1985	Addition 500,000 b/d
Iron-steel expansion[a]	1990	Convert all sponge iron to steel

Source: *Middle East Economic Digest*, Special report, December 1979, p. 26.
a. Among contingency plans for the industrial complex.

Table 2.9: Planned Industrial Projects in Abu Dhabi

Project	Cost ($ million)	Completion date	Planned capacity	Objective
ADNOC oil refinery	500	1983	230,000 b/d	Meet domestic requirements; export excess capacity.
Cement works	13.5		600 tons/day	Meet domestic requirements.
Flour mill	18		200 tons/day	Meet domestic requirements.
Flour mill and grain silo	26	1978	200 tons/day	Meet domestic requirements.
Petrochemical plant[a]			10,000 tons/yr PVC 15,400 tons/yr caustic soda 9,500 tons/yr dicalcium phosphate	Limited amount of LPG for domestic uses.
Fish meal and oil plants (2), Trawlers (6)	14.5			Modernize fishing fleet, expand processing capacity.
Liquefied natural gas	300		3 million tons/yr	Entire output to be exported.
Associated gas plants (3)	650	1980		Utilize gas which is currently flared off.
Fertilizer plant	580			Furnish urea and ammonia.
Sponge-iron plant[b]		1983		
Desalination plant[b]	53			
Power station	20		17-MW units (3)	Supply domestic requirements.

Table 2.9: Continued

Project	Cost ($ million)	Completion date	Planned capacity	Objective
Power station	1,500	mid-1980s	2,000 MW	Supply domestic requirements.
Desalination	19.7			Supply domestic requirements.
Crude oil export terminal	750		40,000 b/d	Export crude from Dalma, Satah and Jarnain fields from Dalma Island.
Airport Al-Ain	132	1981 +		Service Al-Ain.
Pipeline	48.2		99-mile pipeline	Transport water from Umm Al-Nar Island to Al-Ain.
Pumping stations and reservoirs	35.2			To facilitate flow of water along 99-mile pipeline.
Refinery extension		1983 +	60,000 b/d	Supply domestic requirements.
Polypropylene	6.8			
Television microwave network	8.1			Improved communications.
Desalination	14.8 – 16.9			To supply Abu Dhabi Marine Areas Operating Company offshore fields from Das Island.

Sources: *Middle East Economic Digest*, various issues; *Middle East Economic Survey*, 19 November 1979.
a. The French firm Compadec has obtained an unreported participation percentage.
b. Joint UAE-Indian project.

Table 2.10: Planned Industrial Projects in Other Emirates

Emirate	Project	Cost ($ million)	Completion date	Planned capacity	Objective
Dubai	Aluminium smelter	500	1979-80	20,000 tons/yr 135,000 tons/yr	80% of production to be exported, the remainder to meet domestic requirements.
Dubai	Aluminium extrusion plant	8.6		3,000 tons/yr	To be ancillary to the smelter project noted above.
Dubai	Desalination plant	85.5	1978 +	670,975 ft^3/day - 4,979,341 ft^3/day	Supply fresh water.
Dubai	Electrical station			400 MW	To power the smelter and desalination plants.
Dubai	LPG plant[a]	400			Export output.
Dubai	Cement works	26	1978	1,400 tons/day	Supply domestic requirements.
Ras Al-Khaimah	Cement works			200,000 tons/day	
Sharjah	Cement works				
Ajman	Power station expansion	14.8			To treble present capacity.
Dubai	Soda-ash plant	130	1980 +	150,000 tons/yr	Employment and to supply manufacturers and industries in area.
Fujairah	Cement works	92.9	1980 +	520,000 tons/yr	Domestic supply and export.
Umm Al-Quwain	Asbestos plant	21.9		40,000-50,000 tons/yr	Domestic supply and export.

Sources: *Middle East Economic Digest*, various issues; *Middle East Economic Survey*, 25 June 1979.
a. Sunningdale Oils of Canada has 20% participation.

provide little more than cursory and statistical information.

These sectors include:

Oil Refining and Petrochemical Plants. The ADNOC oil refinery listing in Table 2.9 clearly establishes the importance of this project in strictly monetary terms — a $500 million investment. In 1976 it began limited production (15,000 b/d of crude on the average in that year) and to supply a portion of domestic requirements.

In addition to the ADNOC refinery, Abu Dhabi has begun the construction of another petrochemical plant in a joint venture between its government and Compadec of France. Further exploitation of the petrochemical and refinery sector is virtually certain to continue given the investible surpluses accruing to the UAE and the salient characteristics of the petrochemical and refining industries, four of which are noted below:

(1) The highly capital-intensive nature of petrochemical and refinery operations.
(2) The advanced technological state of this industry which allows the UAE to establish modern and efficient plants with great rapidity.
(3) The increasing returns to scale available in the petrochemical industry, i.e. unit cost of production tends to decline as production increases.
(4) The profitability of the indirect products of petrochemical processing.[41]

Liquefied Natural Gas Projects and Gas Liquefaction Plants. Both utilize recently perfected technology and substantial amounts of capital to garner sizable profits from a petroleum product once designated waste and flared off at the well-head.[42]

The gas liquefaction plant currently produces for a market limited to the UAE and the other Gulf states while the major LNG plant in Abu Dhabi exports its entire annual output of 3 million tons to the Tokyo Electric Power Company, Inc. under terms of an exclusive 20-year contract.[43] Exports will soon increase substantially with the construction of two new LNG facilities. In Abu Dhabi, $650 million in contracts were let during the month of April 1977, for the construction of three associated gas plants at Ruwais — 100 miles west of Abu Dhabi City. At about the same time, Dubai entered into a joint venture (80-20 per cent) with Sunningdale Oils of Canada for the erection of a similar LPG facility in Dugas. As noted above, both plants will export their production.

Feasibility studies elsewhere in the UAE have disclosed extensive fields of natural gas. For example, four inland fields in Abu Dhabi are estimated to have reserves in excess of seven (US) trillion cubic feet. The exploitation by the UAE of the wealth represented by such a figure is likely to continue to accelerate and to provide an increasing portion of national income over the course of the next decades.

Tanker Companies. ADNOC recently purchased two oil tankers — the first the firm has owned. Should ADNOC choose to augment its fleet, the vertical take-over of oil production in the UAE by its government will have commenced in earnest in all phases of production and distribution.

Aluminium. The smelter under construction at Jebel Ali in Dubai by British Smelter Construction is likely to remain unique in the UAE. It will be managed by an American firm, the Southwire Company, and is co-owned by the Dubai Aluminium Company or Dubal (80 per cent), Southwire (7.5 per cent), Nissho-Iwai of Japan (7.5 per cent) and local interests (5 per cent). The first aluminium was poured in late 1979, and by mid-1981 the venture should be producing 135,000 tons per year. The smelter has spawned three ancillary industries which collectively represent an investment in excess of $100 million — an aluminium extrusion plant, a desalination plant, and a 400 MW power station. The contracts for the ancillary industries were split between British Smelter Construction and Southwire. Similarly, Southwire and Nissho-Iwai share the contract for marketing the estimated 80 per cent of the production which is destined for foreign consumption.

Cement Plants. In years past, the UAE imported all of its cement primarily from Kenya, Japan, West Germany and Belgium. When cement requirements reached in excess of one million tons in 1974, Pakistan, Egypt, Romania and the Philippines likewise began to export cement to the UAE.

Economic Development Policies

Since construction activity in the UAE will require increasing supplies of cement to maintain a growth rate that is among the world's highest, and since the UAE as a whole on the average demands 10 per cent of the product annually, the development of a native cement industry is considered advisable. As cement prices continue to rise rapidly due to worldwide shortages such a development plan, if feasible, appears to be imperative. The foundation for a domestic cement industry has already been effected in Abu Dhabi. Dubai, Ras Al-Khaimah, Sharjah and Fujairah also possess the necessary raw materials and have cement works planned or under construction. With an expanding market to exploit and a national goal of self-sufficiency in this commodity, cement production and the facilitation thereof is likely to remain one of the most important of the short-run industrial projects in the UAE.

Selected Domestic Industries. The UAE plan for self-sufficiency in certain areas of its economy includes a few other sectors worthy of note here. For example, flour mills recently constructed in Abu Dhabi will eventually be expanded to enable it to satisfy the domestic requirements of the entire UAE. Similarly, the construction of thermal insulation material-producing plants is presently under consideration due to the ready availability of raw materials for this oil-based industry and the burgeoning domestic demand for such products which reduce the costs of air conditioning. Since thermal insulation materials are typically low in value and high in volume and therefore extremely expensive to import, the establishment of such an industry will be most beneficial to the UAE and its economy.[44]

The need for specialized repair machine shops in the Emirates has recently been recognized by its government. The UAE became a member of the Arab Company for Shipbuilding and Repair which was initially capitalized in March 1972 at $100 million, this cost to be borne by the UAE and the six other OAPEC countries which comprise its membership. The intent of this co-operative enterprise is to minimize the heretofore high rate of machine failure, to maximize the generally low utilization rates and to extend the currently short life of machinery in the Gulf region. Other transportation facilitating ventures are also under consideration.

In another co-operative venture — this one with India — $580 million has been spent on the construction of two concerns. One, a fertilizer plant, will supply the UAE with domestically produced urea and ammonia in quantities sufficient to satiate the needs of the nation's agricultural enterprises. The other joint India–UAE facility will produce sponge-iron. Both plants will be located in the Emirates.

Four desalination plants are also under construction. Agriculture will be a prime beneficiary of the subsequent expansion of the freshwater supply. Some industrial ventures will either be expanded or founded upon the increased availability of domestic water. IHI of Japan holds the $53 million contract for the four nascent plants. Other desalination projects will follow unless a feasible alternative source of fresh water is discovered.

The relative abundance of information on the development plans and planning of Abu Dhabi has precluded more than a cursory mention of the other six emirates and their complementary endeavours. These endeavours are not dissimilar in their approaches to development as they too emphasize the same petrochemical and refining, cement and construction material industries which have proved to be the staples of the Abu Dhabi plans as well.

However, because Dubai has the second largest population of the seven emirates and a concomitantly greater human resources base, its development planning encompasses more and diverse industrial projects than those of the five less populous emirates. In monetary terms, Dubai ranks behind only Abu Dhabi in importance with the Dubai government estimating the value of projects in the construction or planning stage as of 1976 at Dh 11.228 million (or $2.848 million). Table 2.11 apportions this total among the 13 major projects officially sanctioned by Dubai at that time.

Among the projects listed the dry dock is perhaps the most important. When completed the newly expanded facility will accommodate up to eight supertankers as well as ships of one million tons or less. This port expansion will cost the Dubai government £91 million sterling and will be discussed at greater length in the economic infrastructure section of this volume. The airport expansion, hospital construction and extension, and Port Rashid ventures also listed in Table 2.11 are infrastructural in nature as well and will be covered later in similar fashion.

The other entries in Table 2.11 — natural gas, aluminium and (by

Economic Development Policies

Table 2.11: Dubai Development Expenditure for Planned Projects and Projects Under Construction (in millions of Dh)

Project	Value
Natural gas project and petroleum refinery	2,600
Aluminium smelter	2,400
Steel plant	1,400
Drydock	1,320
Extension to Port Rashid	1,000
Expansion of Dubai International Airport	800
Dubai International Trade Centre	600
New 600-bed hospital	500
Dredging and reclamation of Dubai creek	300
Water and electricity supply	120
Extension of Rashid Hospital	120
Housing schemes	50
Bridges	10
Total	11,220

Source: *Middle East Economic Digest*, 14 May 1976, p. 34.

inference) steel — have been dealt with previously in the paragraphs devoted to the seven major industrial project types currently favoured by the United Arab Emirate planners. The National Cement and Asbestos Company (which operates in other Gulf states as well) is of this type as is the planned expansion of its facilities through the construction of a plant capable of producing up to 500,000 tons of cement annually. Smaller-scale construction-material plants already manufacture a variety of building items ranging from bricks and waffles (corrugated moulds of concrete) to asbestos and fibreglass pipes. Other manufacturers of water tanks, detergents, metal furniture and even 'Kleenex' tissues have recently commenced production as have enterprises which serve the interests of conservation as well as those of the UAE by recycling scrap metal and aluminium. The projections for the immediate term call for similar small-scale manufacturing ventures and for the establishment of a free-trade zone and an industrial city. The latter is to be located at Jebel Ali, a previously virtually unpopulated tract about 17 miles from

Dubai City. The industrial city will function as a free zone for both industry and labour as foreign workers from Arab and Asian countries will be allowed to enter the designated area without a visa. However, these workers will not be allowed to leave the zone without a contract for employment elsewhere in the federation. A steel plant, aluminium smelter, oil refinery, LPG plant, fertilizer factory, and a cable-manufacturing plant are examples of projects already planned for the site.[45] In contrast to the industrial city, the free-trade zone will allow the participation of both foreign labour and expertise and of foreign capital. All will enhance to a greater or lesser extent the economic prospects of the state of Dubai and those of the United Arab Emirates as well.

The other five emirates in the federation have drafted relatively modest but similar plans for industrial development. All tend to follow the Abu Dhabi/Dubai pattern within the parameters of resource availability, efficiency in the allocation thereof, and contribution to the national welfare. Sharjah, for example, plans to set up an oil refinery and a sodium chloride and sulphuric acid plant. It has established several oil-based industries, owned by the National Industrial Corporation of Sharjah, within the past few years, their foundation attributable to the growth of the local petrochemical industry and the consequent greater availability of raw materials. Some of these new ventures have already commenced production including a rope factory which manufactures 80-mm ropes. A plastics factory producing door and window frames has likewise drawn from the same resource pool and recently began to cater to the domestic market for such products. Many of the new industrial ventures will be acquired by Sharjah's $76 million Industrial Investment Company. This company will also engage in the acquisition or establishment of other industries manufacturing basic and finished products.

Ras Al-Khaimah and Ajman with even fewer resources at their disposal have drawn up less ambitious plans more suited to their needs. In Ras Al-Khaimah the central government has initiated the construction of a cement project capable of producing 200,000 tons per year. Ajman, famous for its fine marbles, plans to enlarge its marble manufacturing plant. Other activities of this more modest scale and scope are now being drafted by the two respective emirates.

A new federal law has been proposed that would require every new industrial scheme of any type or size to obtain a federal licence before it can be implemented. The main objective of the law is to ensure that new schemes serve the interests of the federation as a whole rather than only those of an individual emirate. The law would also prevent unnecessary duplication of industrial projects within the federation.

A similar, non-legislative, co-ordinating proposal for the entire Gulf region has been approved by Industrial Ministers from Iraq, Saudi Arabia, Bahrain, Oman, Kuwait, Qatar and the UAE. The ministers met in Doha to establish the Arabian Gulf Organization for Industrial Consultancy. This organization encourages co-ordination between the states of the Arabian Gulf in their respective plans for economic/industrial development. Here again the intent was to avoid unnecessary duplication of projects. The organization will also review industrial development projects and provide technical assistance in the preparation and evaluation of such schemes. An anticipated ancillary benefit will eventually accrue from the formation of this Arab Gulf Organization in the form of reduced dependence on foreign consultancy companies.

The UAE also participates in another multinational planning organization — the Arab Industrial Investment Company (AIIC). Originally founded by Iraq and Egypt in November 1974 to co-ordinate production of tractors, trucks, buses, cars, and other vehicles, the AIIC now includes Qatar, Syria, Saudi Arabia, Kuwait, Jordan, and UAE as well. The $500-million organization, based in Baghdad since its establishment primarily exists to promote complementarity in the Arab motor industry.[46]

Impediments to Industrial Development

Manpower and Skills. The majority of developing countries are confronted with a shortage of skilled manpower alone and not of labour itself. However, in the Gulf states the labour problem assumes quantitative as well as qualitative dimensions. Native Gulf-state labour is scarce and will remain so as long as the region as a whole is under-populated relative to any ambitious industrial programme. Also, the industrially skilled workforce upon which such a programme must rely is virtually non-existent.

The active promotion of capital-intensive industries may ameliorate to some extent the quantitative shortage of (unskilled) labour, but will certainly exacerbate the shortage of skilled workers so necessary to the efficient operation of such industries. Clearly the encouragement of skill or capital-intensive enterprises will rectify the labour imbalance only in the long run.

In the short run the adoption of a liberal immigration policy is a feasible, if partial, solution to the labour shortage. Various states in the Gulf, including the UAE, have already chosen such a policy and are prepared to confront the risks it entails to the small indigenous populations. This influx of foreign workers has and will continue to encounter political and social constraints which will eventually place limits on immigration and diminish its effectiveness in this regard.

The openings of two vocational training centres in Abu Dhabi and Sharjah are recent manifestations of a more visionary, again albeit partial, solution to the labour shortage – specifically the skilled labour shortage – which relies on the efficacy of education and technical training. To effect this educational revolution the government of the United Arab Emirates has implemented an ambitious educational and technical programme which provides its citizenry with a system of primary and secondary schools, and support to those who seek to acquire skills and education abroad. The UAE has entered into co-operative agreements with several other countries which provide its nationals with further exposure to necessary skills and expertise. (See Appendix II – Special Educational Programmes.)

Transportation and Logistics. Rapid development in the Gulf is also hindered by inadequate or antiquated transportation facilities. The traditional and virtual absence of major roads or adequate ports is a consequence of both the desert nature of the terrain and the clustering pattern of the population. Facilities necessary to high-volume, world-wide trade such as storage, handling and refrigeration were not so necessary as recently as a generation ago. An impressive installation is the cold-store terminal operated by Intergulf Cold Storage Services, supplying three controlled temperature chambers totalling 630,000 cubic feet of storage and a 144,000 cubic foot air lock. This infra-structural shortfall has locked the country and its development drive in the midst of an acute logistical snarl. In the Gulf and the UAE in particular, the bottleneck remains despite determined efforts to ameliorate the situation. In Abu Dhabi and Dubai, roads and seaport enlargement and construction and international, modern and large airports

Economic Development Policies

continue to expand. This activity will eventually culminate in an advanced road and telecommunications network as well as larger and more servicable harbours. However, the immediate logistical problems of the UAE will remain due to the not inconsiderable lag between effort and effect which is necessarily involved in constructing an efficient distribution system virtually from scratch.

The Size of the Market. The size of a market is usually determined by three statistical indices — the nation's population, *per capita* income and ability to export or to otherwise supplement the domestic market. The UAE is fortunate with regard to the latter two indices as it possesses one of the world's highest *per capita* incomes and an essentially unhindered export capability with regard to its greatest resource — oil. None the less, the force of numbers, or more correctly the absence thereof, of native citizenry restricts to an inordinate degree the market upon which the nation can depend and develop. The nature of the economy is such that the types of industries suitable to the economy require population bases nearly six times that which is presently indigenous to the former Trucial States. For example, the capital-intensive petrochemical industry generally requires a population base of approximately three million to justify the construction of efficient plants which take full advantage of economies of scale. Clearly, the UAE must seek to augment the markets available to it either through more liberal immigration or export policies. Both policies require long-range planning and co-ordination with both domestic realities and those of affected foreign nations or nationals.

Notes

1. K.G. Fenelon, *The Trucial States* (London: Longman Publishers, 1973), p. 29; also his book *The United Arab Emirates: An Economic and Social Survey* (London: Longman Group Ltd, 1973), Chapter 7.
2. Fenelon, *Trucial States* pp. 30-1.
3. Ibid., p. 31; Donald Hawley, *The Trucial States* (London: George Allen and Unwin Ltd, 1971), pp. 105-6, discusses the gold trade.
4. Hawley, *Trucial States*, p. 205.
5. Ibid., p. 229. The £ = $2.80 at that time.
6. Fenelon, *Trucial States*, pp. 144-6. The Bahraini Dinar (BD) was adopted in 1966 by the Trucial States, only to be dropped in 1973 for the dirham (Dh), valued then at 0.25Dh = $1.00.

7. Ibid., p. 146. The actual distribution of the 1969 capital expenditures of the Trucial States Council was: (in BD 000's) Inter-State Projects 689.0, Sharjah 325.0, Ajman 79.0, Umm Al-Quwain 118.0, Ras Al-Khaimah 289.0, Fujairah 330.0, and Dubai 10.5. The total allocations were 1,843.5.

8. Ragaei El Mallakh 'Challenge of Affluence: Abu Dhabi', *The Middle East Journal*, spring 1979, p. 144.

9. Ibid., p. 145.

10. *Middle East Economic Digest, Special report*, December 1979, p. 9 (hereafter *Middle East Economic Digest* will be cited as *MEED*.)

11. *Middle East Economic Survey*, 11 December 1979, p. IV. (Hereafter *Middle East Economic Survey* will be cited as *MEES*.)

12. Ibid., pp. 1, 3.

13. *MEED*, 4 June 1976, p. 27.

14. *MEES*, 17 January 1977.

15. United Arab Emirates (UAE), Currency Board, *Bulletin*, December 1978, p. viii. Development expenditures, excluding equity participation, foreign aid, and investment fund transfers, were budgeted at Dh 6,900 million and Dh 7,453 million for 1978 and 1979, respectively. Ibid., June 1980, p. 147.

16. *MEED*, 22 April 1977, p. 40.

17. *MEES*, 19 November 1979, p. 3.

18. Henley Centre for Forecasting, *Middle East Prospects: Forecasts to 1985* (London, 1975).

19. Fenelon, *United Arab Emirates*, pp. 51-2.

20. United Arab Emirates, Ministry of Information, *United Arab Emirates, Third Anniversary*, 2 December 1974, p. 2.

21. *Ras Al-Khaimah* (Beirut: Middle East Media, 1971).

22. Fenelon, *Trucial States*, p. 239.

23. *MEED*, Special Report, December 1979, p. 62.

24. *United Arab Emirates, Third Anniversary*, p. 24.

25. *The Times* (London), 21 December 1971. The project, initially funded by the Abu Dhabi government and the Rockefeller Foundation, has been under the direction of a team from the University of Arizona.

26. *MEED*, 14 May 1976, p. 15.

27. *United Arab Emirates, Third Anniversary*, p. 25.

28. An economic base activity may be defined as:

$$\frac{\text{total employees in the particular industry}}{\text{total UAE population}} = \frac{\text{total number of world employees in the industry}}{\text{world population}}$$

29. Fenelon, *Trucial States*, p. 35. A variety of fish inhabit the Gulf, the most abundant being kingfish, rock-cod, snapper, tuna, crayfish, and Red Sea bream. The coastal waters of the Gulf of Oman have an unusual abundance of tuna, Spanish mackerel, bonito, jacks, snailfish, amrin, sardines, and anchovy.

30. Ibid., p. 36.

31. Two sheikhdoms, Fujairah and the enclaves of Sharjah, face the Gulf of Oman and are, therefore, the most probable shrimp industry sites, if and when such a venture is promoted.

32. Mana Saeed al-Otaiba, *The Economy of Abu Dhabi, Ancient and Modern* (Beirut: Commercial and Industrial Press, 1971), pp. 40-4. The author is Minister of Petroleum and Mineral Resources of the UAE.

33. Ibid., p. 45.

Economic Development Policies

34. UAE, Currency Board, *Bulletin*, December 1978, p. 160.

35. Ibid., pp. 161-2. The definition used for an establishment is that one or more than one building fully devoted to (1) one economic activity, e.g. industry, transport, etc., (2) rendering services, e.g. medical, social, etc., (3) run at least by one person, (4) run for profit or non-profit purposes, (5) owned by one proprietor, e.g. government, company, more than one individual. Excluded were foreign embassies, regional and international organizations' offices in UAE, and all establishments with military barracks, stores, and animal and poultry sheds.

36. Adapted from Arthur D. Little Company, *Industrial Development Opportunities for Abu Dhabi: Final Report*.

37. A mineral study under the auspices of the United Nations Industrial Development Organization located deposits of bauxite, iron, copper, and uranium; whether these resources are sufficient to allow for feasible commercial development remains in question.

38. If water and power projects are excluded, the percentage will be only 5.8. Such a low percentage is a result of the fact that the bulk of funds is allocated for the various surveys and studies that are being undertaken.

39. United Arab Emirates, Ministry of Finance, *Industry and Plans of Industrial Development in UAE*, a paper presented to the Third Arab Industrial Development Conference, held in Tripoli, Libya, in April 1974, pp. 13-14. (In Arabic.)

40. Anthony McDermott, 'United Arab Emirates', *Financial Times*, 23 June 1980, p. 3.

41. Ragaei El Mallakh, *Economic Development and Regional Cooperation: Kuwait* (Chicago: The University of Chicago Press, 1968), p. 113.

42. A related industry with development potential is gas bottling. The feasibility of a UAE bottling plant is enhanced by three factors. (1) Facilities already exist in the Abu Dhabi Shames field for the removal of gas liquids. (2) The Abu Dhabi government, through oil company concession agreements, is able to obtain the gas at production cost, which is near zero – the primary input can thus be obtained at a cost which is lower than most world market prices, a significant competitive edge. (3) The importation of gas cylinders presently used widely for domestic and commercial purposes is expensive. Significant reductions in related transportation costs would ensue if a domestic manufacturing facility was established. Currently, the bulky cylinders are imported from abroad, their costs inflated further by transportation charges which would be obviated if the items were produced locally.

43. The project was undertaken by the Abu Dhabi Gas Liquefaction Company Ltd. The Company is made up of the British Petroleum Company (26-2/3% share), Compagnie Française des Petroles (13-1/3% share), Mitsui and Company (36%), Bridgetsone Liquefied Gas Company, (4%) and the Abu Dhabi National Oil Company (20% share).

44. Little, *Industrial Development Opportunities*, p. 40.

45. *MEED*, 18 June 1976, p. 34.

46. *MEED*, 12 March 1976, pp. 8-9, 23 April 1976, p. 11 and 4 June 1976, p. 25.

3 SOCIAL INFRASTRUCTURE

Education

Until recently the poverty of the UAE was so pervasive that the establishment of a formal, compulsory educational system was virtually inconceivable. Indeed, not until 1953 was there a modern school in the UAE. The marginal status of education in the former Trucial Sheikhdom was accurately reflected in the illiteracy rate which was then well in excess of 90 per cent.[1] Now that education has become one of the more important items in the Emirates' budget, the capital outlays for educational facilities are overcoming the problem of illiteracy. However, educational progress has been understandably and necessarily slow because of the time lag involved in putting a student through primary and secondary schools. And as is clear from Table 3.1, the UAE has a youthful population, both the indigenous, which accounts for the largest proportion of those of 14 years of age and younger, and the expatriate grouping, which obviously swells the ranks of those in the prime working age of 15 to 44 years. Moreover, those in the older age brackets who often require more health care are UAE nationals, since the labour permits restrict residence in the Emirates for expatriates only while employed.

Historically, Kuwait has provided funding for educational facilities and for many essential requirements (desks, books, sometimes operating expenses) in the Emirates with the exception of Abu Dhabi. Teacher trainees from the Emirates were sent abroad for technical training by the Government of Kuwait. Kuwaiti aid has been so effective that educational facilities were considerably increased.

Rapid improvement of human capital is a crucial element in the development process. The long-held notion that capital is the engine of growth has given way to the idea that investment in education and training — both formal and informal — is also a precondition for successful development. Consequently, from the formation of the federation until 1978, education was consistently the highest budgeted

Social Infrastructure

Table 3.1: Estimated Population by Age-Group and Sex, Beginning of 1979

Age group	Male	Female	Total	Per cent
0–4	52,150	49,950	102,100	11.64
5–9	39,360	36,710	76,070	8.67
10–14	32,490	26,450	58,940	6.72
15–24	131,640	47,340	178,980	20.40
25–34	197,230	44,730	241,960	27.57
35–44	103,270	23,760	127,030	14.48
45–54	42,370	13,410	55,780	6.36
55–64	14,270	8,080	22,350	2.55
65–74	5,990	4,370	10,360	1.18
75–84	1,870	1,460	3,330	0.38
85+	230	210	440	0.05
Total	620,870	256,470	877,340	100.00

Source: UAE, Currency Board, *Bulletin*, December 1978, p. 158.

expenditure item in the development plans, next to defence. The 1978 UAE federal budget allocated more than Dh 1,304 million to the Ministry of Education and Youth: a ninefold increase over the amount budgeted in 1975 and nearly 50 times the 1972 expenditure on education.[2] In 1979, Dh 864 million was actually spent by the Ministry of Education and Youth, while the 1980 allocation in the federal budget for that Ministry reached Dh 1,388 million.[3] Of the 1980 figure, about 78 per cent is for current expenditures of the Ministry with the remainder earmarked for development projects, i.e. new facilities, equipment, and the like. More than 96,000 students were enrolled in 370 educational institutions in the UAE in 1980. Such fundamental changes have led the ruler of Ras Al-Khaimah to state that 'the advances in education have been the most important achievement of the Union.'[4]

Abu Dhabi had proceeded on its own path of educational development since the inflow of oil revenues negated the necessity of Kuwaiti aid. Since the accession of Sheikh Zayid Ibn Sultan in 1966, educational development has received high priority.

Educational facilities were greatly improved and increased with the implementation of the First Abu Dhabi Development Plan which allocated Dh 12.14 million ($30.35 million) for the period of 1968 to 1972. In 1966, Abu Dhabi had only five elementary schools — four schools for boys and one for girls — with a total enrolment of 528 students. By 1972-3, the number of schools had increased to 30 with a total enrolment of 13,916. Another 200 students were abroad for special educational training. Fifty-one schools were constructed in 1972 at a cost of Dh 6 million. By 1974 total school enrolment had reached 42,137. Approximately 30 per cent of total enrolment was female, which should be a factor in increasing future female participation in the labour force.

New and developing sectors of the economy require technically trained personnel. The UAE still relies on expatriate labour for skilled (especially technical) positions in all aspects of economic activity. It is thus that the establishment of a university in the UAE can be regarded as one of the most significant developments in the federation. With the establishment of the university at Al-Ain, which emphasizes the training of UAE nationals in all aspects of the oil industry, the Emirates hope to avoid manpower bottlenecks that might occur in the future should the pool of expatriate labour dry up or be drastically reduced. The Trucial States Development Fund, founded in 1967, was established with the objective of reducing the public service reliance on foreign experts by providing overseas training for nationals. With increased educational facilities, nationals are expected to have a larger role in the market for skilled labour.

Consequently, all levels of education are being expanded and teachers have been sent to work with the Bedouin desert tribes. However, despite financial incentives, few students attend vocational training centres after completing secondary education. Instead, after graduation most choose to enter business which is more lucrative.

Adult education has been successful. At present there are 11,000 UAE nationals learning to read and write at evening classes. This is significant to the extent that it compensates for the high dropout rate after secondary education as well as offering literacy training to older citizens who did not have access to formal education in past years.

By 1977 approximately 2,000 UAE nationals were, with the aid of UNESCO, enrolled in foreign universities; more than one-quarter of these students received their advanced education in the United States.[5] UAE students studying abroad are provided with generous scholarships from the government.

The university at Al-Ain promises to help foster the attainment of UAE educational goals. For the 1979/80 academic year, 1,000 students were studying at the university. Located in the Abu Dhabi emirate, the institution is open to students from other emirates as well as to expatriate Arab students and Palestinians.

Technical education has not developed at a rate consistent with development needs. Since technical institutions were first established in the Emirates in 1972 with an enrolment of 258, the enrolment did not reach this level during subsequent years. Indeed, in 1977 only 170 students were enrolled in technical establishments in the UAE. The number of students taking agricultural disciplines fell from 40 in 1972 to 8 in 1977. This state of affairs in technical education is repeated in all other vocational fields of education. These declines in enrolment in technical and vocational schools in the UAE are unfortunate since middle-level manpower is indispensable for industrialization and for the expansion of the absorptive capacity of the Emirates. Recently the federal government has directed greater efforts and funds to this critical sector of education.

The majority of teachers in the UAE are Egyptians. Through these educators, Egypt has supported education in the Gulf for over half a century.[6] The number of school teachers in the federation was about 5,500 in 1979 (out of which only 361 were UAE nationals). This is an increase of 650 teachers over the previous year and is to cope with the rise in the number of students, partially due to the influx of families escaping the civil conflict in Lebanon. The UAE hopes to attract 7,000 teachers by the early 1980s.[7] Both Egypt and the Gulf countries see such an exchange of factors of production as mutually beneficial. Despite efforts to train more UAE teachers, Egyptian teachers will continue to have a place in UAE's educational development. Perhaps the most difficult task facing the educational authorities in the UAE is to 'produce students qualified to run a rapidly changing society without sacrificing traditional values.'[8]

Health

Along with education, health services are considered a fundamental means of upgrading and developing human resources in the federation. Prior to the oil boom, health facilities were nearly non-existent in the UAE. The Trucial States Council Capital Works Programme initially allotted Dh 345,350 to establish health centres. Most of the early financing for Trucial sheikhdoms' health facilities, however, came as aid through Kuwait's specialized economic assistance agency for the Gulf, known later as the General Authority for the South and Arabian Gulf States.

Abu Dhabi and Egypt reached an agreement whereby Egypt supplied the former with all the medical requirements for its health services, including equipment, medicines and surgical instruments, experts to run hospitals, and medical advisers. Patients from Abu Dhabi who could not be treated locally were sent to Egyptian hospitals. Special women's wards in Al Maktoum Hospital, a clinic and maternity ward in Umm Al-Quwain, and clinics in Fujairah and Ras Al-Khaimah were built. In addition, Abu Dhabi's first 5-Year Development Plan allocated Dh 6,510 million to health services and facilities, a relatively substantial amount which greatly improved the quality of health facilities.

Thus Abu Dhabi has shown signs of catching up with Dubai, which has long been the leading health centre in the UAE. In 1980 Dubai was forging ahead to complete a $60.7 million, 325-bed maternity and pediatric hospital. This will be additional to the existing 120-bed Corniche maternity hospital which began operation in February 1977. The Corniche maternity unit is managed by the United Kingdom Allied Medical Group and delivers an average of 6,500 babies annually, reflecting the high birth-rate.

The provision of quality health care is viewed by the government of the UAE as serving a number of goals. It is an effective means of enhancing the welfare of the population. Better health conditions, like education and training, upgrade the quality of the labour force, thereby increasing the indigenous supply of workers needed for the development process. And comprehensive, free health care for UAE citizens is, in a sense, a positive distributive measure, a method whereby oil-generated revenues accruing to the government can be disseminated to the population. The manner in which a government moves to distribute

Social Infrastructure

wealth and income can have serious side effects: for example, direct subsidies to citizenry as contrasted to social infrastructure investment, among other results, can cause a diminution of the relationship between effort and economic reward.

Given the burst of hospital and health facility construction of recent years, it comes as no surprise that the lion's share of the 1980 UAE federal budget allocation to the Ministry of Health of Dh 1,314.7 million (over 80 per cent) went to current expenditures. New projects accounted for less than 20 per cent of the 1980 federal health allocation. Yet it is critical to note that of the total development expenditures (as contrasted to current) in the 1980 federal budget, health ranked fourth with 12.7 per cent, after the Ministries of Public Works and Housing (18.5 per cent), Education and Youth (16 per cent), and Electricity and Water (12.8 per cent).[9] In short, social infrastructure, including health, continues to dominate development expenditure priorities in the UAE.

The provision of health services is now rather extensive. Hospitals are located in every major urban area and clinics in the smaller towns and rural areas. The federation provides complete coverage of medical care within the UAE for every citizen, free of charge. Treatment for patients referred to foreign hospitals is paid for by the federal government.

One of the largest projects is a 520-bed hospital at Mafraq, located about 25 miles from Abu Dhabi. It is being built especially for the presidential court at an estimated cost of Dh 262 million ($71 million). Facilities include equipment for radio-therapy, nuclear medicine, traumatology, and animal research. The animal-research facilities will be unique in the entire Middle East. The staff of the hospital could number as many as 1,500. The Mafraq would, in part, claim some of the overload from the central hospital at Abu Dhabi. When finished, it will be one of the best-furnished facilities in the region.

A proposed 200-bed hospital at Fujairah will help fill the health-care gap on the east coast of the UAE. The hospital will cost an estimated Dh 150 million ($40.5 million).

Originally the federal government had planned to provide a 500-bed hospital at Sharjah. However, these plans were reduced to a 320-bed hospital. The 1980 budget provided for more spending on hospitals in other areas as well. These projects include: (1) a 150-bed Saif

Ibn-Ghobash hospital in Ras Al-Khaimah; (2) completion of the second and third phases of the Kuwaiti hospital at Dubai (350 beds); (3) a 320-bed hospital at Umm al-Quwain; and (4) the completion in Jumairah, outside Dubai, of a 100-bed psychiatric hospital.

Authority over hospital care is somewhat diffuse in the UAE. Besides the Federal Ministry of Health, at least three groups of government authorities have taken responsibility for the provision of hospitals. As already mentioned, the presidential court has taken the initiative to establish the hospital at Mafraq. The defence system controls its own hospitals. And the government of Dubai has a hand in hospital provision.

Two examples reflect the Dubai government's role in this area. It is supervising a contract given to a hospital management company from the United Kingdom for the Corniche maternity hospital. The other example of Dubai's activity in hospital care is its projected $67-million hospital at Zabeel East. When complete, this hospital will have 324 beds and will emphasize maternity and pediatric care.

Emirates-wide integration of health care in the UAE has yet to be realized. The expanding private health-care facilities require integrative attention. In Sharjah, a former hotel will soon be converted to a 100-bed private hospital. And some businessmen have considered the possibility of a private hospital close to the Dubai Hilton.

Housing

Given the rapid economic growth of the country, the UAE is not unexpectedly experiencing a housing boom. The Federal Council of Ministers approved Dh 275 million for housing development projects in the UAE in 1978. These funds were used for the construction of low-cost housing units, utility services, and various public works projects. Additionally, plots of land are provided by the government for citizens to build on. Interest-free loans are offered to UAE citizens working in government departments to assist in construction of their own homes. Under this scheme, plots are allotted by the Municipal and Town Planning Departments. In order to ensure effective utilization of the loan and to prevent this programme from falling prey to real-estate speculation, the conditions for the loan include that: (1) houses must be built to meet certain standards; (2) the scheme's beneficiaries will

Social Infrastructure

not get housing allowances until the loans (which are for 20 years) have been repaid; and (3) the houses, when built, are not resaleable, but must remain within the family.

A federal fund of $52.7 million in 1979 has been established to make soft loans to nationals for residential construction. In addition, it has been announced that the government plans to build 1,400 low-cost homes in the Al-Ain area.

In the 1980 federal budget, some Dh 406.5 million were designated for the Ministry of Public Works and Housing (less than 1 per cent of the total budget allocations). However, almost 87 per cent of the Ministry's allocation was earmarked for development expenditures. In fact, of the total funds in the federal budget designated for development spending, public works and housing ranked first.[10]

In the 1970s, particularly in the latter half of the decade, a great deal of investment flowed into the construction of apartment and office buildings. Yet in spite of the building boom in Abu Dhabi, rents continue to be high, regardless of the level of availability. Some building owners prefer vacancies to lowering rents. A three-bedroom apartment in 1980 was renting for $21,000 per year, over $5,000 per year more than the year before. But in Dubai, rents actually declined by 25 per cent in the two years prior to 1980. Sharjah, in late 1980, was providing housing at bargain prices. In Abu Dhabi, villas rent at $35,000 − $50,000 per year, but in Sharjah, for only $11,000 per year.

Not only is residential housing booming, but construction of hotels has skyrocketed also. Hotel construction includes: a new 360-room hotel in Abu Dhabi costing Dh 23 million in a joint venture agreement between the government and Gulf Air. The new hotel will have a 600-seat conference hall and is the second project for Abu Dhabi of this nature. Another venture is a $50 million contract to Intercontinental Hotels of the United States; Gulf Air, in which the UAE has a quarter share, is to hold 10 per cent of the hotel's equity with the other 90 per cent being controlled by the new Abu Dhabi National Company for Hotels, a similar arrangement to that governing the Intercontinental contract. As of 1979, there were 66 hotels in the UAE. Thirty-eight were located in Dubai, thirteen in Sharjah and three in Ras Al-Khaimah and Fujairah.

In conclusion, the UAE has tried to expand its absorptive capacity by increasing investment in social infrastructure. This is an area of investment which the social rate of return, though difficult to quantify, may be high enough to warrant future massive investment. The fact that return from education, health, and the like is slow in coming should not be a reason for reduced government efforts at achieving improvements in the social welfare of the people in the UAE. Indeed, in most cases investment in social infrastructure is the quickest and least disruptive way to ensure that the large oil revenues which accrue are disbursed to as wide a spectrum of the population as possible.

Notes

1. K.G. Fenelon, *The Trucial States* (London: Longman Publishing Co., 1973), p. 23. In 1975 it was estimated that only 41.6 per cent of the male and 61.9 per cent of the female population over 15 years of age were illiterate. United Nations, Economic Commission for Western Asia (ECWA), *Demographic and Related Socio-Economic Data Sheets for Countries of ECWA* (Beirut: ECWA, January 1978).

2. Donald Hawley, *The Trucial States* (London: George Allen & Unwin Ltd, 1971), p. 238.

3. United Arab Emirates (UAE), Currency Board, *Statistical Supplement* March 1980, p. 24. *Middle East Economic Digest*, Special report, October 1980, p. 27 (Hereafter *Middle East Economic Digest* will be cited as *MEED*.) In the 1980 federal budget the Ministry of Education and Youth ranked third, after defence and interior.

4. *Middle East Annual Review 1978*.

5. *Middle East Economic Survey*, 31 March 1972, p. 4. Although most countries would prefer to have their own institutions of higher learning for prestige, reasons of proximity, and as a source of advisory and technical skills, such a nationalistic policy would result in duplication and undue competitiveness at the university level. Saudi Arabia, for example, already has a University of Petroleum and Minerals while Kuwait has a medical school. Co-ordination of higher education to avoid misallocation of resources – both intellectual and material – appears to be an advisable and desirable alternative in the Gulf and is currently under consideration by the Gulf States.

6. *MEED*, 18 June 1976, pp. 11, 36. *MEED* issues dated 30 April 1976 and 25 June 1976, as well as that of 18 June 1976 are noteworthy sources of information on the UAE with respect to its current and projected social and educational systems.

7. In 1976 only 365 out of 1,000 male students entering the first grade completed the 12-year primary school education. The number for girls is higher, 490, giving an average drop-out rate of 57 per cent. Also, out of 1,000 male students only 23 made it to a secondary school without repetition of a grade; the number for girls was 62. *Financial Times*, 23 June 1980.

8. Ibid.

9. *MEED*, Special report, October 1980, p. 27. The allocation to the Ministry of Public Works and Housing includes both economic (in the public works) and social (housing) infrastructure components, while the Ministry of Electricity and Water is largely of an economic or physical infrastructure nature.
10. Ibid.

4 ECONOMIC INFRASTRUCTURE

Economic infrastructure, particularly transport and communications, looms large in the economic activities and planning of the UAE for several reasons. First, the physical size of the federation is relatively vast, yet the UAE is sparsely populated with the urban centres widely dispersed; for example, the distance between the cities of Abu Dhabi and Ras Al-Khaimah is substantial. Secondly, prior to federation, the Trucial sheikhdoms were administratively fragmented, fiercely independent of one another, and often had better and more direct communications with Great Britain than with either the other sheikhdoms or Arabian peninsula states. Recent investment in economic infrastructure in the UAE stands in part as an attempt to remedy this situation. Thirdly, due to oil-generated revenues and massive capital surpluses (especially after 1974 and again after 1979), financial constraints did not exist — a condition opposed to that of most other nations, developing and developed alike — and economic infrastructure projects could go forward quickly.

Thus, the government of the UAE has opted to expand investment in economic infrastructure such as roads, airports, radio, television, postal and telephone services. The importance attached to developing this sector by the governments is exemplified in the allocations earmarked in the earlier Trucial States Council Capital Works Programme (Dh 3.9 million, or 28 per cent of the total) and in the Abu Dhabi First 5-Year Development Plan (with Dh 710.3 million, or 24 per cent of total expenditures). Actual expenditures in the UAE on communications have risen from Dh 96.5 million, or 11.8 per cent of federal expenditures in 1968 to Dh 3,908.4 million or 14.2 per cent in 1978. In 1979, the UAE federal budget provided more than Dh 151.6 million for the Ministry of Communications, for the following year (Table 2.2), the federal government allocated over Dh 300 million.

Economic Infrastructure 75

Airports

Dubai has a modern and efficiently constructed international airport with a capacity to accommodate the jumbo Boeing 747. Abu Dhabi has built an international airport with a runway of 10,500 feet which will similarly handle the largest jet planes. By 1980, two more airports — one civil at Al-Ain and one military, a little further inland from the new civil airport under construction — had been planned by Abu Dhabi at a total cost of $225 million ($150 million for the military facility and $75 million for the civil airport). Ras Al-Khaimah's new airport is the UAE's third international airport.

On 1 January 1977, the fourth airport in the Emirates was opened. The facility is located 7.5 miles from Sharjah. Several phases of construction have been contracted since then, designed to increase the capacity of the airport to 10 million passengers a year. When two new airports, one at Abu Dhabi to replace the present facility and the other at Fujairah are completed, the UAE would have five airports of international standard serving a population of about one million and an area of 32,046 square miles.

An initial impression might be that the UAE is overbuilt in airports. However, three factors figure in this spate of airport construction. First, the very nature of the early attitudes by the Emirates toward the federation itself heightened the desire for each sheikhdom to have, among its achievements, its own prestigous airport. Some airport plans were under way prior to federation. Secondly, with the very high *per capita* income in the UAE, travel is rapidly evolving into an integral part of the life-style, whether for business, pleasure, health or educational motives. During the very warm summer months a sizable migration occurs. Thirdly, now that the UAE has a number of international airports, some facilities, such as Dubai's, can challenge other major international airports in the region. The Dubai International Airport in 1979 matched the level of passenger traffic of the well-established Bahrain facility. In 1980, as many as 2.6 million passengers (more than double the entire population of the UAE) were expected to use the Dubai airport. Nor is the air travel international only; intra-Emirate air flights are increasing, used mainly by businessmen and a growing number of government officials. Further, air transportation is essential not only for regular and emergency passenger service, but for commercial purposes such as the movement of perishable goods and, of course, mail.

Roads

Internal transportation in the UAE in the past was limited to movement through the desert or on coastal tracks. Along with economic growth and federation came the need to establish an efficient road network capable of supporting interregional economic activity. The need was quickly recognized at the onset of economic growth by all the sheikhdoms. In both the Trucial States Council Capital Works Programme and the Abu Dhabi Development Plan, generous allocations were made to establish the necessary internal road systems. One of the largest internal construction programmes links Ras Al-Khaimah to Qatar. The section which links Ras Al-Khaimah to Dubai was completed in the spring of 1970. The 80-mile section linking Dubai and Qatar was funded largely by Abu Dhabi.[1] The Abu Dhabi government also led in the construction of a Dh 26-million road linking the cities of Abu Dhabi and Tarif, which greatly reduced travel time between the individual sheikhdoms and, in turn enabled the UAE to integrate its social and economic life-styles.

A second major road linking the east and west coasts of the UAE via the Wadi Hamand further integrated the east with the western regions.[2] In the event that a major fishing industry is established in the Gulf of Oman, the road will provide a quick and economical means of transporting the fish to a marketable location. The latter project was one of the largest funded by the Trucial States Development Office, the institution which has played a vital role in the development of the Emirates in the past.

In addition to the large road projects, town transportation systems were being vastly improved. Prior to the discovery of oil, it was rare to find even a single asphalt-covered road. Automobile travel was slow and burdensome due to these poor conditions. With increased economic activity, however, the road network has been vastly improved and extended, making it easier to transport goods and cargo from one point in the Emirates to another. Presently, the road links between major towns in the Emirates can be described as excellent.

Road transportation is vital to the Emirates because it is the most efficient form of moving goods, with the exception of the airways. Thus the objective of road development in the UAE has been to open up the country by making as much of the desert hinterland as accessible as possible. With oil revenue and increased income comes urbanization, which necessitates the provision of an efficient transit system. Improvement of urban transportation also has been an objective of the transportation strategies of the federation. However, the future transit system should necessarily take into account the congestion and pollution problems which result from the increased use of automobiles.

Port Facilities

One of the physical bottlenecks associated with the process of economic development in surplus funds countries is port congestion. Rising oil revenues since 1973 had initiated increased imports of both capital and consumer goods in most of the Gulf countries. Consequently, the port facilities came under a severe strain in the effort to handle efficiently the increased volume of trade.

Dubai, traditionally a major trading centre and an entrepôt for the Emirates before the unification, already had relatively sophisticated port facilities to help handle this increased volume of imports.

In order for Dubai port facilities to continue to play a vital role in the development of the Emirates, elaborate development programmes have been carried out to expand the shipping facilities in that emirate. Begun in 1968, 1.9 miles of coastline were pushed 438 yds out to sea, with fill obtained from dredging the basin and levelling the sandhills which had impeded the expansion of the town. The harbour was dredged to accommodate ships with draughts of up to 30 feet and consisted of 15 alongside-berths for cargo-passenger ships and one oil tanker berth. This harbour was served by a vast network of roads and had internal port services to provide bunkering, watering, and ship chandlering. Twelve huge transit sheds were also erected to handle the ever-increasing cargo pouring into Dubai. Total storage facilities now cover an area almost as large as that of the old town of Dubai.

The port city of Dubai has provided a centre for transit trade, notably in gold, as mentioned earlier. Owing to this historical background

Dubai continues to act as the main locale in the UAE for importation of commercial and consumer goods. Offshore bunkering has been available since the government of Dubai established general maritime services to vessels in port and offshore. In May 1974, the first motor tanker, the 20,000-ton *Said* began supplying bunkering oil to supertankers and ships offshore Dubai. *Said* has a fuel oil capacity of 19,000 tons and its use obviates the need for ships to put into port merely for refuelling. Dubai's Port Rashid facilities have been expanded so as to allow larger tankers, particularly those hauling oil, to dock in the area. The extension scheme added new berths (bringing the total to 30 general cargo berths) which are 30 feet long and can handle roll-on, roll-off container ships. In addition, 15 transit sheds were constructed on reclaimed land, together with additional buildings for the port authorities and container berths. In 1978, the port handled 5.3 million tons of cargo and its capacity was increased to 6 million tons in 1979. In the first seven months of 1980, Port Rashid handled 1.8 million deadweight tons (dwt).

Growth in port facilities at Dubai has been rapid. This rapid growth can be partially gauged by the increased throughput of containers at Port Rashid where, in 1976, yearly container throughput registered only 4,530 20-foot equivalent units (TEUs); in 1978, 120,000 TEUs; and in 1980, estimates were that throughput would reach 200,000 TEUs.

Work began in January 1974 on the Dubai dry dock and was completed in 1979. The new dry dock, constructed by a joint venture of two British civil engineering companies, is one of the largest ship repair facilities in the world, and is capable of catering in particular to the needs of the ever-increasing number of large oil tankers in the Gulf. The complex is situated alongside Port Rashid and is comprised of three dry docks, the largest capable of docking vessels up to 1 million dwt.

A tanker-cleaning berth and five moorings enable the facilities at the dry dock to handle virtually all types of repair, fabrication, and maintenance. The total cost of the shipyard complex, including the construction of a breakwater and pre-operation financing, was in the region of $162 million and when fully operational the dry dock will provide work for 4,000 persons of various trades.

The construction of the Dubai dock has seemingly resulted in a regional clash of economic interests. Dubai had planned for its $27 million dry dock to be partially paid for and used by the Organization of Arab Petroleum Exporting Countries (OAPEC). For a number of economic and political reasons, OAPEC opted to support the construction of a superdry dock in Bahrain which also already possesses outstanding harbour-repair facilities. Because of OAPEC's move, Bahrain and Dubai will be faced with vigorous competition over those tankers in transit. The economic confrontation in shipping between these two sea-faring sheikhdoms will undoubtedly continue (as now appears to be similarly occurring in airport service). Meanwhile, Abu Dhabi also is expanding its port facilities, increasing its number of berths by three (for a total of 21) to supplement Dubai facilities.

To prevent the further erosion of the Deira coastline at the mouth of Dubai Creek a seawall is currently being constructed. The 4 mile-long corniche from Ras Deira to Hamriya will encompass, upon completion, more than 1 square mile of land reclaimed from the sea, yielding valuable space for large-scale commercial and residential development. The total cost of the project is in the region of $19.4 million. This project was extended to include a small fishing harbour and marina at Hamriya, which was recently completed. Three similar fishing harbours have also been constructed along the Jumeira beach. The marina planned to be built at the head of Dubai Creek will involve dredging the open tidal flats and reclaiming banks to establish an inland lake, a marina and a new residential area. The project has been estimated to cost Dh 350 million and will include the establishment of a tourist centre with two artificial islands, casinos and other recreational facilities.

Whereas the port facilities at Dubai may be adequate to handle the import trade, locational factors do not make it feasible for Dubai to handle the large volume of the Emirates' exports, made up almost exclusively of crude oil. Additionally, as downstream operations in the oil industry widen, the need for expanded port facilities to export refined and other petrochemical products will become imperative.

Also located in Dubai are the port facilities of Jebel Ali. It is hoped that the establishment of a free zone at Jebel Ali will attract trade to its facilities, perhaps even drawing trade from the nearby Port Rashid. The volume of merchandise handled at Jebel Ali was 6.1 million tons of cargo in 1979, and customs-released cargo valued at $28.6 million. The port here has 66 berths and was constructed at a cost of $1.6 billion (US). While Port Rashid has the advantage of being close to the major city of Dubai, Jebel Ali's port is part and parcel of the industrial, free-trade zone complex built from scratch, so to speak. Located in this industrial site is Dubal (Dubai Aluminium Company), where the $1.4 billion (US) smelter has a 1981 capacity of some 140,000 tons per year. Other industries at Jebel Ali provide built-in customers for the port.[3] Moreover, such support or secondary facilities and services include the Dubai International Trade and Exhibition Centre, where regional offices of British Petroleum, Union Carbide, and Leyland Vehicles Export are headquartered. The Jebel Ali Port Authority's offices are in the Trade Centre. Thus, while Port Rashid is heavily import and re-export oriented, Jebel Ali aims at both import and export trade, the latter of locally produced items.

Turning to Abu Dhabi, this Emirate also has continued to expand and modernize its port facilities. By 1984 the number of berths at Mina Zayed will expand from its present 21 berths to 29. In addition, the new industrial port at Ruwais handles LPG carriers, oil tankers, and fertilizer bulk carriers. This port is especially suited to the recent 1980 doubling of Ruwais oil-refining capacity and the construction of the Ruwais fertilizer complex whose first phase of construction will cost an estimated $200 million.

Sharjah, as of December 1980, was constructing a large container-port at Khor Fakkan on its Gulf of Oman coast. This is virtually an expansion of Khor Fakkan's natural deep water harbour into a two-berth port. The objective for the expansive form of port facilities in Sharjah is to avoid congested Gulf ports where waiting time can reach 100 days. The cost of transporting containers by road from Khor Fakkan to the main centres of the Gulf should be cheaper than paying the present surcharges imposed at Gulf ports. The Fakkan mostly receives commerce provided by Indian routes, but the port offers the entire region an alternative route of access to the Gulf, should the vulnerable Strait of Hormuz ever be closed.

Moreover, Sharjah has modified its tariff to attract regular and large-volume users to its 12-berth Port Khaled. The tariff cuts have been as high as 25 per cent in some cases. The volume of Sharjah's Port Khaled rose in 1979 to 2.5 million tons from 1.75 million tons in 1978. Port Khaled has many attractive features and outstanding characteristics, including the free-zone facilities. BP Marine International Bunker service provides shippers with bunkering facilities. The port has the busiest ro-ro (roll-on, roll-off) transhipment terminal in the Gulf. A special ro-ro berth is able to handle vessels up to 771 ft in length. The port has 538,000 ft^2 of covered storage space. And merchants can avail themselves of the free-zone development area at the in-bond area of the port.[4]

Although Ras-Al-Khaimah's Mina Saqr handles over a million tons of cement per year, the second phase of its construction has been halted by lack of funds and diminished prospects of added business. Its two ro-ro berths have had very little business since it was built.

The intensity of competition among UAE ports is not insubstantial. By and large, shippers opt for but one stop within the UAE given rising operating expenses for the larger vessels. And the type of merchandise offloaded is important as well — the majority is destined for re-export and/or transhipment elsewhere in the Gulf, frequently to Iran, using auxiliary means of trucks and smaller ships. As the 1980s opened, the UAE boasted 133 berths in the various ports (excluding Khor Fakkan): 100 in Dubai's Port Rashid and Jebel Ali, 21 berths in Abu Dhabi, and 12 in Sharjah (Port Khaled).[5]

To further aid development of port facilities, the UAE became a member of the United Arab Shipping Company (UASC) based in Kuwait and established in January 1976. Saudi Arabia, Iraq, Qatar, Kuwait, and Bahrain, in addition to the UAE, formed the company with an authorized capital of KD (Kuwaiti dinars) 500 million, divided into 50 million shares of KD 10 each, and a subscribed capital of KD 180 million, 50 per cent of which was to be paid immediately.[6] Participation by the founding states in the subscribed capital is set at KD 6 million for Bahrain, and KD 34.8 million each for the remaining five member states. The objectives of the company are (1) to run regular shipping services between Arab and international seaports; (2) to engage in all shipping activities itself or on behalf of other parties; and (3) to acquire, sell and operate all kinds of vessels.

Managers from the UAE, Bahrain, Iraq, Kuwait, Oman, Qatar, and Saudi Arabia also have agreed to establish a permanent bureau at Dammam, Saudi Arabia, to co-ordinate efforts to ease shipping congestion in Gulf ports. This decision was reached at a special shipping conference in Abu Dhabi. The conference members also decided to remove surcharges on ships given priority in unloading at Gulf ports. Such co-ordination is needed to reduce excessive competition and wasteful duplication.

Public Utilities

Perhaps one of the factors which cause the absorptive capacity of oil-producing countries to expand at an accelerated rate is the phenomenal demand for public utilities. With development comes urbanization and industrialization resulting in rising consumption of social and public services. Water supply, electricity, and other utilities are provided by the government through public corporations.

In both the Abu Dhabi and the former Trucial States Council plans, there have been substantial allocations for sewage and water facilities.[7] In Abu Dhabi, a major desalination plant was constructed which distills two million gallons per day and produces 96,000 kilowatts (kW) of electricity. However, as water becomes more and more essential to the economic growth of the UAE for industrial and agricultural development, needs for municipal improvements and for increased demand because of population increases, allocations for further water and power facilities are bound to rise. The projects in this area in the federation include the following.

(1) Construction of a power and desalination plant at Umm al-Nar is under way. The plant, which will be gas-powered, will have a total electrical capacity of 115-120 megawatts (MW), and its water output will be nearly 6 million gallons per day. Power units began operating in 1978. The desalination plant will be linked by pipeline to an existing desalination plant at Mina Zayed, so that water from both plants can be fed simultaneously into Abu Dhabi City's water distribution system.

(2) The 140-MW power plant at Mina Zayed in Abu Dhabi would virtually double the Emirate's electrical capacity. Work began in August 1975 on the six turbines and boilers and the first stage of the construction was completed in 1976.

(3) The supply and installation of three 15,700-kW generators at Al-Ain in Abu Dhabi are to augment Al-Ain's present power output of 65,000 kW.

(4) The expansion of the Jebel Ali power plant began with construction on the first phase of the project which came on stream in 1979; the whole project was completed in 1980. Also located at

Jebel Ali is Dubal (Dubai Aluminium Company) which, in addition to the production of aluminium, functions as a public utility. An output of some 25 million gallons of water daily will be made possible through utilization of waste heat from the smelter's boilers. Depending on the capacity of the Dubal plant, water output could be expanded to as much as 40 million gallons per day.

(5) In July 1980 Abu Dhabi hired Electrowatt of Switzerland to study a proposed UAE national power grid. The study will determine the cost and capacity of the proposed $1 billion (US) power station. By mid-1985, the first 300-MW unit could be operational. Eventually, the entire project could provide a 1,500 MW capacity.

Major projects are being undertaken to improve the Emirate's sewage capabilities. First is the building of a sewage treatment plant in Abu Dhabi. The facility, to be located at Mafraq some 20 miles east of Abu Dhabi City, will treat 14 million gallons per day of sewage. Secondly, Dubai City's sewage treatment plant is to be extended. The expansion will mean that the present plant, built to handle a population of 25,000, will be capable of servicing at least 100,000. This treatment plant complex includes the re-use of treated effluent for horticultural and industrial development. Thirdly, Ajman, Umm Al-Quwain, and Fujairah will be beneficiaries of a $53.5-million sewage scheme to be financed by the federal government.

Telecommunications

The UAE has a modern and efficient telecommunications system. The development of the system has been very rapid by any standards. From only 40 international circuits available to telephone subscribers in 1972, 758 were available by the end of March 1980. In this latter year, direct dialling to more than 30 countries existed, including the United States, United Kingdom, and Japan. It is predicted that by the end of 1981 the number of countries will increase to 40. In March 1980, there were ten times as many domestic circuits and direct exchange lines as existed seven years earlier. The telex industry has similarly boomed. There were in 1980 some 4,000 subscriber lines and 460 international circuits as compared to 1,500 lines and 142 circuits four years earlier.

84 *Economic Infrastructure*

At the Ruwais complex, the latest in telephone technology has been installed. The system enables a person who may be located 100 km in the desert to call directly to the United States.

An efficient communication system enhances business and commerce. To this end, a digital telephone exchange with 42,000 lines and digital transmission systems has been planned. A computer-controlled switching system, to be in operation in the Dubai international telephone facilities by 1981, will facilitate international communication. The satellite system in the Emirates is used for international telephone communication but it also affords the television system in UAE the luxury of bringing international events into UAE homes.

Industrial Zones

Abu Dhabi and Dubai have both placed considerable hopes in the development of two of their industrial zones. These projects are essential foundation-stones of the UAE's long-term industrial strategy, i.e. diversification by increasing downstream petroleum operations and branching into non-oil sectors. Details on the actual industries and enterprises at these industrial complexes were noted in Chapter 2.

The Ruwais complex is located 260 km (162 miles) west of Abu Dhabi. Total investment in the project will eventually reach $20 billion (US) and will not be finished for 10 to 12 years. The complex will take advantage of UAE's comparative advantage in petroleum endowments, that is, crude oil, natural gas, and gas liquids for use as feedstock and fuel. Projects in this complex are numerous: a 2 x 40-MW power complex; a Dh 50 million ($13.5 million) seawater desalination plant; a 120,000 barrels per day refinery to come on stream in 1981; a plant to separate natural gas liquids into butane, propane, and condensates; a petrochemical plant; tremendous infrastructural work to support not only the main projects of Ruwais but also diversified private and state industries in the future; a 1,000-unit housing project; and a fertilizer firm (Abu Dhabi Fertilizers Company) with one of its plants capable of producing 1,000 tons per day of ammonia and a second some 1,500 tons per day of urea. Moreover, liquids extracted by Gasco's plants at the Bu Hasa, Asab, and Bab fields will be processed further at Ruwais facilities.

Given this level of activity it is understandable that port facilities near Ruwais are expanding. Only 20 miles east of Ruwais at Jebel Dhanna is the crude oil loading terminal which is capable of loading 1.2 million barrels per day. A continuous flow of tankers, approximately 40 each month, keeps the port busy. The construction of two twin bulk cargo berths is under way to serve the urea fertilizer plant. Plans for an iron and steel plant at Ruwais were to be held in abeyance until a joint sponsor could be found.

Continued expansion of the Jebel Ali complex near Dubai will tend to ensure Dubai's competitive commercial status in the Gulf. The port facilities are enormous, 66 berths at a cost of about $1.6 billion (US).

The Dubai Aluminium Company (Dubal) hopes to produce 140,000 tons of aluminium at full capacity in 1980. Its electric generating potential is huge. The Dubai smelter is furnished with five of the world's largest gas-fired turbines (100 MW each). A by-product of the aluminium smelter, as noted earlier, is potable water — 25 million gallons per day, with a potential of up to 40 million gallons.

Built near the perimeter of the Jebel Ali complex is the Gulf Norbuild prefabricated housing plant whose output will help to lessen the housing crunch in many Emirates. Nearby is an insulated-cable manufacturer (Dubai Cable Company) that makes, among other things, power cables insulated with polyvinylchloride (PVC) and cross-linked polyethylene-insulated power cables. Both products are widely used in providing the electrical infrastructural materials in demand in the Gulf region and other developing nations. The cost of this plant was approximately Dh 60 million ($16.2 million).

Another prosperous plant at Jebel Ali that has already begun to export is the Cleveland Bridge and Engineering Factory. In 1979 alone the company exported 5,000 tons of fabricated steel, with projected output in 1980 of 15,000 tons for export. Steel is considered to be important to many infrastructural development projects.

Jebel Ali may benefit by a move by such oil field service and fabricator firms as Halliburton, International Marine Services, and McDermott Dubai from the Dubai City-Port Rashid area to its industrial complex. Due to its duty-free trade-zone status, Jebel Ali is likely to attract additional traffic in the form of storage awaiting transhipment to destinations elsewhere in the Gulf.

As elsewhere in the Gulf, the concept of industrial complexes as the core of economic diversification into and within that sector seems well established. Kuwait has its Shuwaiba; Saudi Arabia its Jubail and Yanbu. And a sufficient level of economic infrastructure to provide requirements in water, electricity, communications, ports, and storage must be provided in order to lure foreign ventures and investment as well as ensuring the viability of governmental industrial enterprises.

Construction

Expenditures for construction continue to be large. The Abu Dhabi government — the largest spender on construction in the UAE — plans sizable expenditures for 1980. Projects include expenditures for transport and communications at Dh 2,620 million ($710 million); for sewage at Dh 817.8 million ($221.6 million); for housing at Dh 473.7 million ($128.3 million); for electricity at Dh 1,240 million ($336 million). A glance at the map makes it abundantly clear why construction and infrastructure (especially in road systems) hold a high priority in Abu Dhabi's spending: Abu Dhabi is some ten times the combined size of the other six emirates.

Moreover, Abu Dhabi stands as the major oil producer within the UAE. Both its proven reserves and crude output levels figure in the range of oil-related projects completed or under way, including several of the Abu Dhabi National Oil Company. ADNOC plans to build a liquefield natural gas (LNG) tank farm costing an estimated $500 million at the Das Island oil-field complex. Sadiyat Island, next to Mina Zayed, has received attention from the oil industry; Abu Dhabi Drilling Chemicals Products (ADDCAP) located there has begun production and a shipyard may be built as well. Sadiyat Island will be attached to the mainland once the construction of a bridge is complete.

The need for suitable water provision has provided, and will likely continue to provide, opportunities for the construction industry. Contracts for a 93-mile pipeline from the main desalinating complex at Umm Al-Nar Island to other areas of Abu Dhabi have been let. And for 1980, Abu Dhabi will support water resource development to a sum of Dh 770 million ($208.6 million).

Dubai is also bustling with construction activity. In 1979 approximately Dh 454.1 million ($123 million) was spent on construction.

Construction items receiving attention in 1980 encompass 1,400 homes, 164 schools, a cabinet ministries complex, a building to house the advisory assembly, headquarters for the Ministry of Finance and Industry, and expansion of hospitals and roads.

Infrastructural development has been one of the most rapidly expanding economic activities in the UAE. To this extent, it has tended to put pressure on the government budget and hence, has provided avenues for increased absorption of oil revenues. Although some facilities have been over-ambitious, the provision of excess capacity is generally preferable to bottlenecks such as those experienced in the late 1970s in port facilities. Generally, the UAE has been able to postpone serious physical bottlenecks in the development process.

Notes

1. *Arab Economic Review*, January–February 1972, p. 4. The highway section linking Ras Al-Khaimah and Sharjah has been named in honour of the former King of Saudi Arabia, Faisal Road, whose government financed that segment of the project.

2. K.G. Fenelon, *The Trucial States* (London: Longman Publishers, 1973), p. 19.

3. Among the other industries located at Jebel Ali are Gulf Norbuild (a prefabrication factory and joint venture between the government of Dubai and Norcem of Oslo), the Dubai Cable Company and the Cleveland Bridge and Engineering facility. It should be noted that the Iran–Iraq hostilities in 1980 increased usage of all UAE ports because of 'distress' storage of products diverted from Iran and Iraq and that some transhipment was possible, particularly from Dubai, to the originally planned destination using smaller, local vessels.

4. Among the more specialized products in Port Khaled's trade traffic are the car terminal handling some 1,500 vehicles monthly destined for final delivery throughout the Gulf region and the export of locally manufactured styrene by Dow Chemicals.

5. The effect of shipping dislocations resulting from the Iran–Iraq conflict is analyzed in *Middle East Economic Digest*, Special report, October 1980, p. 51. (Hereafter, *Middle East Economic Digest* will be cited as *MEED*.)

6. The 1980 exchange rate was approximately 1 KD = $3.4.

7. *MEED*, 2 April 1976, 4 June 1976, and 25 June 1976, are particularly informative on public utilities development in the UAE.

5 FUELLING UAE DEVELOPMENT: OIL

The Development of the Oil Industry

The discovery of oil in the United Arab Emirates is undoubtedly the single most dynamic force in the changes within the Trucial region. Government revenues are skyrocketing as a result of this resource's exploitation and oil revenues are stockpiling, overwhelmingly from production in Abu Dhabi and, to a much lesser extent, Dubai and Sharjah. The first involvement of the Trucial States in petroleum exploration was in October 1935. Petroleum Concessions Ltd, a subsidiary of Iraq Petroleum Company, formed a new company — the Petroleum Development (Trucial States) Ltd, commonly referred to as PDTC. PDTC immediately contacted the individual sheikhdoms, offering arrangements for concession rights to explore for oil and to develop production should oil be found.[1] In 1938 the sheikhs of Dubai, Sharjah, Ras Al-Khaimah and Kalba (an independent sheikhdom which in 1952 was incorporated as an integral part of Sharjah) signed agreements to give concessions in return for rentals which were to commence immediately. Later, Abu Dhabi granted concessions to PDTC in January 1939 which were to last 75 years and included all territorial islands and waters.[2]

After World War II, the exploration drive by PDTC in the Trucial region declined. Exploration in Qatar fields first received attention by PDTC parent companies as more investment had been done in this area prior to the war and exploration activities received more advanced consideration. Oil was first exported from Kuwait in 1946 and Qatar in 1949, but success was not attained by PDTC in the Trucial States until 1960. At that time oil was found in commercial quantities in Abu Dhabi at the Murban field onshore south of Tarif.[3]

Under pressure, particularly from the rulers of Sharjah and Ras Al-Khaimah, PDTC relinquished its concessions in all the sheikhdoms except Abu Dhabi and Dubai shortly after the discovery of oil. The rulers of the other five sheikhdoms felt multi-company competition

Fuelling UAE Development: Oil

for concessions would lead to more rapid and extensive exploration of their regions. Further, in 1963 PDTC relinquished its concession in Dubai to concentrate its efforts in Abu Dhabi; PDTC became the Abu Dhabi Petroleum Company (ADPC).

During the 1940s and 1950s a new concept of territorial ownership was also under way which widened the boundaries of the coastal sheikhdoms. This concept marked the continental shelf as the territorial boundary and meant that more oil concessions could be granted for further exploration. ADPC objected to this move, claiming it, and not other oil companies, should have the jurisdiction over the recently obtained offshore territory. In order to settle this dispute both Abu Dhabi and ADPC went to Paris to present their cases before a board of arbitrators in 1951. The board ruled in favour of Abu Dhabi, stating that the concessions granted to ADPC contained only land under control of the sheikhdom at the time of the initial settlement.

As a result of the arbitrators' decision, Abu Dhabi granted a concession to the International Marine Oil Company (IMOC) which was to cover the newly acquired offshore territory.[4] After IMOC completed a small amount of exploration without positive results, they relinquished their concessions in 1953. Another concession of 12,000 square miles was then granted to the Abu Dhabi Marine Areas Ltd (ADMA). Two-thirds of ADMA was owned by British Petroleum (BP) and one-third by Compagnie Française des Pétroles (CFP) at that time. (See Appendix III for a listing of oil companies working the UAE, their ownership and area of activity.)

ADMA was actually the first company to strike oil in commercial quantities in the Trucial States, two years before PDTC (renamed ADPC), the first concessionaire holder. In 1958 its drilling barge struck oil at 5,500 feet at Umm Shaif, which is located 80 miles into the Gulf near Das Island. July 1962 was important not only to ADMA but to all the Trucial sheikhdoms, as it marked the first commercial shipment of oil from that region. That first shipment was loaded from Das Island, which has since developed into a major oil depot.

Abu Dhabi Marine Areas (now Abu Dhabi Marine Operating Company or ADMA-OPCO) is Abu Dhabi's major offshore operator with production in 1977 amounting to 194 million barrels of oil, an increase of 25 per cent over 1975.[5] Current production averages around 450,000 barrels per day (b/d).

At the end of 1972, BP sold 45 per cent of its two-thirds stake to the Overseas Petroleum Corporation (OPC) of Japan, which formed a company called the Japan Petroleum Development Company (owned by OPC and a group of Japanese oil-development companies) to look after its interests. BP received $780 million for the agreement. The government of Abu Dhabi demanded compensation for the deal, and following lengthy discussions it was agreed that BP would finance for the Abu Dhabi National Oil Company (ADNOC) the $35 million oil refinery which was built by Kellogg International Corporation of Britain on Umm Al-Nar island off Abu Dhabi.[6] As settlement, BP also agreed to provide the government with a $50 million interest-free loan repayable in 50 instalments beginning in January 1975.

ADMA has spent a significant amount of money over the past few years in developing its oil installations on Das Island. A seawater desalination plant, oil and gas-processing facilities and other oil installations were built by international companies with further expansion expected. The trend in the company's agreement was for higher per unit government revenue and greater control over the speed with which a concession was exploited, as illustrated by the 14 May 1968 concession granted to a Japanese consortium, Middle East Oil Company Ltd, concerning inland acreage relinquished by the Abu Dhabi Petroleum Company. The Middle East Oil Company undertook exploration 6 months after signing the concession, with drilling commencing within 2 years from the signature date. The company also pledged to expend no less than $24 million in the first eight years plus an initial payment to the government of $1.65 million. Once oil was located in commercial quantities, a raft of payments was scheduled as certain production levels were reached.[7]

The Abu Dhabi Petroleum Company (also known as Abu Dhabi Company for Onshore Oil Operations or ADCO) is presently the largest operating oil company and is owned jointly by BP, Shell, CFP, Near East Development Corporation — a joint venture of Exxon Corporation and Mobil Oil — and Participations and Explorations Corporation. Under the participation agreement of 2 September 1974, the Abu Dhabi Government acquired a 60 per cent undivided interest in the assets and concessions formerly held by ADPC (see Appendix III for present ownership shares). Crude-oil production has been reduced over the past few years totalling 373,984,000 barrels in 1977 and 315,434,000 barrels

Fuelling UAE Development: Oil

in 1979 (total Abu Dhabi output was 533,275,000 barrels in 1979). ADPC (now ADCO) operated onshore concessions in Abu Dhabi, and oil was struck in the Murban field in 1960. Japan is ADPC's largest customer, followed by Europe, North American and other Eastern hemisphere countries (see Table 6.4).

Abu Dhabi's concessions with other oil companies in the territory previously relinquished by ADPC and ADMA and recent discoveries include the following:

(1) Phillips, Aminoil, and Agip signed an agreement with Abu Dhabi on 21 January 1967, covering 4,994 miles^2. To date no commercially exploitable quantities have yet been found.

(2) The Middle East Oil Company, mentioned earlier and which is owned by Mitsubishi of Japan, was granted a 35-year concession on 14 May 1968, of 2,498 miles^2. Like the Phillips, Aminoil, and Agip con-concession, Middle East Oil Company has yet to discover commercially exploitable oil.

(3) Oil was discovered in the Mubarraz field in 1971 and the 996 square miles concession began to yield oil in the autumn of 1972. Oil from the field has a very low sulphur content and ADOC agreed on a sulphur premium to be added to the posted price, a proposal which was strongly resisted by the other foreign oil companies. A port was also built at the Mubarraz field and exports, beginning at a rate of 50,000 tons per year, rapidly grew to 200,000 tons per year. The company consists of the three Japanese firms of Maruzen Oil, Darkyo Oil, and Nippon Mining with the government of Abu Dhabi holding a 51 per cent interest.

(4) Pan Ocean, Wingate, and Syracuse were granted a concession on 17 June 1970 that included 1,216 miles^2. This group has since been expanded to include Amerada Hess and Houston Oils.[8] Currently, the company is developing commercial production near Arzanah.

(5) Gas potential in Abu Dhabi was greatly increased by a major gas discovery in early 1979 deep in the Rhuff zone under the Umm Sharif oil field, about 22 miles east of Das Island. The consortium, ADNOC and ADMA-OPCO, made the discovery, which tested out at 80 million cfd (cubic feet/day). In 1980 a survey was under way of the lower formations of Umm Shaif.

(6) Adding to its already large concessions in UAE petroleum, the Japanese firm Abu Dhabi Oil Company (ADOCO) obtained additional

acreage in Abu Dhabi in early 1979 totalling 611 miles^2. A previous 1967 agreement had given ADOCO entitlement to part of the 20,000 barrels per day flow from the Mubarraz oilfield. ADOCO has contracted to spend at least $16 million of exploration on the new acreage over the five years following 1979. Bonus payments will be made to the government concurrent with increased evidence of commercial feasibility: $1 million within 60 days after signing the contract, $2 million upon discovery of commercial quantities, $3 million if and when exports reach 100,000 barrels per day. Rent will be $100,000 each year and the Abu Dhabi government retains the option of acquiring up to 60 per cent of the venture.

(7) A $230-million secondary recovery programme will be undertaken at the troubled Bunduq field by the largest concessionaire in the Bunduq Company, the Japanese firm United Petroleum Development. In October 1979, the field was closed down due to reservoir-pressure maintenance problems. Qatar and Abu Dhabi split oil revenues on a 50-50 basis. The recovery programme, it is hoped, will generate a flow rate of 25,000 b/d at peak rate after April 1983 when the injection recovery will be under way.

(8) ADNOC, the wholly state-owned national oil company, announced in early 1980 that it planned to build a gasline from Abu Dhabi to the Jebel Ali industrial area to supply Dubai's aluminium smelter and to supply the proposed Abu Dhabi-Dubai border power plant.

(9) ADNOC and Japan Oil Development Company (JODCO) in 1980 signed a $700 million agreement to develop the Satah, Dalma and Jarnain fields. Sixty per cent of the concession is owned by ADNOC and 40 per cent by JODCO. The jointly owned ADNOC-JODCO company Umm Al-Dalkh Development Company (UDECO) will construct a 40,000 b/d export terminal at a total cost of $700 million on Dalma Island some 31 miles south of Satah. Oil is expected to begin flowing by 1984 at an initial level of 30,000 to 40,000 b/d. Satah is thought the most promising field, with reserves estimated at around 100 million barrels.

(10) ADNOC announced the successful completion of an exploratory offshore well at Bu Tinah, some 35 miles from the Abu Dhabi coast and about 16 miles south of Zirku. Although the reserves may be in the area of 1,000 million barrels, additional wells must be drilled to ascertain the field's actual size.

Fuelling UAE Development: Oil 93

(11) A new onshore concession was signed with Amoco (Standard Oil Company of Indiana) in October 1980 covering 965 miles^2 north of Al-Ain city. Amoco is committed to invest $55.5 million in exploration during the first eight years with a number of bonuses upon signature ($5 million), discovery of oil in commercial quantities ($2 million), when output reaches 50,000 b/d ($2 million), when exports amount to 100,000 b/d ($4 million), and when those exports reach 200,000 b/d ($6 million). Taxes and royalties will be paid as laid down by the Abu Dhabi government.

(12) Drawn much along the lines of the Amoco concession, the second agreement in the Al-Ain area (3,012 miles^2 east and south of the city) was concluded with a Canadian consortium.[9] Some $70 million is earmarked for exploration during the first ten years with bonuses on signature ($4 million), when commercially exploitable oil is discovered ($5 million), when output reaches 50,000 b/d, 100,000 b/d, and 200,000 b/d ($10 million at each level). Again, the royalty and tax payments by the consortium will be those set by the government.

(13) A new concession agreement was concluded in November 1980, for exploration in two onshore areas covering 1 million acres near the Bu Hasa, Asab, and Bab fields southwest of Abu Dhabi City. The consortium of firms includes Amerada-Hess (50 per cent), Occidental Petroleum (33.3 per cent), and Alpha Oil of London (16.6 per cent). The terms call for $100 million to be spent over the first eight years with the usual bonuses structure: on signature ($4 million); on discovery of oil in commercial quantities ($5 million); when production reaches 50,000 b/d ($4 million) and 200,000 b/d ($6 million). Moreover, an annual rent of $100,000 was set. The consortium is to pay taxes and royalties as laid down by the government. Moreover, any associated natural gas found is to belong to the government.

(14) The Umm Al-Nar refinery's capacity will be expanded fivefold, from 15,000 b/d to 75,000 b/d, by early 1983. The expansion, coupled with the coming on stream of the 120,000 b/d refinery at the Ruwais complex early in 1981, should allow the UAE to become totally self-sufficient in gasoline and other products. Consumption of petroleum products in the UAE as a whole has been in excess of the output of Abu Dhabi's Umm Al-Nar refinery. For 1980, the Emirates' demand for petroleum products was estimated at between 80,000 and 100,000

b/d. Even when the Ruwais refinery comes on stream in August 1981, the UAE will still continue to import some products since a full range of refined items may not be either produced by or produced in sufficient quantities by that plant. In addition, should marketing demand greater refining capacity in the UAE, the Ruwais facility could be expanded to 250,000 b/d capacity in the future.

In late 1972, Abu Dhabi joined Saudi Arabia and other Gulf states in the Organization of Petroleum Exporting Countries (OPEC) to formulate an agreement which would give the producing nations a share in the capital of concessionaire companies' interest within their own countries. The first day of January 1973 marked the first day of the enforcement of this agreement from which the Abu Dhabi government acquired an initial 25 per cent interest in the major Western oil companies — ADPC and ADMA. This share progressively increased until it reached 60 per cent in 1975. The government of Abu Dhabi originally had the right to sell back to the companies any oil in excess of its own requirements, but in February 1973 the government signed an agreement with the Japanese oil tanker company, Japan Line, under which the company agreed to purchase crude oil directly from it. Japan Line made a down payment of $150 million and planned to import 83.9 million barrels of crude oil during the first three years of the agreement, rising to higher levels by 1980.

By retaining its former concessionaire companies as equity holders in the operating enterprises (as, for example, ADMA-OPCO and ADOC), Abu Dhabi stands out as the only member of OPEC in the Gulf to keep this arrangement. The government take per barrel in revenues is one issue; another that has arisen concerns the profit margins of equity holders. This margin is derived as the difference between the official selling price of crude as set by the government and the equity holders' tax-paid cost on their crude entitlement (40 per cent for foreign participants, 60 per cent ADNOC) or their share of oil produced. The tax-paid cost to the companies includes the government take (85 per cent tax based on posted prices and a 20 per cent royalty) in addition to the production costs. Since 1978 when the participation equity holders' profit margin was some 65 cents/barrel, that margin has more than doubled, rising to about $1.60 per barrel by mid-1980. It should be kept in mind that foreign companies as equity holders are still responsible for sharing in required investment in operations. An agreement on this issue was concluded in the autumn of 1980 whereby the companies' profit margin for 1980 will be limited to 40 cents/barrel (that is, $1/barrel on the equity holders' 40 per cent entitlement). The new arrangement will turn over the 60 cents/barrel added profit, which would have resulted in 1980 from application of the old tax-paid cost and the official selling price, to the government of Abu Dhabi as a 'make-up' payment. Henceforth, an annual review of the equity companies' margin will be carried out.

The Abu Dhabi government also formed a state company, ADNOC, to administer the government's undivided interest in the foreign companies. In late 1978 it was agreed to form an operating company, ADCO (owned 60 per cent by ADNOC and 40 per cent by BP, CFP, Participations and Exploration Corporation or Partex, Shell, Exxon, and Mobil), to carry out operations for the joint concession holders. On 1 July 1973, ADCO (formerly known as ADPC), took over the local distribution of all petroleum products, after taking over all petrol stations in the state earlier that year. The joint concessions, however, are administered by joint management committees consisting of representatives of the government and the companies. ADCO has contracted with France's CFP to carry out a 500,000 b/d development of the offshore Upper Zakum oil field.[10] In addition, the national company is responsible for carrying out plans to set up both oil-based industries and a college to train staff. Furthermore, Abu Dhabi seeks to use the experience which it is gaining in the oil industry not only in other domestic undertakings but to assist in development projects in other countries. The truly vital place of petroleum in Abu Dhabi's — and by extension, in the UAE's — economy is evident in the area of revenue; in 1978, roughly 88 per cent of the Abu Dhabi government's revenues were derived from oil production (refer to Tables 2.4 and 2.6).

Dubai is the other main oil-producing UAE sheikhdom. When ADPC relinquished its Dubai concessions in 1963, that territory was granted to Continental Oil, the principal owner of Dubai Petroleum Company. The offshore concessions were originally granted to Superior Oil Company in 1954 and later were taken over by Dubai Marine Areas Ltd, which is jointly owned (50-50) by CFP and Hispanoil. In short, the exploration and production concession offshore Dubai is shared equally by Dubai Marine Areas Ltd and Dubai Petroleum Company Ltd.[11]

Fuelling UAE Development: Oil

Oil in commercial quantities was originally struck offshore Dubai in July 1966 which enabled production to begin in the following year. Exports commenced in 1969 when 3.8 million barrels were produced. In 1978, crude-oil production reached its highest level of 131.8 million barrels (see Table 5.2 for UAE oil production since 1962).

Oil reserves for Dubai were estimated to be 1,300 million barrels as of 1 January 1978, which is relatively small by comparison to the reserves of Abu Dhabi, put at 30,000 million barrels for the same date. Sharjah's reserves were about 16 million barrels. None the less, Dubai ranks tenth among Middle East producers and Abu Dhabi fifth. Combined total reserves for Dubai and Abu Dhabi were 30,850 million barrels, accounting for 8.5 per cent of the total Middle East proven reserves of 369,996 million barrels.[12]

A 35-year oil exploration agreement has been initiated with a group of five United States firms covering 1 million acres in Dubai's Jebel Ali area. The American firms participating in the venture are: Texas Pacific Dubai (50 per cent), United Texas Dubai (25 per cent), Louisiana Land and Exploration (12.5 per cent), Thomas of Dubai (5 per cent), and Quintanan (7.5 per cent). Seismic operations began in April 1975 and drilling followed shortly thereafter.

In addition, plans to expand offshore drilling by 22 more wells in Dubai in its Fateh and Southwest Fateh offshore fields raised total daily output from roughly 250,000 barrels in 1975 to 400,000 barrels in 1976. Nine wells were sunk at Fateh, where 34 have been brought into production since 1969; the number at Southeast Fateh was to be increased from the present 16 to 25. Table 5.3 gives technical details on not only Dubai's Fateh field but Abu Dhabi's and Sharjah's fields.

Dubai recently signed a 35-year agreement with Atlantic Richfield. The agreement entails the study of petroleum potential of a 1,180-square mile tract of land. The terms of the agreement require that Atlantic Richfield drill at least one exploratory well each year for five years beginning in 1983. A résumé of well completions in Abu Dhabi, Dubai, and Sharjah is given in Table 5.4.

The remaining sheikhdoms, with the exception of Sharjah and recently Ras Al-Khaimah, have not been as fortunate as Abu Dhabi and Dubai in their quest for oil. Even after extensive exploration, which is still being undertaken, no oil in commercially exploitable quantities has been found. However, in mid-1977 Ras Al-Khaimah tested its first offshore well which is flowing at 2,750 b/d with 44° API oil along with a considerable amount of gas. In that same year, Umm Al-Quwain, which possesses a partial interest in Sharjah's oil field, has announced the discovery of significant gas reserves.[13] Actual production in Sharjah started in May 1974, from the Mubarak offshore field at Abu Musa. The field produced an average of close to 40,000 b/d for the first six months of 1975 and storage facilities were provided by the 640,000-barrel tanker *Baraka I*. The Buttes Gas and Oil Company is the operator for the Abu Musa project under a participation agreement giving 55 per cent of all oil lifted to Sharjah. West of Mubarak, Sharjah granted two United States firms, Pinnacle Gas and Oil and Nicklos Drilling, the oil exploration right on 386 miles^2 of acreage located in the western part of Sharjah which was recently relinquished by Crystal Company. Under the agreement Sharjah will receive 60 per cent (its 'participation' share) and the companies 40 per cent of any oil discovered and produced; the companies will invest $12 million in the first three years and drill 316,000-foot wells over a period of 30 months at the rate of one well every 10 months.[14] In addition, Reserve Oil signed an agreement with the ruler, Sheikh Sultan, for exploration rights in the Eastern sector. A concession in the western portion of Sharjah involves Amoco. The results of the seismic testing in 1979 have led to exploratory drilling in 1980. There is optimism that petroleum will be discovered in commercial quantities; in fact, a 16,656-foot exploration well in the Sagga field has reportedly tested out at 4,650 b/d of high-gravity crude as well as associated gas of 50 million cfd.[15]

Sharjah sold its participation crude to Japan Line at a rate of 2.2 million barrels in 1974, with a planned increase in sales to 11 million barrels by 1978. Based on the expectation of oil exports, Sharjah was able to get a $20 million loan from a group of Japanese banks.[16]

Early in 1980 London and Scottish Marine Oil Company and Forman Exploration of New Orleans discovered natural gas at a test well at Hamriyyah, about 20 miles offshore from Sharjah in two zones. Total flow was registered at 14.4 million cubic feet daily (cfd).

Ras Al-Khaimah granted an offshore concession in 1964 to Union Oil Company (80 per cent) and Southern National Gas Company (20 per cent), which joined together to form the Ras-Al-Khaimah Oil Company. The oil discovered offshore Ras Al-Khaimah in January 1972 by Union Oil Company of California was originally thought to be exploitable. However, after extensive studies had been made, the oil was found to be of insufficient quantity. The company, despite its insufficient find, is continuing its search.

Shell Oil Company was granted an onshore concession on 15 March 1969, totalling some 375 miles^2. The area held by Shell and the John Mecom Corporation was later concessioned to Peninsula Petroleum, a subsidiary of the US California Time Group. Peninsula began seismic work in February 1974.

Vitol Exploration of the Netherlands was also awarded a concession in Ras Al-Khaimah. In addition, Gulf Oil has taken an active interest in the exploration for petroleum in Ras Al-Khaimah. Early in 1980, Gulf completed seismic onshore surveys of the Emirate and drew maps of the area. Gulf's initial investigation at Khatt, only 12 miles from the Ras Al-Khaimah airport, was promising enough that plans had been drawn up to drill its first well ever in Ras Al-Khaimah.

Other oil concessions in Sharjah, Umm Al-Quwain, and Ajman were granted to John W. Mecom and Pure Oil Company; Bomin Bochumer Mineralgesellschaft won the concession rights in Fujairah.[17] The first reports of the efforts of United Refinings (URC) and the Occidental Petroleum Company in concessions offshore Umm Al-Quwain and Ajman are encouraging, with Fujairah hoping to benefit from the latest exploration rights granted to Reserve Oil and Gas. United Refining is sharing its concession in Umm Al-Quwain with three Canadian companies — Canadian Superior Oil, Zapata Exploration, and Kewanee Overseas Oil. URC also won a 35-year hydrocarbon exploration and production concession from Ajman. Further, in 1976 Umm Al-Quwain signed an exploration and drilling agreement with Houston Oil and Minerals which covers the emirate's onshore area. Later, Texaco took part in the same concession.

In high hopes of discovering its own petroleum, Ajman granted exploration rights in 1978 for a 55,000-acre tract offshore to Forman Exploration of New Orleans. Forman later (in 1979) sold 50 per cent of its lease to the UK firm, London and Scottish Marine Oil Company Ltd. The lease is for 35 years during which time $10 million is to be spent. In September 1980 Reynolds Diversified Corporation of Denver, Colorado, acquired an 80 per cent interest in the offshore oil and gas concession held by Northland Minerals of Australia. Reynolds is scheduled to make a $100,000 payment to the government of Ajman

Fuelling UAE Development: Oil 99

and to underwrite the costs of a geographical survey to be completed by the spring of 1981 at a cost of $300,000. When the survey is completed, Reynolds retains the option to acquire an additional 15 per cent in the concession for which the company must finance the cost of two exploration wells. The concession area lies only 12 miles from Sharjah's Mubarak field.

An oil concession at Fujairah was further opened to participation when Mitsubishi acquired a 10 per cent portion of it from Getty Oil. Denison Mines of Canada along with 15 other companies also participate in the 700,000-acre offshore concession. Mitsubishi set up a branch company, Fujairah Oil Exploration and Development Company, especially to further its oil interest. The company was capitalized at $3.3 million at its outset in mid-1980.

The most sweeping development in the UAE's recent oil history is the establishment of the ADNOC. This move is very much in line with other Middle Eastern, North African, and OPEC producers which have instituted national petroleum companies such as Lipetco (Libya), Kuwait National Petroleum Company, and Petromin (Saudi Arabia). The purpose of the newly formed company was outlined in its founding document.

> The objective of the company shall be to engage in the petroleum industry in Abu Dhabi as agreed and to operate in any of the stages of this industry including exploration and drilling for oil, natural gas and other hydrocarbon substances, and the production, refining, transportation and storage of the afore-mentioned substances or their derivatives and products and distribute, sell and export them.[18]

Article IV in the document further continues:

> In order to achieve its objectives, the company may undertake the following:
> (1) The establishment of companies, by itself or jointly with others, or participation in existing companies.
> (2) The conclusion of contracts for cooperation in various forms with companies or organizations engaged in operations related to its objectives and the purchase or affiliation of such companies or organizations.
> (3) All legal actions necessary for the good performance of the

company's operations.[19]

The national company was officially established on 28 November 1971 by Sheikh Zayed Ibn-Sultan al-Nahayyan. The company was designed so that it could eventually take over a sizable share of Abu Dhabi's oil industry; OPEC has urged such a path. With control of the oil now primarily in government hands, attention is on investment in future oil and gas projects and in continuity in the supply of essential technical and managerial talents. The second factor of skilled manpower is a major reason why Abu Dhabi officials prefer to retain international companies as equity holders in oil and gas ventures in the current 60/40 partnership. This is seen as a means to maximize the benefits from the companies, know-how and expertise. Still, an abiding concern among officials is that Abu Dhabi's income per barrel of exported oil should be on par with that of the neighbouring countries. The government also feels that a 60 per cent government participation is sufficient to ensure in practice total control over key policies as output levels by the state. Observers view two things as possibly curbing the long-term continuation of the 60/40 formulation: (1) build-up of grass-roots political pressure as a result of a 100 per cent takeover in neighbouring countries, and/or (2) international companies concerned with profitability may back out if return on investment is inadequate.[20] ADNOC markets a portion of its share of crude directly to both public (government-owned) and private companies. For example, crude supplies to India from the UAE will be raised from an annual level of 1 to 1.5 million tons to nearly 2.5 million tons. As something of a *quid pro quo*, India has agreed in principle to import some 40 per cent of the projected output of Abu Dhabi's Nitrogenous Fertilizer Industries Company (an ADNOC joint venture with CFP).

Abu Dhabi's buy-back arrangements for 1976 were based on liftings of 70 per cent of output by the companies (40 per cent equity and 30 per cent buy-back) and 30 per cent by ADNOC. This compares with a split of 80 per cent for the companies (40 per cent equity and 40 per cent buy-back) and 20 per cent for ADNOC in 1975. For their 1976 and 1977 liftings, the ADPC (now ADCO) partners onshore and the ADMA group offshore, purchased the equity crude at tax-paid cost and the buy-back at government market prices, i.e. 93 per cent of posting.[21] The government selling prices (as of July 1977) for the

Table 5.1: UAE Oil Prices by Fields and Gravity, 1978-80 (in US $/barrel)

	31 Dec. 1978	1 Jan. 1979	15 Feb. 1979	1 April 1979	17 May 1979	1 July 1979	1 Nov. 1979	1 Jan. 1980	1 Feb. 1980	1 July 1980	1 Sept. 1980
Abu Dhabi Murban-39° (850,000 b/d)[a]	13.26	14.10	15.12	17.10	17.90	21.56	27.56	29.56	29.56	31.56	33.56
Zakum-40° (300,000 b/d)[a]	13.17	14.01	15.03	17.01	17.81	21.46	27.46	29.46	29.46	31.46	33.46
Umm Shaif-37° (200,000 b/d)[a]	13.04	13.78	14.62	16.88	17.68	21.36	27.36	29.36	29.36	31.36	33.36
Abu Bukhoosh-32° (70,000 b/d)[a]	12.65	13.28	14.12	16.29	17.09	20.75	26.75	28.75[b]	28.75[b]	30.75[d]	32.75[d]
Mubarraz-38° (20,000 b/d)[a]	13.08	13.92	14.76	16.92	17.72	21.59[b]	27.40[b]	29.40[b]	29.40[b]	31.40[d]	33.40[d]
Dubai Fateh-32° (355,000 b/d)[a]	12.64	13.27	c	16.286	17.086	19.93	25.93	27.93	27.93	29.93[d]	31.93[d]
Sharjah Mubarak-38° (15,000 b/d)[a]	13.29	14.13	15.15	17.13	17.93	21.62	27.62	27.62	27.62[b]	29.62[d]	31.62[d]

Sources: *Middle East Economic Survey*, 19 February 1979, p. 3; 9 April 1979, p. 3; 2 July 1979, p. 4; 17 December 1979, p. 3; 14 July 1980, p. 6; 20 October 1980, p. 6; *Petroleum Intelligence Weekly*, 3 March 1980, special supplement, p. 3.
a. Estimate of overall supply potentially available.
b. *Petroleum Intelligence Weekly* estimate.
c. March 1 price of $13.78; March 10 price of $14.27.
d. Assumes $2 increments in line with those for Abu Dhabi's Murban, Zakum, and Umm Shaif.

various crudes were $13.26/barrel for 39° API Murban (onshore); $13.17/barrel for 40° API Zakum and $13.04/barrel for 37° API Umm Shaif (offshore). Table 5.1 gives UAE oil prices by fields and gravity for 1978-80 indicating the price escalation in 1979. Credit terms were 60 days for ADPC and 90 days for ADMA, the extra allowance for ADMA being in the nature of a compensation for its high investment requirements (with costs which ran at over $1/barrel).

The allowable output for the two ventures for 1976 was set at 1 million b/d for ADPC (now ADCO) onshore and 450,000 b/d for ADMA offshore. This assumed the 1976 lifting would be made up as follows: ADPC — 700,000 b/d for companies and 300,000 b/d for ADNOC; ADMA — 315,000 b/d for the companies and 135,000 b/d for ADNOC. Since that time, the allowable production levels have reflected a number of factors: demand (either shortages or gluts); political decisions in an effort to reinforce pricing stances within OPEC; and the very real need to conserve the petroleum resources. The output ceiling from all of Abu Dhabi's fields indicates the growing concern to conserve oil reserves, down from 1.355 million b/d to 1.275 million b/d as of 1 August 1980, with a further lowering of the ceiling as of 1 January 1981, to 1.195 million b/d.[22] None the less, the allowable output is not immutable; it can be and is changed, although the changes tend to be in response to special or immediate requirements. For example, following the disruption of oil exports from Iraq during the autumn 1980 conflict with Iran, Abu Dhabi jacked up offshore production, albeit understood on a temporary basis, by 50,000 b/d. The additional output was for sale to CFP and Elf/Aquitaine of France to offset lost deliveries from Iraq.

Nor is Abu Dhabi the only major oil exporter to impose production-conservation ceilings. All have moved in this direction, although the allowable output levels are more flexible in some than in other producing countries. Kuwait, Libya, and Qatar have relatively long-established conservation of production policies as reflected in their ceilings. Similarly, non-OPEC exporters Mexico and Norway have production policies which have upper limits on output under normal conditions. Saudi Arabia's self-imposed 8.5 million b/d ceiling is among the more flexible, often being increased (as during the Iran–Iraq conflict) to about 10 million b/d to meet special needs.

Table 5.2: Production of Crude Oil, 1962-80 (in millions of barrels)

	Abu Dhabi[a]	Dubai[b]	Sharjah[c]	Total
1962	6	—	—	6
1963	18	—	—	18
1964	69	—	—	69
1965	103	—	—	103
1966	131	—	—	131
1967	139	—	—	139
1968	182	—	—	182
1969	219	4	—	223
1970	253	31	—	284
1971	341	46	—	387
1972	384	56	—	440
1973	476	80	—	556
1974	515	88	9	612
1975	513	93	14	620
1976	580	115	14	709
1977	603	116	—	719
1978	528	132	8	668
1979	533	129	5	667
1980	504	128	4	636

Sources: UAE, Currency Board, *Bulletin*, May 1975 and December 1978; UAE, Currency Board, *Statistical Supplement*, March 1980; Shell International Petroleum Co., Ltd, *Information Handbook 1980-81* (London: Shell International Petroleum Co., Ltd, 1980), p. 26; United Arab Emirates, Ministry of Petroleum and Mineral Resources, *Annual Report, 1980* (1 May 1980), p. 176 (in Arabic); *Oil and Gas Journal*, 29 December 1980, p. 78.
a. Including Abu Bukhoosh which started production and exports in July 1974, and Bunduq which started in November 1975.
b. Dubai started production and export of crude oil in September 1969.
c. Sharjah started production and export in July 1974.

Total production for the Emirates is presented in Table 5.2; Tables 5.3 to 5.5 give more detailed information regarding the status of oil and gas operations in the UAE.

The discussion on oil in the UAE would be incomplete without some reflections on the pricing policies and the role which the federation has

Table 5.3: Details of UAE Crude Oil Production

	Name of field, discovery date	Depth, feet	Number of wells Flow	Number of wells Artificial lift	Number of wells Shut-in	B/d average first 6 months 1980	Cumulative barrels to 1 July 1980	API gravity
Abu Dhabi	Arzanah, 1973	8,000	8	—	—	22,000	7,250,000	43.4-44.4
	Asab, 1965	7,500	—	—	—	300,000	—	38.0-40.0
	Abu Bukhoosh, 1969	7,900	20	—	—	75,000	155,000,000	32.1
	Bab (Murban), 1960	8,500	—	—	—	54,000	—	38.0-40.0
	Bu Hasa, 1962	7,500	293[b]	—	38[b]	365,000	3,592,000,000	38.0-40.0
	Bunduq, 1965[a]	8,500	(shut in since 1979)			—	3,300,000	40.0
	Mubarraz, 1971[a]	11,000	20	—	11	22,000	50,800,000	37.8
	Sahil, 1970	7,500	—	—	—	20,000	—	40.0
	Umm Shaif, 1958[a]	9,150	—	—	—	250,000	—	37.0
	Upper Zakum, 1964[a]	9,500	—	—	—	48,000	2,021,000,000	39.8
	Lower Zakum, 1964[a]	9,100	—	—	—	200,000	—	
	Total Abu Dhabi		341		49	1,356,000		
Dubai	Fateh, 1966[a]	7,600-9,000	16	26	4	151,712	560,239,330	31.8
	S.W. Fateh, 1970[a]	7,500-9,000	5	23	6	182,165	387,169,570	30.3
	Falah, 1972[a]	8,100	1	6	—	9,479	5,290,267	25.5
	Rashid, 1973[a]	9,400-11,500	2	—	1	1,589	889,741	38.0
	Total Dubai		24	55	11	344,945	953,588,908	
Sharjah	Mubarak, 1972[a]	12,650-12,990	3	1	—	10,000	60,685,000	27.0

Source: *Oil and Gas Journal*, 29 December 1980, pp. 87, 96, 121.
a. Offshore.
b. Estimated.

Table 5.4: Well Completions

	Total wells 1978	Producers 1978	Total footage 1978 (1,000 ft)	Total wild-cats 1978	Discoveries 1978	Total wells 1977	Total wells 1975	Total wells 1970
Abu Dhabi	78	77	761	19	1	67	49	7
Dubai	12	7	80	5	0	31	17	0
Sharjah	0	0	0	0	0	0	2	0

Source: *Oil and Gas Journal*, 31 December 1979, p. 207.

Table 5.5: Summary Statistics of Oil and Gas in the UAE

Estimated Proved Reserves, 1 January 1981

	Oil (1,000 barrels)	Gas (10^9 cu. ft)
Abu Dhabi	29,000,000	20,000
Dubai	1,400,000	775
Sharjah	10,000	–

Oil production

	Producing wells 1 July 1980	Estimated 1980 (b/d)	Per cent change from 1979
Abu Dhabi	341	1,380,000	–5.7
Dubai	79	350,000	–1.1
Sharjah	4	10,000	–23.1

Refining capacity (b/d) 1 January 1980

	Number of refineries	Crude	Catalytic cracking	Thermal cracking	Reforming
Abu Dhabi	1	13,500	–	–	2,500
Dubai	–	–	–	–	–
Sharjah	–	–	–	–	–

Source: *Oil and Gas Journal*, 29 December 1980, p. 78.

played in the OPEC decision-making process. The UAE has traditionally taken a moderate position at OPEC meetings. The country has co-operated with Saudi Arabia to adopt a more conservative attitude *vis-à-vis* some other OPEC members, i.e. the so-called price hawks. Like Saudi Arabia, however, it has shown the ability to adjust to prevailing market conditions, although invariably among the reasons given for price increases include the argument that it is desirable to realign UAE prices with those of the other members of OPEC. See Table 5.1 for the prices of UAE crude oil, which does not include the increment decided upon at the December 1980 OPEC meeting held in Bali. At those sessions, Saudi Arabia headed the moderates in seeking a $2/barrel increase, raising the price of OPEC's marker (or benchmark) crude to $32/barrel (Saudi Arabian Light 34° API). Other OPEC members will be charging anything from the market price to the ceiling of $41/barrel, depending on individual government decisions and on premiums and other differentials for lighter/low or sulphur crudes and/or locational advantages.

The UAE has played its part in the process of alleviating the strain and stresses which have characterized OPEC meetings. Being a 'low absorber' capital-surplus country, its moderate position at these meetings is understandable. With the exit of Iran from the moderate camp early in 1979, Saudi Arabia viewed its co-operation with the UAE as more critical than ever to maintain a moderate pricing movement within OPEC. In this regard, the future will likely see the UAE in a continuing significant role.

Utilization of Natural Gas Resources

The UAE possesses gas reserves amounting to 21.6 trillion (US) cubic feet (tcf) as of 1 January 1978, of which the lion's share belongs to Abu Dhabi (20 tcf) with Dubai's estimated at 1.6 tcf.[23] Natural-gas utilization, however, is still very limited, but it will increase as development proceeds and the petrochemical and energy-intensive industries planned and/or being constructed come on stream. (See Table 5.6 for gas production and utilization statistics.)

Das Island, lying approximately 137 miles northwest of Abu Dhabi city, is developing as a highly sophisticated processing, storage, and tanker-loading terminal for the offshore fields at Umm Shaif, Bunduq and Zakum operated by ADMA-OPCO. It accommodates 1,000 highly skilled experts and technicians who live at and work on the site, joined by 2,500 live-in workers and another 2,500 travelling to the site daily — a substantial work force for completion of the giant liquefied natural gas plant in March 1977.

The Abu Dhabi Gas Liquefaction Company (ADGLC) is a driving force behind what must be termed an ambitious undertaking in the energy history of the UAE. With a total capitalization of $105 million, the consortium is owned by ANDOC (51 per cent), BP (15.33 per cent), CFP (8.16 per cent), Mitsui and Company (22.05 per cent), and Bridgestone Liquefied Gas Company (24.6 per cent).[24] When fully operational, the production flow of gas is some 550 million cfd. The

Table 5.6: Abu Dhabi Production and Utilization of Natural Gas, 1975-9 (in million cubic feet)

Company	1975 Production	1975 Utilization	1976 Production	1976 Utilization	1977 Production	1977 Utilization	1978 Production	1978 Utilization	1979 Production	1979 Utilization
ADCO[a]	275,599	34,498	325,613	44,525	313,839	74,383	249,188	59,540	278,651	—
ADMA[b]	149,690	31,918	158,433	55,226	211,804	107,699	211,584	109,025	202,504	—
ADOC[c]	3,083	327	5,384	532	4,950	453	5,532	340	4,671	—
TABK[d]	9,569	9,569	13,182	200	47,186	7,992	12,328	642	12,036	—
Amerada-Hess	—	—	—	—	—	—	—	—	9,471	—
Total	437,941	76,312	502,612	100,483	577,779	190,527	478,632	169,547	507,333	—

Source: Organization of Arab Petroleum Exporting Countries, *OAPEC Bulletin*, December 1980, p. 31.

a. Abu Dhabi Company for Onshore Operations, formerly Abu Dhabi Petroleum Company.
b. Abu Dhabi Marine Operating Company, since 1978 abbreviated as ADMA-OPCO.
c. Abu Dhabi Oil Company Ltd (Japan).
d. Total-Abu Al Bukhoosh (subsidiary of Compagnie Française des Pétroles).

Fuelling UAE Development: Oil

Table 5.7: Abu Dhabi Exports (Das Island Plant) of Liquefied Natural Gas (LNG) and Liquefied Petroleum Gas (LPG), 1977–80 (in metric tons)

		LNG	LPG		
			Propane	Butane	Pentane
1977[a]	Second quarter	56,213	–	–	–
	Third quarter	208,204	11,087	8,749	–
	Fourth quarter	229,278	6,802	4,497	–
	Total	493,695	17,889	13,246	–
1978	First quarter	282,489	42,970	17,023	16,836
	Second quarter	358,556	53,266	47,297	–
	Third quarter	358,903	51,615	37,978	22,936
	Fourth quarter	316,382	57,890	50,299	25,815
	Total	1,316,330	205,741	152,507	65,587
1979	First quarter	198,913	53,088	38,046	21,084
	Second quarter	268,302	79,997	57,411	22,036
	Third quarter	416,723	80,265	57,463	29,306
	Fourth quarter	489,955	86,909	60,746	26,642
	Total	1,373,893	300,259	213,666	99,068
1980	First quarter	439,506	78,805	65,771	37,805

Source: UAE, Currency Board, *Bulletin*, December 1979, p. 147, and *Statistical Supplement*, March 1980, p. 20.
a. UAE (Abu Dhabi) gas exports commenced in April 1977.

plant on Das Island produces nearly 3 million tons a year of LNG (2.2 million tons) and LPG (800,000 tons), all for export and almost totally destined for Japan as part of a 20-year contract with Tokyo Electric Company (TEPCO). Four 786,000-barrel/tankers have been chartered for LNG transportation and three 503,000-barrel/ships were under construction in Japan for LPG transportation. Table 5.7 depicts the level of exports from the ADGLC Das Island plant since the beginning of its operations. By 1980, ADGLC's operations were reducing the amount of gas flared and, along with re-injection to maintain pressure in the oilfields, upwards of 300 million cubic feet of high- and low-pressure natural gas was being utilized. With completion of a second gas-gathering system in 1980, more than 90 per cent of the gas produced will be used.

Near the close of 1975, the first stages of a massive natural-gas utilization project began as part of the Ruwais industrial complex. Natural gas fuels the infrastructure of the complex in the areas of power generation and water supplies (desalination). But natural-gas utilization goes beyond these applications as production starts up of the $2 billion onshore gas project of GASCO. One of ADNOC's largest subsidiaries, Abu Dhabi Gas Industries Company (GASCO) is empowered to exploit the natural gas liquids produced from the onshore fields of Asab, Bu Hasa, and Bab (operated by ADCO). The gas is treated at the fields then moved by pipeline to Ruwais for processing (fractionation), followed by storage (sometimes at temperatures of $-44°C$), and finally loading at the dock into specialized marine carriers. The original shareholders in GASCO, aside from ADNOC (68 per cent), are CFP (15 per cent), Shell (15 per cent), and Partex (2 per cent).

The GASCO facility has the productive capacity for an annual output of 1.23 million tons of propane, 1.41 million tons of butane and 2.11 million tons of natural gasoline, that is, the extraction of liquefied petroleum gas (LPG). The Das Island plant output, by contrast is predominantly of LNG (liquefied natural gas). Onshore natural gas will offer the feedstock for the Abu Dhabi Fertilizers Company (a joint venture between ADNOC and CFP), the contract for which was awarded in 1980. The two plants at Ruwais will produce 1,000 tons/day of ammonia and 1,500 tons/day of urea, respectively.

On the basis of oil production at full rated capacity of 1.28 million b/d from the three onshore fields, the output of associated gas would average around 1,070 million cfd from which 185,000 b/d of NGL could be extracted. The breakdown of the 185,000 b/d of NGL projected for the associated gas from the Bu Hasa, Bab and Asab oil fields is as follows:[25]

	Bu Hasa	Bab	Asab	Total
Oil production (thousand b/d)	690	130	460	1,280
Associated gas (million cfd)	550	120	390	1,070
NGL output (thousand b/d)				
LPG	56	6	52	114
Natural gasoline	34	4	33	71
Total	90	10	85	185

Fuelling UAE Development: Oil

The Government of Abu Dhabi commissioned the French Institute of Petroleum to carry out a feasibility study on the maximum utilization of natural gas throughout the area. The conclusions were: (1) natural gas from the various plants could be readily on tap for piping to the bigger industrial and public utility complexes; (2) bottled LPG would be available for distribution for the domestic and small industrial consumption throughout the immediate area and the UAE; and (3) LNG would be exported to countries in urgent need of clean fuel.

The Thamama F gas plant which ADCO operates on behalf of ADNOC supplies power stations in Abu Dhabi city and Umm Al-Nar. Currently, power generation, crude sweetening, and oil pumping are uses made of associated gas from the area.

Dubai is also moving swiftly ahead to make use of the energy at present flared off into the atmosphere. Future industrial expansion will be in urgent need of every type of fuel. Sunningdale Oils of Canada has been granted a 15-year concession to exploit the natural gas potential of the Fateh and Southwest Fateh fields. The Dubai government owns 55 per cent of the joint venture and a feasibility study is already under way. In April 1980 Dubai officially opened the Dubai Natural Gas Company which processes gas from offshore and supplies Dubai's aluminium smelter. The availability of natural gas at reasonable costs is critical in allowing Dubal (Dubai Aluminium Company) to compete internationally, in large part because aluminium smelting is so energy intensive.

Sharjah's plans for natural gas usage include the probability of a production and storage complex similar to Abu Dhabi's Das Island, depending on thorough studies of existing reserves and the potential in other areas as yet under-exploited.

A law recently issued by the Abu Dhabi government makes all natural gas reserves in the emirate the sole property of the state. The law also covers associated gas from Abu Dhabi's oil fields which at the moment are owned by the government in partnership with Western oil companies. The state-owned ADNOC has been given the right to exploit all the emirate's gas reserves; however, it will be able to set up joint ventures as long as it retains a 51 per cent controlling interest. Under the new law, ADCO, the emirate's main onshore oil producer, and its offshore producer, ADMA-OPCO, will be able to use, free of charge, all the gas they need for their oil-output operations.[26] (See Appendix

IV for further details of this law.)

The role of natural gas in development plans to accelerate industrialization and to upgrade agriculture in the arid lands of the Emirates could be a vital one. Natural gas is an attractive fuel — clean burning and an inexpensive replacement for oil. Roughly speaking, estimates of the total reserves of natural gas are three times those of oil. And the vast petrochemicals industry, especially fertilizer production, uses natural gas feedstock.

The advantages of gas utilization in agricultural development are obvious. The UAE's drive to make the area as self-sufficient as possible in fresh foods would quicken with the provision of a readily available easily stored and flexible alternative to oil, capable of powering the generators necessary for soilless and hydroponic culture, greenhouses, and experimental farms.

For many years, associated gas was simply flared off at the wellhead since the costs of processing into transportable form (NGL, LNG), plus the high cost of pipelines and/or specialized tankers for transportation, made natural gas economically unviable. Even re-injection programmes were not deemed cost effective. However, rising demand domestically and for export, the burgeoning petrochemical industries within the oil-producing countries, and new technologies have combined to raise the price for liquefied natural gas. Effective 1 January 1980, Abu Dhabi instituted a new LNG price to Japan of $4 million per BTU (cif Japan), a 70 per cent increase. Moreover, this new price will be indexed against the official price for Murban crude oil. Formerly, the LNG price was indexed against the average level of delivered prices for all crudes imported into Japan during the previous year.

Notes

1. K.G. Fenelon, *The Trucial States* (London: Longman Publishers, 1973), p. 32. Technically, the Iraq Petroleum Company established Petroleum Concessions Limited as a subsidiary initially capitalized at £100,000.
2. Ibid.
3. Shell International Petroleum Company Limited, *Information Handbook 1972-3* (London: Shell International Petroleum Co., Ltd, 1972), pp. 19, 35, and 41. The ownership of Abu Dhabi Petroleum Company and Qatar Petroleum at that time was identical, involving 23.75 per cent each for Shell, CFP, British Petroleum, and Near-East Development Corporation (jointly owned by Mobil

Fuelling UAE Development: Oil

and Exxon) and 5 per cent for Participation and Exploration owned by Gulbenkian.

4. Fenelon, *Trucial States*, pp. 32-4.

5. United Arab Emirates (UAE), Currency Board, *Bulletin*, November 1977, p. 116.

6. The refinery's capacity is 15,000 b/d.

7. Mana Saeed Al-Otaiba, *The Economy of Abu Dhabi, Ancient and Modern* (Beirut: Commercial and Industrial Press, 1971), pp. 174-9.

8. Ibid., pp. 169, 174-9.

9. The consortium is headed by Sceptre Resources; other participants include Bow Valley Industries of Calgary, Western Mines of Toronto, and Scarboro Resources of Vancouver. See *Middle East Economic Survey*, 20 December 1980, pp. 2-4 for Oil Minister al-Otaiba's description of Abu Dhabi's massive exploration drive for the 1980s. (Hereafter *Middle East Economic Survey* will be cited as *MEES*.)

10. *MEES*, 28 February 1977, p. 8. To summarize, the companies and the fields under their operation are: ADCO, Bu Hasa, Asab, Bab, and Sahil; ADMA-OPCO-Umm Saif, Lower Zakum, and Upper Zakum (ADNOC); CFP – Abu Bukhoosh; Amerada-Hess – Arzanah.

11. The partners in the Dubai Petroleum Company are: Continental Oil Company (Conoco), 60 per cent; Texaco, 20 per cent; Sun Oil, 10 per cent; and Wintershall, 10 per cent.

12. *Oil and Gas Journal*, 25 December 1978, p. 102.

13. *Middle East Economic Digest*, 10 June 1977, pp. 41-4 and 1 July 1977, p. 34. (Hereafter *Middle East Economic Digest* will be cited as *MEED*.)

14. *MEES*, 31 May 1976, p. 3.

15. United Arab Emirates, Ministry of Petroleum and Mineral Resources, *Annual Report 1980* (1 May 1980), p. 184 (in Arabic); *MEES*, 15 December 1980, p. 7.

16. *Quarterly Economic Review*, no. 1, 1974, p. 23.

17. Donald Hawley, *The Trucial States* (London: George Allen and Unwin Ltd, 1971), p. 223.

18. *MEES*, Supplement, 10 December 1971, pp. 1-2.

19. Ibid.

20. From a report by *MEES* new editor Ian Seymour entitled 'Abu Dhabi: The Oil and Gas Scene', *MEES*, 12 April 1976, pp. i-v.

21. As 1980 drew to a close, ADNOC announced very sizable cuts in 1981 sales, specifically to the foreign equity holders. Most foreign equity holders will get entitlements only in 1981, marking the end of buy-back contracts. The volume involved in their terminated contracts is approximately 70,000 b/d; deliveries to Japanese customers (including equity-holding JODCO) will be cut back by 28 per cent (some 94,000 b/d) of which Japan Line's reduction will be the greatest (from 60,000 b/d slashed to 15,000 b/d). Several reasons have been offered for these moves: the overall production cutback; the rising requirements to supply the 120,000 b/d Ruwais refinery coming on stream in mid-1981; the critical supply needs of the oil-importing developing countries' draw-off deliveries which would otherwise go to the Japanese buy-back group and equity holders. *MEES*, 24 November 1980, p. 7 and 8 December 1980, pp. 3-4.

22. *MEES*, 8 December 1980, p. 3. The following table indicates which companies and fields will absorb the cuts in allowable production (in b/d).

Company and field	1 Jan. 1981	1 Aug. 1980	Pre-Aug. 1980
ADCO:			
Bu Hasa		295,000	365,000
Asab		300,000	300,000
Bab		50,000	50,000
Sahil		25,000	25,000
Total	600,000	670,000	670,000
ADMA–OPCO:			
Umm Shaif	250,000	250,000	250,000
Lower Zakum	200,000	200,000	200,000
Upper Zakum (ADNOC)	30,000	40,000	50,000
Total	480,000	490,000	500,000
Total-Abu Al Bukhoosh:			
Abu Bukhoosh	75,000	75,000	75,000
ADOCO:			
Mubarraz	20,000	20,000	20,000
Amerada-Hess:			
Arzanah	20,000	20,000	20,000
Total	1,195,000	1,275,000	1,255,000

The above figures exclude the 50,000 b/d offshore production for two French companies to offset loss of Iraqi deliveries in the autumn of 1978.

23. *Oil and Gas Journal*, 25 December 1978, p. 102.

24. *MEED*, special report, July 1977, p. 10. Gas liquefaction plants produce two fuel types — liquefied natural gas (LNG) and liquefied petroleum gas (LPG). LPG is known to users in many countries for light industries, domestic use, greenhouses, and for other purposes where a clean and easily transportable fuel is needed. LNG, on the other hand, presents some costly production-technique problems to the producer; yet with the change in world prices and the massive demand for fuels with a low pollution content, the production of LNG is becoming more profitable.

25. *MEES*, 12 April 1976, pp. 1-2, and *MEED*, 23 April 1976, p. 30.

26. *MEED*, 12 March 1976, p. 28, and *MEES*, 5 March 1976, p. 7.

6 THE FOREIGN TRADE SECTOR

The linchpin of life in the UAE is oil. Almost all the petroleum produced is exported in its crude form. Exports other than oil are negligible, and consist mainly of re-exports. However, in the future liquefied natural gas, fertilizers, plastics, and other petrochemicals and oil derivatives, along with products in which the energy component is as substantial as aluminium, may assume importance on the export list.

While it was originally assumed that the oil producers of the Middle East would never be able to import up to the level of their exports, this assumption can no longer be automatic or all-inclusive. The dominance of oil in combination with the theory of absorptive capacity brings the issue of internal spending of the region's wealth to the forefront. In the long run, it is felt that the possibilities for consumption and investment in the Middle East will certainly be capable of absorbing a major part of the oil revenues and surpluses which may accrue. In the short run, foreign entrepreneurs and governments are still offered investment schemes in industry, infrastructure and agriculture, despite the existence of logistic, administrative, managerial, labour and cultural impediments.

Countries such as the United Arab Emirates have been labelled 'low absorbers,' for they exhibit a disproportionately large oil-income compared to their small-sized population and national economy. With a limited domestic market and an inadequate labour supply, the UAE has an inherent tendency to amass huge surpluses of unspendable oil-income (as indicated in Table 2.6).[1] The necessity of assessing the economy's absorptive capacity has thus become the object of intense study due to the increasing awareness on the part of the international business community of the opportunities and financial potential of this burgeoning market.

In general, the expenditure pattern for the UAE is concentrated in the areas of improving social welfare services, infrastructure, downstream petroleum industries, defence, agriculture and other industrial developments. Deceleration of expenditures on consumer and conspicuous goods in favour of increased spending on planned industrial commitments should eventually be the emerging pattern.

Composition of Imports

Imports to the United Arab Emirates significantly increased in the 1970—9 period. The rise was especially marked for manufactures and transport equipments. Table 6.1 shows the evolution of importation to the UAE as well as projected imports for 1985. Table 6.2 presents a more concise summary of the UAE's imports for 1970—9.

Food and live animal imports consist of livestock, canned meat, fresh fruits, frozen meat, sugar, canned foodstuffs, canned fish, wheat flour and frozen vegetables. This category has shown rapid expansion over the years. Beverages and tobacco imports also demonstrated considerable rates of growth, especially in Dubai. Beverages, followed by liquor and wine, canned juice and cigarettes, lead in the group sales.

Imports of fertilizers and crude materials (group 2) to Abu Dhabi registered a brisk expansion in the 1970s; and in Dubai, the large increase in the crude-materials category arose from a near doubling of general building materials. Group 4, encompassing animal and vegetable oils and fats, constituted relatively small sales to the United Arab Emirates. The chemicals group principally consisted of higher imports of medicines, toilet preparations and paints. During 1978 import levels of groups 1, 2 and 3 declined. Whereas the decline in the first two groups of imports can be explained only by several conditions (high stocks, regional instability in Iran resulting in some greater financial caution, general global economic slowdown), the decline in group 3 should be expected since it is the results of increased domestic production of lubricants.

Projections to 1985 expect the first three commodity groupings (groups 0, 1 and 2) to maintain the 1975 percentage share of total imports while group 3 (mineral fuels, etc.) will exhibit a declining percentage share of total imports as new plants processing these commodities come on stream. The 1975 percentage shares of animal and vegetable fats and oils and chemical imports are foreseen to continue at the same rate until 1985. With a larger area and population than some of the other Gulf states, the UAE should experience little difficulty

Table 6.1: Commodity Classification of Imports (Abu Dhabi and Dubai), SITC-adjusted (millions of Dh)

Group	1971	1972	1973	1974	1975	1976	1977	1978	1979a	1985
0 Food and live animals	183.1	245.5	344.7	822.3	1,020.8	1,250.3	1,440.1	1,689.7	1,036.5	2,044.8
1 Beverages and tobacco	48.1	58.4	75.5	112.0	152.2	198.8	218.3	214.3	211.2	228.9
2 Crude materials, inedible, except fuels	33.4	39.0	86.4	146.2	147.8	305.9	339.8	280.7	123.4	225.0
3 Mineral fuels, lubricants and related materials	—	111.6	159.6	537.3	780.9	930.8	1,216.1	729.9	137.4	1,361.9
4 Animal and vegetable oils and fats	45.1	5.5	6.0	36.8	18.0	28.8	31.7	44.2	23.5	—
5 Chemicals	48.4	60.5	100.7	212.5	404.5	474.6	641.9	736.3	420.1	—
6 Manufactured goods, classified chiefly by materials	331.2	511.3	866.1	1,857.4	2,834.1	3,351.0	4,417.1	4,431.2	2,610.9	5,901.5
7 Machinery and transport equipment	349.9	632.8	1,001.2	2,186.7	4,388.2	5,733.6	7,749.4	8,532.0	4,385.2	8,171.3
8 Miscellaneous manufactured articles	249.8	309.9	414.6	681.7	1,051.7	1,203.0	1,904.8	2,166.6	1,188.2	2,269.8
9 Commodities not classified according to kind	18.4	35.0	24.4	48.2	112.0	123.9	130.7	190.0	98.2	225.0
Oilfield materialsb	74.9	174.9	165.3	272.8	412.2					1,361.9
Total	1,482.3	2,175.0	3,352.1	7,053.5	10,910.1	13,600.8	18,089.7	19,015.1	10,234.6	22,698.0

Source: UAE, Currency Board, *Bulletin*, November 1977, p. 126 and December 1979, p. 156. Projections of total imports for 1985 were derived from regression analysis conducted by the International Research Centre for Energy and Economic Development. The breakdown of imports were forecasted in light of the historical experience and anticipated change in the UAE's industrial structure in the next decade.
a. For first half of 1979 only. b. From 1976 reclassified to other groups.

Table 6.2: Commodity Classification of Imports, Major Groups (Abu Dhabi and Dubai)[a] (in millions of Dh)

	1970		1971		1972		1973		1974	
	Value	%	Value	%	Value	%	Value	%	Value	%
Consumer goods (of which foodstuffs and tobacco)	744.6 (203.1)	57.7 (15.7)	817.3 (236.3)	55.1 (15.9)	1,130.6 (309.4)	52.0 (14.2)	1,706.9 (426.2)	50.9 (12.7)	3,510.2 (934.3)	49.8 (13.2)
Intermediate goods	124.1	9.6	121.8	8.2	211.1	9.7	346.7	10.3	896.0	12.7
Capital goods	330.3	25.6	349.9	23.6	632.8	29.1	1,001.2	29.9	2,186.7	31.0
Oilfield materials	74.9	5.8	174.9	11.8	165.3	7.6	272.8	8.1	412.2	5.8
Others	16.6	1.3	18.4	1.2	35.0	1.6	24.4	0.7	48.4	0.7
Total	1,290.5	100	1,482.3	100	2,175.0	100	3,352.1	100	7,053.5	100

	1975		1976		1977		1978		1979[b]	
	Value	%	Value	%	Value	%	Value	%	Value	%
Consumer goods (of which foodstuffs and tobacco)	5,076.8 (1,173.0)	46.5 (10.8)	6,031.9 (1,477.9)	44.4 (10.9)	9,028.2 (1,944.8)	44.7 (9.6)	9,538.3 (2,341.6)	45.7 (11.2)	5,675.0 (1,640.3)	50.7 (14.7)
Intermediate goods	1,333.2	12.2	1,711.3	12.6	2,404.8	11.9	1,970.1	9.5	776.0	6.0
Capital goods	4,388.2	40.2	5,733.7	42.2	8,649.9	42.8	9,142.8	43.9	4,635.5	41.4
Oilfield materials	–	–	–	–	–	–	–	–	–	–
Others	111.9	1.1	123.9	0.9	134.2	0.6	193.4	0.9	99.6	1.0
Total	10,910.1	100	13,600.8	100	20,217.1	100	20,844.7	100	11,186.1	100

Source: UAE, Currency Board, *Bulletin*, November 1977, p. 127, and December 1979, p. 156.
a. Imports of consumer goods are taken generally to comprise SITC groups 0, 1, 4, 6 and 8 of which foodstuffs and tobacco are included in items 0, 1 and 4. (Separate figures for tobacco imports are not available.) Intermediate goods roughly comprise groups 2, 3 and 5, while group 7 is taken to reflect imports of capital goods. Oilfield materials are classified into respective categories since 1975. b. For first half of 1979 only.

The Foreign Trade Sector

utilizing these steady increases, with the exception of group 3, to the mid-1980s.

Groups 6 to 8, including the manufacturing and transport categories, largely reflect the UAE's massive spending for development projects. Group 6 has grown largely as a result of a greater need for building materials in the numerous construction activities. It is expected that demand for such commodities will rise slightly until 1985 and even thereafter, depending upon the speed of implementation of the planned projects. Manufactured goods are expected to take a 26 per cent share of the UAE's total imports by 1985. A steady and notable expansion in import sales of machinery and transport equipment is also anticipated until the mid-1980s.

In the commodity grouping of miscellaneous manufactured goods, a slight decline in the percentage share of total imports was registered for the 1969—75 period. The percentage share in 1985 should remain the same as that recorded for 1975 due to an increasing population requiring such goods as watches and clocks, ready-made garments, furniture, footwear and tape recorders. The demand for these commodities is generally income-elastic and should increase slightly as the Emirates' consumers acquire higher incomes. Increasing purchases of these goods stem also from the UAE's narrow industrial base. Industries have become functional and should continue to function primarily as resource developers rather than as producers of a wide variety of consumer goods.

A major difference in the pattern of importation exists between the largest two emirates. Dubai's composition of imports embodies a substantial amount of re-exports, while Abu Dhabi's trade contains goods primarily for local use. Dubai benefits from its entrepôt position and offers low tariff rates and few restrictions on trade. Customs duties are a minuscule 3 per cent and lower for foodstuffs and goods in transit. Gold bullion and precious metals may be imported and exported duty-free. This trade flexibility has attracted regional merchants from the other Gulf states and the Arabian Peninsula as well as from Iran, Pakistan, India, Afghanistan and the Far East. Much of Abu Dhabi's trade is also channelled through Dubai; however, the expansion of Port Zayed will redirect Abu Dhabi's imports. Abu Dhabi requires large imports of machinery and equipment, building materials, road construction and communications equipment; the other emirates

Table 6.3: Imports by Major Country of Origin: Value and Per Cent (Abu Dhabi and Dubai)[a] (in millions of Dh)

	1974 Value	1974 %	1975 Value	1975 %	1976 Value	1976 %	1977 Value	1977 %	1978 Value	1978 %	1979 Value	1979 %
Western Europe and certain other industrial countries	4,880.7	69.2	8,094.7	74.2	10,130.0	74.5	15,292.1	75.6	16,583.7	79.6	19,250.3	72.3
Japan	1,278.3	18.1	1,735.5	15.9	2,369.2	17.4	3,811.2	18.9	3,813.5	18.3	4,406.5	16.5
United Kingdom	1,092.0	15.5	1,890.4	17.3	2,293.0	16.9	3,588.1	17.7	3,701.3	17.8	4,170.7	15.6
United States	919.8	13.0	1,644.8	15.1	1,825.4	13.4	2,241.0	11.1	2,504.4	12.0	3,453.5	13.0
Federal Republic of Germany	461.7	6.5	751.7	6.9	1,016.1	7.5	1,902.0	9.4	2,170.5	10.4	2,148.5	8.1
France	219.2	3.1	535.2	4.9	530.0	3.9	682.3	3.4	970.4	4.7	1,384.2	5.2
Italy	161.5	2.3	355.2	3.3	386.1	2.8	725.5	3.6	780.4	3.7	1,120.5	4.2
Netherlands	153.5	2.2	262.3	2.4	387.7	2.8	604.0	3.0	978.8	4.7	613.4	2.3
Switzerland	148.9	2.1	133.4	1.2	197.5	1.5	306.1	1.5	271.5	1.3	298.7	1.1
Australia	115.5	1.6	217.2	2.0	224.8	1.7	184.1	0.9	236.1	1.1	–	–
Others[b]	330.2	4.7	568.9	5.2	900.2	6.6	1,247.8	6.2	1,156.8	5.5	1,368.8	5.5
Eastern Europe and China	391.5	5.6	431.2	4.0	559.2	4.1	696.3	3.4	555.0	2.7	636.6	2.4
China	176.4	2.5	226.1	2.1	197.9	1.5	322.8	1.6	299.6	1.4	423.5	1.6
Romania	87.4	1.2	61.1	0.6	164.9	1.2	158.4	0.8	110.3	0.5	48.7	0.2
Yugoslavia	27.9	0.4	37.9	0.4	73.8	0.5	46.4	0.2	18.2	0.1	25.5	0.1
Czechoslovakia	26.9	0.4	29.9	0.3	14.4	0.1	14.7	0.1	55.9	0.3	43.6	0.2
USSR	24.0	0.3	25.7	0.2	19.4	0.1	7.4	–	12.7	0.1	9.5	–
Poland	17.4	0.2	14.8	0.1	49.6	0.4	112.7	0.6	26.9	0.1	32.2	0.1
Others[c]	31.5	0.5	35.7	0.3	39.2	0.3	33.9	0.2	31.4	0.2	53.6	0.2
Arab Countries	538.2	7.6	664.1	6.1	875.0	6.4	1,224.4	6.1	953.1	4.6	2,515.8	9.4
Kuwait	172.2	2.4	184.6	1.7	229.5	1.7	189.3	0.9	145.8	0.7	365.6	1.4
Bahrain	105.7	1.5	158.7	1.5	84.9	0.6	300.7	1.5	198.2	1.0	1,733.1	1.4
Qatar	18.8	0.3	11.0	0.1	7.4	0.1	9.7	–	17.7	0.1	81.6	0.3
Sultanate of Oman	1.6	–	1.9	–	0.3	–	4.0	–	0.5	–	0.8	–
Lebanon	144.1	2.0	187.6	1.7	93.4	0.7	166.0	0.8	181.1	0.9	163.6	0.6
Saudi Arabia	59.2	0.8	78.6	0.7	382.5	2.8	480.3	2.4	284.5	1.4	22.2	4.6
Somalia	10.0	0.2	10.2	0.1	10.4	0.1	9.9	–	13.5	0.1	3.1	–
Jordan	6.3	0.1	10.3	0.1	30.9	0.2	36.5	0.2	61.7	0.3	55.6	0.2

Table 6.3: Continued

	1974 Value	1974 %	1975 Value	1975 %	1976 Value	1976 %	1977 Value	1977 %	1978 Value	1978 %	1979 Value	1979 %
Arab Countries												
Arab Republic of Egypt	6.2	0.1	6.1	0.1	7.6	0.1	8.1	–	20.5	0.1	22.1	0.1
Syria	4.4	0.1	9.8	0.1	12.0	0.1	11.9	0.1	16.6	0.1	23.1	0.1
Iraq	2.9	–	2.6	–	10.7	0.1	2.4	–	6.1	–	–	–
Others[d]	6.8	0.1	2.8	–	5.4	–	5.6	–	6.9	–	36.7	0.1
Selected Asian countries	1,052.6	14.9	1,520.5	13.9	1,846.4	13.6	2,635.3	13.0	2,329.4	11.2	3,652.2	13.7
Iran	282.2	4.0	385.1	3.5	274.7	2.0	250.5	1.2	110.0	0.5	131.9	0.5
India	217.6	3.1	339.0	3.1	614.4	4.5	826.0	4.1	614.9	3.0	711.7	2.7
Hong Kong	141.3	2.0	202.1	1.9	201.7	1.5	287.5	1.4	305.1	1.5	532.6	2.0
Pakistan	156.5	2.2	161.7	1.5	116.4	0.9	144.7	0.7	151.9	0.7	290.9	1.1
Singapore	83.1	1.2	166.5	1.5	224.8	1.7	318.9	1.6	386.6	1.9	717.9	2.7
Korea, South	72.3	1.0	95.5	0.9	104.8	0.8	247.2	1.2	271.5	1.3	453.9	1.7
Taiwan	43.9	0.6	89.4	0.8	165.6	1.2	321.5	1.6	281.2	1.3	464.6	1.7
Thailand	34.8	0.5	29.2	0.3	42.1	0.3	75.0	0.4	113.0	0.5	200.4	0.8
Malaysia	20.8	0.3	52.0	0.5	101.9	0.7	164.0	0.8	95.2	0.5	148.3	0.5
Other countries	190.5	2.7	199.6	1.8	190.2	1.4	369.0	1.8	423.5	2.0	587.4	2.2
Kenya	34.2	0.5	33.9	0.3	37.1	0.3	81.0	0.4	40.8	0.2	21.3	0.1
Mozambique	5.2	0.1	–	–	10.0	0.1	2.8	–	47.3	0.2	38.7	0.1
Others	151.1	2.1	165.8	1.5	143.1	1.0	285.2	1.4	335.4	1.6	527.3	2.0
Total	7,053.5	100	10,910.1	100	13,600.8	100	20,217.1	100	20,844.7	100	26,642.4	100

Sources: UAE, Currency Board, *Bulletin*, December 1979, pp. 158-9 and *Middle East Economic Digest*, Special report, October 1980, p. 67.

a. Includes transit trade as separate data are not available, and also imports to Sharjah ports.
b. Includes Austria, Belgium, Canada, Denmark, Finland, Greece, Ireland, Luxemburg, Norway, Portugal, Spain, Sweden and Turkey.
c. Includes Albania, Bulgaria, Cuba, German Democratic Republic, Hungary, North Korea and North Vietnam.
d. Includes Algeria, Libya, Morocco, Sudan, Tunisia and Yemen (North and South).

Table 6.4: Destination of Crude Oil Exports (in thousands of barrels)

	From Abu Dhabi[a]						From Dubai				UAE[b]			
	1977		1978		1979		1977		1978		1977		1978	
	Amount	%	Amount	%	Amount	%	Amount	%	Amount	%	Amount	%	Amount	%
Japan	187,727	31.5	170,044	32.7	163,561	31.2	4,932	4.3	5,615	4.2	192,659	26.7	175,659	26.5
United States	101,601	17.0	69,992	13.4	64,190	12.2	10,108	8.8	1,725	1.3	121,806	16.9	79,327	12.0
France	73,405	12.3	61,193	11.8	55,677	10.6	20,335	17.8	30,986	23.1	93,739	13.0	92,179	13.9
Netherlands	41,712	7.0	65,111	12.5	38,404	7.3	8,451	7.4	18,214	13.6	50,163	7.0	83,325	12.6
United Kingdom	25,840	4.3	16,683	3.2	9,221	1.8	17,396	15.2	18,104	13.5	43,236	6.0	35,192	5.3
Federal Republic of Germany	32,736	5.5	11,665	2.2	28,320	5.4	14,920	13.0	12,556	9.3	47,656	6.6	24,221	3.7
Italy	12,575	2.1	14,412	2.8	7,605	1.4	6,283	5.5	5,708	4.2	18,858	2.6	20,120	3.0
Netherland Antilles	48,769	8.2	34,368	6.6	52,465	10.0					4,769	6.8	34,368	5.2
Switzerland	11,899	2.0	6,356	1.2	8,928	1.7					11,899	1.7	6,356	1.0
Pakistan	7,258	1.2	7,568	1.4	9,060	1.7					7,258	1.0	7,568	1.1
India	7,185	1.2	6,691	1.3	12,503	2.4					7,185	1.0	6,691	1.0
Poland	6,614	1.1	3,283	0.6	1,316	0.3					6,614	0.9	3,283	0.5
Brazil	1,794	0.3	6,013	1.2	6,981	1.3					1,794	0.2	6,013	0.9
Curacao	583	0.1	3,722	0.7							583	0.1	3,722	0.6
Bahamas	1,698	0.3	875	0.2	562	0.1					1,698	0.2	875	0.1
Norway									684	0.5			684	0.1
Thailand	2,560	0.4	3,918	0.8	4,826	0.9					2,560	0.4	3,918	0.6
Sweden	7,355	1.2	9,474	1.8	8,772	1.7					7,355	1.0	9,474	1.4
Bangladesh	4,546	0.8	4,460	0.9	4,504	0.9					4,546	0.6	4,460	0.7
Senegal	847	0.1	575	0.1					372	0.3	847	0.1	947	0.1
Belgium							3,050	2.7	2,889	2.2	3,050	0.4	2,889	0.4
Austria														
Spain	319	0.1	1,602	0.3	1,503	0.3	26,996	23.6	36,243	27.0	27,315	3.8	37,845	5.7
Canada														
West Indies	9,085	1.5	406	0.1							9,085	1.3	406	0.1
Ivory Coast	553	0.1			205						553	0.1		
Kenya	1,267	0.2	1,452	0.3	2,398	0.5					1,267	0.2	1,452	0.2
Yemen South					2,014	0.4								
Australia	2,080	0.3	5,946	1.1	9,201	1.8					2,080	0.3	5,946	0.9

Table 6.4: Continued

	From Abu Dhabi[a]						From Dubai						UAE[b]			
	1977		1978		1979		1977		1978				1977		1978	
	Amount	%	Amount	%	Amount	%	Amount	%	Amount	%			Amount	%	Amount	%
Singapore	882	0.1	695	0.1	1,218	0.2	449	0.4	–	–			1,381	0.2	695	0.1
Portugal	–	–	–	–	3,479	0.7	–	–	–	–			–	–	–	–
Trinidad	–	–	446	0.1	–	–	1,521	1.3	916	0.7			1,521	0.2	1,362	0.2
Mozambique	–	–	–	–	200	–	–	–	–	–			–	–	–	–
Tanzania	2,007	0.3	2,181	0.4	2,361	0.4	–	–	–	–			2,007	0.3	2,181	0.3
Ireland	1,169	0.2	1,986	0.3	14,014	2.7	–	–	–	–			1,169	0.2	1,986	0.3
Madagascar	1,421	0.2	–	–	–	–	–	–	–	–			1,421	0.2	–	–
Taiwan	388	0.1	3,850	0.7	4,666	0.9	–	–	–	–			388	0.1	3,850	0.6
Guinea	410	0.1	–	–	–	–	–	–	–	–			410	0.1	–	–
Egypt	–	–	5,782	1.1	4,136	0.8	–	–	–	–			–	–	5,182	0.9
Philippines	–	–	–	–	–	–	–	–	310	0.2			–	–	310	–
Virgin Islands	–	–	–	–	719	0.1	–	–	–	–			–	–	–	–
Morocco	–	–	–	–	1,512	0.3	–	–	–	–			–	–	–	–
Ethiopia	–	–	–	–	199	–	–	–	–	–			–	–	–	–
Total	596,285	100	520,746	100	524,720	100	114,491	100	134,322	100			720,873	100	663,083	100

Source: UAE, Currency Board, *Bulletin*, December 1979, Table 0.7.
a. Qatar's share in the exports of Bunduq crude is excluded.
b. Including Sharjah exports which amounted to 10 million barrels in 1977 (all going to the United States) and 8 million barrels in 1978 (7.6 million to the US and 0.4 million to the UK).

Table 6.5: Non-oil Exports and Re-exports by Major Country of Destination: Value and in Per Cent[a]
(in thousands of Dh)

	1974		1975		1976		1977		1978	
	Value	%	Value	%	Value	%	Value	%	Value	%
Iran	84,590	25.0	211,352	35.1	249,093	20.7	489,701	33.2	575,352	32.0
Sultanate of Oman	67,926	20.0	113,449	18.8	132,179	11.0	39,532	2.7	25,768	1.4
Other Far Eastern countries[b]	42,364	12.5	31,258	5.2	10,669	0.9	9,800	0.7	14,988	0.8
Qatar	33,781	10.0	67,534	11.2	257,502	21.4	281,036	19.1	249,624	13.9
Saudi Arabia	24,206	7.1	67,781	9.6	358,231	29.8	348,033	23.6	445,224	24.7
Kuwait	23,939	7.1	47,449	7.9	66,046	5.5	62,279	4.2	69,930	3.9
Bahrain	21,043	6.2	35,736	5.9	51,799	4.3	29,745	2.0	35,736	2.0
Iraq	15,152	4.5	6,573	1.1	3,489	0.3	1,847	0.1	15,322	0.9
Arab Republic of Egypt	6,503	1.9	1,143	0.2	5,106	0.4	2,883	0.2	6,786	0.4
Pakistan	5,708	1.7	11,155	1.9	9,314	0.8	17,371	1.2	37,774	2.1
Lebanon	5,374	1.6	6,222	1.0	3,321	0.3	14,298	1.0	18,157	1.0
Somalia	3,100	0.9	4,195	0.7	2,619	0.2	10,969	0.7	15,741	0.9
United States	700	0.2	585	0.1	3,657	0.3	8,254	0.6	3,354	0.2
Federal Republic of Germany	503	0.1	5	—	232	—	2,069	0.2	3,256	0.2
United Kingdom	477	0.1	58	—	14,887	1.2	9,654	0.7	6,385	0.4

Table 6.5: Continued

	1974		1975		1976		1977		1978	
	Value	%	Value	%	Value	%	Value	%	Value	%
Jordan	416	0.1	1,746	0.3	5,302	0.4	6,488	0.4	14,572	0.8
Syria	154	—	929	0.2	4,611	0.4	2,129	0.1	4,663	0.3
Yemen North	38	—	671	0.1	11,868	1.0	95,924	6.5	225,786	12.5
Sudan	8	—	10	—	1,389	0.1	4,415	0.3	8,727	0.5
France	—	—	14	—	2,445	0.2	2,089	0.1	2,972	0.2
Yemen South	2,023	0.6	4,487	0.8	3,565	0.3	5,340	0.4	10,502	0.6
Belgium	—	—	11	—	2,195	0.2	21,915	1.5	2,060	0.1
Others	1,008	0.4	466	—	4,636	0.3	9,468	0.6	6,620	0.3
Total	339,013	100	602,829	100	1,204,155	100	1,475,239	100	1,799,299	100

Source: UAE, Currency Board, *Bulletin*, December 1979.
a. Recorded figures exclude inter-emirate trade as well as trade in gold and silver. Subtotals may not add up because of rounding.
b. Including Bangladesh, China, India and Japan.

require similar imports though on a smaller scale.

Direction of Import Trade

The composition of imports to Abu Dhabi and Dubai by major country of origin is illustrated in Table 6.3. The industrialized (OECD) countries supply nearly three-quarters of the total bill, with Japan and the United Kingdom vying for the largest share of the market. Japan's success may be attributed to the persistence and shrewdness of its salesmen and to the accommodating attitude of its businessmen. Japan leads in most exports to the UAE, but the United Kingdom still maintains an edge in machinery sales. Britain, however, may lose its commanding position to Japan, and it is expected that sales in the areas of textiles and electrical goods will suffer some additional decreases. It seems evident that Britain and the other industrial countries, excluding Japan, will find limited opportunities to increase their market share in the UAE and that changes in the shares of these countries among themselves will occur as sales competition increases. Nevertheless, the United Kingdom should continue to be the principal supplier of processed foodstuffs and construction equipment, while the United States will predominate in sales of oil-industry equipment and motor vehicles. India and Pakistan are beginning to show interest in the Gulf area, taking advantage of their geographical proximity; Australia has also increased sales to the region. At present Australia exports mainly foodstuffs to the Emirates but plans to promote a much broader variety of goods. The Eastern bloc countries, particularly Romania, Czechoslovakia and Hungary, are considering expanding their limited Gulf sales and China is selling significant exports of consumer goods.

Composition and Direction of Exports

Crude oil is by far the major export of the United Arab Emirates. Total oil exports grew from 138 million barrels in 1967 to 440 million in 1972, and increased to a peak of 721 million barrels by 1977. In 1978 exports decreased to 633 million barrels but rose somewhat in 1979 and 1980, in large part as a result of the Iranian cutbacks and the later

Iran–Iraq conflict. Abu Dhabi is accountable for 79 per cent of the 1978 total with Dubai responsible for most of the remaining export. Japan is the largest importer of the UAE's crude, followed by France and the United States. Together they received 57.9 per cent of Abu Dhabi's oil exports in 1978. The Netherlands, United Kingdom, West Germany, Switzerland, Norway and Italy are the other major buyers (see Table 6.4). The relative shares of UAE oil importers remained generally unchanged throughout 1979 and the first half of 1980.

Non-oil exports and re-exports, excluding transactions of gold and silver, inter-emirate trade, and transit trade, are mainly conducted through Dubai's ports. Table 6.5 shows non-oil exports and re-exports for 1970–8 for both Abu Dhabi and Dubai. The total value of non-oil exports and re-exports for the UAE for 1976 was over Dh 1.2 billion (US). The largest components of non-oil trade are food and live animals and crude materials with dry fish, hides and skins traded in significant quantities. In 1978, Dh 1.8 billion (US) non-oil goods were exported or re-exported.

The exports and re-exports were directed primarily to neighbouring countries, in particular Iran, Oman, Qatar, Saudi Arabia, Kuwait and Bahrain. Table 6.5 also illustrates the direction of the UAE's non-oil exports and re-exports by country. In 1979, the various destinations of UAE non-oil and re-exports retained the shares of the preceding year.

The Tourist Trade

The archaeological finds of the past 15 years have made the United Arab Emirates a more attractive area to visit. Although only a beginning has been made to uncover the traces of civilizations dating to almost 3000 BC, archaeologists point to the existence of settled communities such as the burial chambers on Umm al-Nar Island, circular structures built of limestone. Excavations at Mileiha in Sharjah and Hili and Bint Saud near Al-Ain have led to increased interest in other emirates, and there is little doubt that intensive exploration will reveal much to students of early and pre-history.

Climatic conditions in the UAE, especially from the end of October to mid-April, are also attractive features for tourists. Colourful market places, mountains, oases and deserts, coastal beaches, traditions, culture and way of life are fascinating experiences for most travellers. Museums, enshrining the history of the area, are located in Dubai — where an old fort[2] has been adapted to house an impressive array of antiquities — and at Al-Ain in Abu Dhabi. The Al-Ain facility, recently built on the initiative of the Ruler, Sheikh Zayed, is being extended as new exhibits flood in from archaeological sites in and from the surrounding area. All new town-development plans include museums as part of future amenities, notably in Abu Dhabi and Sharjah; their completion is considered necessary to preserve the minutiae of a present way of life which is rapidly being overtaken by modernity as well as to portray the newly revealed past. Khor Fakkan and Dibba, which is located north of Khor Fakkan, are distinct tourist areas and trading centres for Sharjah.

The seas around the coast of the UAE offer bathing, boating and water sports, including such activities as water skiing, skin-diving and spear-fishing.

With these attributes in its favour it seems unusual that the UAE is not an expanding tourist centre. The need for both accommodation and social-life facilities are the urgent considerations required to activate its tourism which is now placed high on the list of priorities for funding. Abu Dhabi, with three major and several minor hotels, is assessing its requirements for the future, and in Dubai three international hotel chains add well over 1,000 rooms to the many existing hotels offering first class accommodation.[3]

Dubai has the largest transient population of all the Emirates' towns. Its commercial character was emphasized in the plan to finish a Dh 500 million trade centre. John Harris and Associates (UK) are consultants and Bernard Sunley (UK) is the contractor for the centre, which will be owned by the Dubai government. The trade centre encompasses hotel and restaurant facilities and includes exhibition areas, international banks, insurance offices and many areas of tourist and commercial interest in its 33 storeys. A multi-storey car park has been constructed adjacent to the centre to help alleviate the heavy traffic load. In addition, two artificial islands to offer hotels with restaurants, night clubs and swimming pools and marinas planned for boating, fishing and water skiing will be located in Dubai Creek. Sharjah has embarked on similar construction activities.

In an effort to spark the tourist sector, the Abu Dhabi government has commissioned the international consultants, Tourism Planning and Research, to conduct a survey whose findings will be equally applicable to the Emirates as a whole. The recommended strategy involves a programme to utilize the inherent attractions in the area and to create tourist amenities, i.e. develop accommodations, places of interest, excursions and planning of sporting and recreational facilities of all kinds. Major operators will introduce multi-destination, inclusive tours and stopover packages for the European-Far East trade. Special-interest tours will be arranged for people with a leaning towards archaeology, water sports, fishing and history, and the Emirates can be included in round-the-world tours. No difficulty is envisaged in attracting visitors from the major markets, especially Western Europe, North America, Australia, and Japan.

Alternative accommodations, such as camping, caravan parks and rest houses, in places such as the Liwa oases are also planned, as the proposed highway construction in the UAE will open up such areas for the tourist industry. A proposal to designate the beautiful Old Palace, Al-Husn, as a National Visitors' Centre is another imaginative tourist idea. The plan is to restore the building as a focal point for visitors and residents, emphasizing the traditions of Arab hospitality and offering modern facilities amidst ancient surroundings. Sadiyat Island is also considered to present an opportunity for tourist village development, with a jetty and yacht marina for marine recreation and activities.

Another project sought is the construction of a tourist zone near Al-Ain, to be called Jebel Hafit, which will encompass a range of inland amenities, including clay pigeon shooting, picnic areas, a complete recreational village and well-established tourist activites such as the Dubai Museum, the Eastern Fort, and Ain al-Faydah.[4]

Taking a broad view of tourism, the UAE government regards it as a means for enriching and diversifying the economy and of opening up the natural attractions of the country for visitors as well as to their own citizens and those living and working in the federation. The government has time to forge a vacation facility to take full advantage of its unique appeal and to call heavily upon international talents, before it begins the campaign to attract the business and pleasure-seeking visitor. There are obstacles, of course, to attracting a sufficient level of tourists other than predominantly business visitors on expense accounts. The high cost of living, specifically lodging, would tend to dampen the appeal for middle-income tourists. Given the climatic conditions, tourism would have a seasonal basis as a winter resort for the northern hemisphere. Finally, industrial development of the UAE should not proceed without serious consideration of the environmental concerns in retaining the clean beaches and invigorating desert air.

Notes

1. While the UAE is consistently within the capital-surplus category within OPEC, not all 13 members of that organization are similarly endowed. The Table below reflects several elements. First, the decline in the current account surplus (or rise in current account deficits) during 1977 and 1978 can be traced to the stability in the price of OPEC crude, an ongoing level of spending by the oil-exporting governments on imports, the impact of inflation, and a levelling-off of global demand for crude oil. The oil-price upheavals caused by a contraction in oil supply due to Iranian cutbacks in 1979 can be seen in the reversal of the earlier trend by 1979 and 1980. It should be recalled that the current account surpluses differ somewhat from investible surpluses.

Current Accounts of OPEC Members, 1977–80 ($ US billions)

	1977	1978	1979[a]	1980[a]
Saudi Arabia	12.8	0.8[a]	15.3	40.4
Kuwait	4.8	6.2	14.2	16.1
United Arab Emirates	2.9	2.6[a]	6.7	12.2
Iraq	4.6[a]	4.0	13.0	19.6
Iran	5.1	−0.7[a]	11.7	0.9
Qatar	0.3[a]	0.9[a]	2.0	3.2
Algeria	−2.3	−3.5	−0.8	0
Libya	2.9	1.8	6.0	9.1
Nigeria	−1.0	−3.8	3.0	7.2
Gabon	−0.1	0.1	0.5	0.8
Indonesia	−0.1	−1.5	1.2	1.6
Venezuela	−3.1	−5.4	−1.5	1.8
Ecuador	−0.3	−0.6	−0.4	−0.5
Total	26.4	0.9	70.9	112.5

Source: *MEES*, 18 August 1980, p. II.
a. Estimated on accrual basis.

2. Department of Information, Municipality of Dubai, *Dubai: Pearl of the Gulf* (France: Editions Del Roisse), p. 59. Run by the city of Dubai and opened in May 1971, the historic Al Finhaidi Fort gives residence to the Dubai Museum. Built in 1800, the fort is the oldest building in the area. Its major function was to protect the town of Dubai from attacks by neighbouring tribes; however, the fort was also the seat of the government. The present aim of the museum is to provide a record of the old way of life in the UAE, particularly in Dubai. Omani, Iranian, Indian, Pakistani, and East African cultures are represented in the museum. Sections of the museum include architecture, weaponry, costumes and jewelry, household items, fishing, pearling and falconry.

3. United Arab Emirates, Ministry of Information, *United Arab Emirates, Second Anniversary*, p. 44.

4. Ibid., p. 47.

7 THE FINANCIAL SECTOR

With respect to banking, there was a problem of establishing a unified currency among the UAE members. Prior to the federation's establishment, Abu Dhabi's official currency was the Bahrain Dinar (BD) while the remainder of the sheikhdoms used the Qatar/Dubai Riyal (QDR).[1] Soon after the UAE became a member of International Monetary Fund (IMF) in 1972, legislation establishing the Currency Board was drafted with the technical assistance of that international body. The Board was charged with the issuing and management of the national currency and the promotion of a healthy financial system in the Emirates. On 19 May 1973 the Currency Board was officially established.[2] On the same day the new currency, the Dirham (Dh), divided into 100 fils and having an initial parity value of 0.186621 grams of fine gold, was put into circulation. This initial par value corresponds to Dh 4,76190 per SDR (or 0.210 SDR per Dh). In November 1973 the dirham became legal tender; on 1 February 1974 the IMF fixed the Dh officially at the initial par values. Since then the dirham has proved to be one of the firmest currencies in the world, backed as it is by the massive oil reserves of the country. As of 4 August 1980, 1 SDR = 4.84 Dh – a decline of only 1.6 per cent compared with initial par value.

Structure of the Banking System

The structure of the banking system and the salient monetary indicators are worth analyzing.

Since 20 March 1976, the Currency Board has stipulated minimum cash reserves and liquidity ratio requirements for commercial banks operating in the UAE. At that time the Currency Board required banks to deposit with them no less than 5 per cent of the banks' current account balances. This reserve requirement was raised to 7.5 per cent in May 1977, in direct response to the banking crisis which resulted in the partial failure of two banks operating in the UAE, the Ajman Arab Bank and the Janata Bank of Bangladesh.[3]

The majority of the banks are joint-stock shareholding institutions, small sized — especially in the case of foreign banks — and concentrated in Dubai and Abu Dhabi. The Currency Board viewed a balanced distribution of banking services throughout the UAE as essential. Therefore, it strove to ensure such a balance in the future.

A draft law has existed for several years which would give the Currency Board a central bank role within the UAE. The Board would then have broad supervisory powers over the Emirates' commercial banking institutions.

In November 1979, plans were approved for the long-awaited Central Bank, which was scheduled to begin operations on 15 December 1980. Sheikh Surour Ibn-Mohammed al-Nahayyan was appointed to serve as the first governor of this new institution, which has an initial capital of Dh 300 million ($81.3 million) subscribed by the government. A seven-member board will oversee bank administration and policy. The Bank's existence should enable a much improved regulation of the UAE money supply and the banking system.

For many years the only bank operating in the region was the British Bank of the Middle East (BBME), joined later by the Eastern Bank (now called the Chartered Bank). The National Bank of Dubai was formed in 1963 under a charter granted by the Ruler, Sheikh Rashid; the National Bank of Abu Dhabi, 85 per cent of which is owned by the National Westminster Bank of Britain and 5 per cent by the Gulf Finance Company, was formed in 1968.[4] By the end of the 1960s, flourishing trade and rapidly expanding oil operations had attracted many foreign companies and there was a boom in banking activity in the lower Gulf. Since then, many foreign banks have opened branches in Abu Dhabi and Dubai, as well as in the smaller emirates.

At the beginning of 1980, 52 fully licensed commercial banks were operating in the Emirates. Of this number, half were locally incorporated while the other half were foreign owned. In addition, two banks from the Gulf (National Bank of Bahrain and Qatar National Bank) had been fully licensed but had not yet begun operation, and five foreign commercial banks were operating in the UAE under restricted licences.[5] The Currency Board's *Bulletin* of June 1980, pp. 181–2, lists the commercial banks and representative offices which were in operation as of 1 January 1980, as follows:

Banks Granted Full Licences and Operating

Locally incorporated (21):
    Al Ahli Bank Limited (CSC)
    Arab Bank for Investment & Foreign Trade
    Bank of the Arab Coast
    The Commercial Bank of Dubai Limited
    Dubai Bank Limited
    Dubai Islamic Bank
    Emirates National Bank
    Emirates Commercial Bank
    Federal Commercial Bank
    First Gulf Bank (opened September 1979, formerly, until 1978, Ajman Arab Bank)
    Investment Bank for Trade & Finance
    Khalij Commercial Bank
    Middle East Bank Limited
    National Bank of Abu Dhabi
    National Bank of Dubai Limited
    National Bank of Ras Al Khaimah
    National Bank of Sharjah
    Bank of Oman Limited
    The Bank of Sharjah Limited
    Union Bank of the Middle East
    United Arab Bank

Foreign (33):
    Algemene Bank Nederland NV
    Arab African International Bank
    Arab Bank Limited
    Barclays Bank International Limited
    Bank of Baroda
    The British Bank of the Middle East
    Banque du Caire
    The Chartered Bank
    Citibank NA
    Bank of Credit & Commerce International SA

The Financial Sector 135

    Bank of Credit & Commerce International (Overseas)
    Distributors Cooperative Credit Bank
    The First National Bank of Chicago
    Grindlays Bank Limited
    Habib Bank AG Zurich
    Habib Bank Limited
    Banque de l'Indochine et de Suez
    Janata Bank
    Banque Libanaise pour le Commerce SA
    Banque du Liban et d'Outre Mer SAL
    Lloyds Bank International Limited
    Bank Melli Iran
    National Bank of Oman
    El Nilein Bank
    Bank Omran Iran
    Banque de Paris et des Pays Bas
    Rafidain Bank
    Royal Bank of Canada
    Bank Saderat Iran
    The Toronto Dominion Bank
    United Bank Limited
    National Bank of Bahrain (granted full licences but not yet operating as of 31 May 1980)
    Qatar National Bank (granted full licences but not yet operating as of 31 May 1980)

Banks Granted Restricted Licences and Operating in the UAE (5)

    American Express International Banking Corporation
    Amsterdam Rotterdam Bank (Amro Bank)
    Banca Commerciale Italiana
    Bank of Nova Scotia (closed August 1980)
    Banco Urquijo SA (of Spain)

International Banks Participating in UAE through Representative Offices (13)

    Chemical Bank
    United California Bank
    Bank of America

Chase Manhattan Bank
Crédit Suisse
Union Bank of Switzerland
County Bank (United Kingdom)
United International Bank (United Kingdom)
Crédit Lyonnais
Banque Nationale de Paris
Banque Bruxelles Lambert
Den Norske Credit Bank
Banco di Sicilia

Among the foreign insurance companies which have been attracted to the region are the Sharjah Insurance Company (with half its initial QDR 2.5-million capital subscribed by the government), and the Abu Dhabi National Insurance Company, of which the Abu Dhabi government holds 25 per cent of its original BD 500,000 capital. The Sharjah company has a local monopoly and the Abu Dhabi National Assembly recently called on the government and local enterprises to use the Abu Dhabi Insurance Company, provided the rates were competitive with those offered by foreign companies. The declared policy of economic diversification combined with increasing oil revenue will create a continuing demand for these and other financial services.

The Abu Dhabi Development Finance Corporation (formerly the Real Estate Finance Corporation) began operation on 14 September 1971 with an initial capital of Dh 20 million. This institution and the UAE Development Banks concentrate on extending long-term credits 'with a view to encouraging and giving impetus to the establishment of "economy-type" residential housing and the diversification of domestic production other than oil.'[6]

A partial listing of other financial institutions in the UAE include: Oryx Merchant Bank Limited and Wardley Middle East Limited – both merchant banks; four finance companies – the Middle East Finance Corporation, Oman Finance Company, Abu Dhabi Development Finance Corporation, and Gulf Citicorp – which provide loan services avoided by most commercial banks, in particular the purchase of consumer durables; two discount houses of Merrill Lynch and Gillet Brothers, which deal in foreign securities and bonds; ten investment institutions such as the Abu Dhabi Investment Authority and Arab

The Financial Sector

Emirates Investment Limited.

The money supply in the narrow definition, i.e. cash outside banks plus private-demand deposits, increased from Dh 1.54 billion at the end of 1974 to 6.27 billion at the beginning of 1980. Most of the growth in money supply was attributed to monetary deposits, reflecting the expansion of the banking habit, the increased level of economic activity and the liquidity of the economy. Table 7.1 gives a monetary survey of the UAE for 1974–9.

Total assets of commercial banks increased from Dh 24.27 billion at the end of 1976 to Dh 43.4 billion at the end of 1979. A substantial portion of these assets are held in foreign currencies and foreign securities. As 1980 began, foreign assets of the commercial banks were Dh 13.39 billion (US) (or 31 per cent of total assets), while foreign liabilities were Dh 15.17 billion (US) or 35 per cent of total liabilities.[7]

Total bank credits to UAE residents amounted to Dh 25,690 million in November 1979, increasing from Dh 21,980 million in December 1978 – an increment of some 17 per cent. Dubai's share in total lending to residents rose from Dh 14,359 million at the end of 1978 to Dh 15,956 million one year later. Credit in Abu Dhabi increased from Dh 7,621 million at the end of 1978 to Dh 9,734.0 million at the end of November 1979. Although Dubai is still the leading sector in terms of credit extended, its relative share in total credit is declining while that of Abu Dhabi has increased for the above-mentioned periods.

Total lending is heavily concentrated in the trade sector, especially wholesale and retail trade, which accounted for close to 38 per cent of all credit granted to residents in September 1979 by local banks. Next to the trade sector is that of construction with over 31 per cent of total credit. Other sectors, including manufacturing, mining and quarrying, transportation, public utilities and agriculture received between 0.3 and 5.5 per cent of total loanable funds. This clearly shows the paramount importance of the trade sector in the economy of the Emirates. (See Table 7.2 for industrial distribution of credits to residents in UAE.)

The UAE's banks lend vigorously, mainly in the short term, in the absence of stringent lending ratios. In general 75 to 90 per cent of a bank's funds is utilized as loans. For Dubai more lending to the private sector has been the pattern due to short-term, import-export lending. Banks finance imports by letters of credit designated in hard currencies

Table 7.1: UAE Monetary Survey, 1974–9 (end of year)

	1974	1975	1976	1977	1978	1979
Assets						
Foreign assets (net)	5,477.1	9,588.8	14,856.7	1,945.9	2,052.6	3,112.5
Foreign assets	6,375.5	11,334.5	19,231.0	11,831.6	14,350.0	20,212.9
Foreign liabilities (—)	898.4	1,745.7	4,374.3	9,885.7	12,297.4	17,100.4
Domestic credit	722.3	−391.0	2,559.6	15,349.1	18,902.6	19,924.5
Claims on the government (net)	−2,687.1	−6,317.3	−8,531.0	−1,426.4	−1,513.7	−2,940.4
Claims	58.2	306.4	1,526.9	2,772.6	3,090.1	4,194.8
Liabilities (—)	2,745.3	6,623.7	10,051.9	4,199.0	4,603.8	7,135.2
Claims on official	8.7	91.2	398.9	735.1	656.7	994.4
Claims on private	3,362.0	5,693.0	10,475.0	15,854.5	19,527.9	21,570.5
Other claims	38.7	142.1	216.7	185.9	231.7	300.0
Liabilities						
Money supply	1,536.2	2,602.9	4,725.1	5,214.6	5,775.8	6,268.3
Currency outside	429.3	627.6	1,077.4	1,392.3	1,703.5	1,965.2
Demand deposit	1,106.9	1,975.3	3,647.7	3,822.3	4,072.3	4,303.1
Quasi money	4,499.3	6,217.3	12,028.5	10,330.5	11,816.8	11,972.8
Other assets	163.9	377.6	662.7	1,749.9	3,362.6	4,795.9
Assets = Liabilities	6,199.4	9,197.8	17,416.3	17,295.0	20,955.2	23,037.0

Source: UAE, Currency Board, *Bulletin*, May 1977, Table 3a, and *Annual Report*, 31 December 1979, p. 38.

The Financial Sector

Table 7.2: Bank Credit to Residents by Economic Activity (as percentage of total)[a]

	1975	1976	1977	1978	1979
Agriculture	0.11	0.11	0.16	0.30	0.26
Mining and quarrying	0.32	0.16	2.09	1.84	2.73
Manufacturing	5.8	5.58	5.67	4.86	5.49
Electricity, gas and water	2.05	1.9	2.09	3.84	3.86
Construction	24.6	25.88	32.42	33.51	31.25
Trade	51.12	48.01	40.12	36.66	37.67
Transport, storage and communication	1.41	2.55	1.92	1.97	2.01
Government	5.74	6.33	8.26	8.68	8.31
Others	8.86	9.48	7.27	8.33	8.43

Source: UAE, Currency Board, *Bulletin*, November 1977, Table 15, and December 1979, Table 10.
a. Columns may not total to 100 per cent due to rounding.

and paid in dirhams, so they can profit from foreign exchange as well as from the charges of financing. Larger projects are generally financed in Eurodollars and US dollars.

A major problem found in UAE bank-loan decisions is informational as no audited accounts were kept until recently. Previously, local borrowers often had no investment portfolios, and their title deeds to property were unregistered since local registration was not required. A recent decree requires that all companies submit audited statements annually to the Currency Board in order to make available a correct accounting of the percentage of participation of local partners in joint ventures with foreign partners. This decree therefore elucidates the question of whether local participants are receiving an adequate share of such undertakings.

With regard to long-term funding for lending abroad, the limited activity of this nature that had been conducted in the past was made by government participation in bond issues or other financial instruments with the assistance of foreign-based institutions. The Abu Dhabi government decided to establish a government investment company to manage its long-term investments, estimated at $2 billion (US). The company

Table 7.3: Basic Data on Investment Companies in the UAE[a]

Company	Location	Date of establishment	Authorized capital (Dh million)	Shareholders
Dubai Union Co. for Investment	Dubai	Established by an Amiri decree of 12 January 1977	1000 (value per share: Dh 100)	10% local (founders), 30% Dubai government, 60% local
Sharjah Group Company	Sharjah	Established by an Amiri decree of 16 November 1976	500 (value per share: Dh 10)	53.6% local and Kuwaiti (founders), 46.4% local and other Arab
Gulf Co. for Investment in Real Estate	Ajman	Established by Amiri decree No. 2/77 of 16 January 1977	300 (value per share: Dh 10)	Local & Kuwaiti (66.7% shareholding by founders of local and Kuwaiti nationality)
Abu Dhabi Investment Co.	Abu Dhabi	Established by Law No. 1 of 24 February 1977	200 (value per share: Dh 100)	60% Abu Dhabi Investment Authority, 10% National Bank of Abu Dhabi, 30% local
National Co. for Investment in Real Estate	Abu Dhabi	Established by Law No. 3 of 4 April 1977	100 (value per share: Dh 100)	85% local (20% by founders), 15% Abu Dhabi Investment Authority
National Industries and Development Co.	Sharjah	Established by an Amiri decree of 28 April 1977	300 (value per share: Dh 10)	50% (by local founders), 50% Sharjah public subscription

Source: UAE, Currency Board.
a. Not included are the Gulf Islamic Investment Company and the two investment institutions of the Abu Dhabi Investment Authority and the Arab Emirates Investment Ltd.

replaces the London-based Investment Board which has directed this emirate's long-term investments since 1967. The decision to dissolve the Investment Board and replace it by a more representative body headquartered in Abu Dhabi was made in May 1976 (see Table 7.3).

Investment abroad of Abu Dhabi's oil revenues has been channelled primarily through Banker's Trust, Morgan Guaranty, and Banque de l'Indochine. Investments thus far have been conservative in the extreme and do not fit a particular pattern as far as the type of property or location are concerned, as long as they offer a maximum hedge against inflation and capital appreciation as well as high current yield. Prime commercial property, completed and tenanted, seems to fit these criteria best. For example, the Abu Dhabi Investment Board directly purchased 44 per cent of Commercial Union Assurance Company in the City of London (July 1974) for Dh 307.8 million. Additional basic information on recently established investment companies operating in the UAE is included in Table 7.3.

Public-sector financial institutions are the UAE Development Bank in Abu Dhabi, Property Development Bank, and the Abu Dhabi Development Finance Corporation. The UAE Development Bank, established on 25 June 1974, drew up policy outlines for future activities aimed at boosting the national economy through financing construction, industrial and agricultural projects. The policies outlined were: (1) giving priority to financing light industry and investment projects based on exploiting fisheries, livestock, resources and other available raw materials; (2) developing and modernizing the agricultural sector with stress on highly productive schemes; (3) development of real-estate holdings and financing the commercial buildings especially for low-income nationals; (4) financing of hotels to promote tourism; (5) giving priority to the northern emirates when financing industry, fisheries and livestock projects. The Bank also adopted a twofold policy in financing projects either through extending loans or participating in some of the projects and by having projects of its own which could later be transferred to joint-stock companies.[8]

The Bank's capital was wholly subscribed by the government; it could borrow funds from the government at 2 per cent and lend to nationals at 4 per cent or less. Among the institution's activities were accepting deposits from customers and extending loans in cash or in kind to individuals, companies, corporations and emirate governments.

It was additionally empowered to participate in the equity capital of a project during its early stage. The Bank is equipped with technical staff to advise the private investors and companies as well as to give needed technical and administrative assistance, and relief on reports from the World Bank (the United Nations' industrial development consulting organisation), the Indian government, and the Arab League Industrial Organization. The UAE Development Bank's lending was regulated as indicated in Table 7.4.

Table 7.4: Regulation Project Lending by UAE Development Bank

Type of Project	Maximum lending as % of the total project value
Private residential housing	60
Commercial real estate	75
Fisheries	75
Industrial projects	80
Agriculture and livestock projects	90

Lending stipulations of the Bank have been as follows: the loan period limited to the economic life of the project, but for no more than 20 years; a 3-year grace period prior to repayment may be granted; the Bank could directly participate in agricultural or industrial projects, up to 50 per cent of the project's capital with a maximum of Dh 2.0 million; and in the public interest, the Board of Directors may modify these limits.

The chief purpose of the UAE Development Bank was to help the establishment of non-oil industries in order to meet local needs as well as provide exports to neighbouring countries. Therefore the Bank has subsidized industries which may utilize local raw materials, i.e. fish, oil derivatives – plastics, detergents, insect repellents, paints – and food industries such as dairy and poultry.[9] In addition, the Bank endeavoured to expand the agricultural sector in co-operation with the Ministry of Agriculture.

Another main concern of this institution, as noted earlier, was encouraging construction of hotels, tourist motels, and other recreational tourist facilities in order to promote tourism while assisting in residential

The Financial Sector

construction and forming marketing centres.

Loan commitments of the Development Bank by November 1975, about a year and a half after its creation, totalled Dh 367 million; over 56 per cent of this amount went for 138 loans for construction or residential housing in the northern emirates and 28 per cent extended for the establishment of eight marketing centres, one in each emirate as well as in Al-Ain. Agricultural projects supported accounted for only slightly over 9 per cent of the total first-year commitments; in contrast, a single hotel undertaking in Fujairah received over 8 per cent. During the next year or so of activity the Development Bank's major loans went for the construction of three hotels in Abu Dhabi, Umm Al-Quwain, and Ajman (over $58 million) and as housing credits to middle-income citizens (over $8 million).[10]

Further, the UAE Development Bank granted Dh 104 million to the Abu Dhabi Cold Storage Company for the formation of a federal trading company to establish fixed price outlets for necessary commodities as an inflation-control measure. Earlier (1974–5), the Bank had given small loans to cold-storage plant and ice-plant projects (totalling Dh 8.9 million). The government's dry cargo shipping company also was a recipient of Bank financing; at that time the government planned to rely more heavily on the Bank as a vehicle for obtaining equity positions in appropriate industries for financing its own industrial companies.[11]

Since its creation the activities of the UAE Development Bank have consistently been weighted in favour of investment and lending in the real-estate sector, whether in individual housing or facilities for trade or other enterprises. Given this lending record, the UAE Council of Ministers approved a loan on 6 October 1980, transforming the UAE Development Bank into a Real Estate Bank to handle all real-estate loans and other related operations in the federation. A public corporation and an independent juristic entity, the new bank is supervised by the Minister of Finance and Industry. Involved is a capital of Dh 1.6 billion ($446 million) earmarked for settlement of real-estate loans made by UAE citizens and some Dh 200 million ($56 million) extended to the National Housing Council for real-estate loans. The loan obligations to be settled were those assumed prior to 1 January 1978, and on real-estate projects which have been constructed within the UAE. The new UAE Real Estate Bank is empowered to grant loans for real-estate projects to UAE citizens and to those companies and enterprises ownership of which is at least 80 per cent held by UAE nationals.[12]

The Sharjah Group is of special interest because of its regional and international flavour. With offices in Sharjah, Kuwait and London, this investment company was incorporated in Sharjah with a capitalization of $125 million. Among the 35,000 Arab institutional and private shareholders, both the ruling families of Kuwait and Sharjah along with leading Kuwaiti business names are well represented in the group of founding shareholders. Initial institutional shareholders included Gulf International Company, United Fisheries Company and United Reality Company. Sharjah Group's objective has been to invest, on its own behalf and for clients, in profitable projects both within the Middle East and in international markets. The company could become involved with international firms planning to operate in the Middle East and which have growth potential, a sound management record and research-proven technology or services. Sharjah Group's investment could take the form of direct equity participation in joint ventures, arrangements of partnerships, and the provision of facilities for industrial and commercial development.

The Property Development Bank, established by Sheikh Rashid in Dubai, has Dh 200 million to lend at a 1 per cent interest rate to individuals for building purposes on their own land.

The Abu Dhabi Development Finance Corporation, established by Sheikh Zayed in 1971, is a real-estate financing corporation specifically for Abu Dhabi for the construction of private housing at low-interest rates with a usual 15-year payout period provision. The Corporation's plans have included the construction of a two or three-storey commercial/apartment building. The limit of Dh 1 million, representing up to 80–90 per cent of the cost of construction, has been designed to cater mainly to owner-occupied, small-scale housing. Among other Corporation projects under study have been a fibre plant, a soap facility, a marble plant, and sponge rubber production.

Not to be confused with either the Abu Dhabi Development Finance Corporation or the Real Estate Bank established in 1980 from the former UAE Development Bank, was the creation (also in 1980) of a real-estate fund by Sheikh Zayed of Abu Dhabi. This Dh 1 billion ($271 million)-fund, geared to absorbing some of the real-estate loans extended to citizens during the mid-1970s construction boom, has done much to strengthen the original lending banks, particularly the smaller

The Financial Sector 145

institutions.[13]

In July 1980 an emiri decree set up a new investment company in Ras Al-Khaimah. The Sahil Investment Company is capitalized at $70 million, 80 per cent subscribed by the founders which include the government of Ras-Al-Khaimah. The remaining capitalization will come from the 14 million shares (with a nominal value of $1 each) offered to citizens of Gulf countries. The company is envisaged as engaging in various investment and commercial activities in Ras Al-Khaimah and abroad.[14]

Finally, in the same year the Abu Dhabi Chamber of Commerce announced its plans to establish an investment company to participate in international investment projects in Arab countries and internationally.[15]

Development as a Financial Centre and an Aid Source

It is possible that the UAE may be developed as a major financial centre in the Middle East somewhat along the lines of Kuwait. With the abundant capital surplus and the expanding banking system, such development appears on the horizon. A move in this direction would help relieve pressure on the already burdensome reliance on the oil sector for capital funds in the future. The surrounding states offer exceptional short and long-run investment opportunities, as the majority of countries in the region are not characterized by capital surplus. The importance to the UAE of maintaining a world position in international banking is therefore exemplified by its increasing regional participation.[16] However, any heavy commitment to the development of the UAE as a major financial centre must be carefully scrutinized as other states, particularly Kuwait, are moving in the same direction.

The establishment of the Abu Dhabi Fund for Arab Economic Development in July 1971 was a giant step toward the promotion of regionalism. The ADFAED enjoys an independent legal status and has the authority to provide aid in terms of loans, participation in shareholdings, or guaranteeing projects, and in certain cases it extends grants. Initially, the authorized capital of ADFAED was $120 million to be paid up by the government, and its explicit domain is defined as fostering development in the Arab countries. Later, however, and as a result of the capital being raised to $500 million, aid was extended to other nations as well. The Fund's Board of Directors agreed in September 1979 to increase the authorized capital to Dh 4 billion.[17] The rules and operations of ADFAED are the following:

(1) It operates on a similar basis as the Kuwait Fund for Arab Economic Development (KFAED) from whose experience it benefited. Today, the two funds stand together as a successful prototype for Arab national aid-extending agencies to assist developing countries.

(2) Like KFAED, ADFAED may participate in any project up to 10 per cent of its capital and may extend any direct loan up to 50 per cent of the total cost of any project. Under certain circumstances, however, the 50 per cent provision can be waived. Like KFAED, again, the standard ADFAED loan is of 10 to 15 years duration and carries 3.5 to 5 per cent interest plus one half per cent as an administration charge. Some credits, however, have carried only 2 per cent interest. The ADFAED requires detailed information on the projects it will help finance and in some cases it requires guarantees by some international or regional organizations. Appendix V presents a concise summary of basic information about the Fund: lending policies, technical assistance, economic research and study, and the Fund's financial status as of 31 December 1979.

Regionally, about three-quarters of the Abu Dhabi Fund loans traditionally have gone to Arab recipients. Tables 7.5 and 7.6 show the regional breakdown of ADFAED loans, while the types of projects receiving financing are contained in Table 7.7.

By 1980, funds administered by ADFAED (but not necessarily provided by that institution) since its establishment reached Dh 4.616 billion ($1.25 billion). Some Dh 2.86 billion ($775 million) had been extended by the Fund itself, while it was administering an additional Dh 1.756 billion ($476 million) in loans extended by the government of Abu Dhabi. Of the Abu Dhabi government's amount, Dh 1.5 billion reflected investment financing for 12 projects in other emirates of the UAE.[18]

In an attempt to establish itself as a source for capital funds, the UAE is beginning to look abroad for viable projects in which it might invest. During 1967 Abu Dhabi pledged $7.2 million to the initial capital of the Arab Fund for Economic and Social Development (AFESD) which was proposed and accepted by the Khartoum Conference

Table 7.5: Geographical Distribution of ADFAED Loans, 1974–9 (in millions of Dh, $1=Dh 3.768)

Arab States	1974	1975	1976	1977	1978	1979	Total
Bahrain	40.0	—	160.0	20.0	—	—	220.0
Egypt	50.0	138.0	18.4	60.0	—	—	266.4
Jordan	21.5	5.0	—	100.0	—	—	126.5
Lebanon	—	—	—	67.8	—	—	67.8
Mauritania	—	—	—	16.0	—	120.0	136.0
Morocco	—	—	110.0	—	—	40.0	150.0
Oman	—	—	60.0	—	663.0	—	723.0
Sudan	—	—	96.5	40.0	4.0	—	140.5
Syria	43.5[a]	8.0	—	56.0	—	—	107.5
Tunisia	51.2[b]	—	—	47.0	—	321.7[c]	419.9
Yemen (Arab Rep.)	4.0	40.0	—	—	45.0	—	89.0
Yemen (Democratic)	—	—	35.7	—	—	—	35.7
Total	210.2[d]	191.0	480.6	406.8	712.0	481.7	2,482.3
Percentage of total[f]	100.0	100.0	71.8	75.5	84.8	95.3	85.0
Non-Arab Asian	—	—	169.0	87.0	68.0	—	316.0
Percentage of total[f]	—	—	25.2	16.1	8.1	—	10.8
Non-Arab African	—	—	20.0	45.2	60.0[e]	24.0	121.2
Percentage of total[f]	—	—	3.0	8.4	7.1	4.8	4.2
Aggregate total	210.2	191.0	669.6	539.0	840.0	505.7	2,919.5

Source: Abu Dhabi Fund for Arab Economic Development, 'Projects Financed by Abu Dhabi Fund for Arab Economic Development, 1974-1979,' mimeographed, pp. 1-3 and *Annual Report, 1978 and 1979.*

a. Under addition in 1975 is Dh 8 million of loan total to Syria of this year.
b. Includes Dh 11 million in equity participation.
c. Includes Dh 102.85 million in equity participation.
d. Including technical assistance.
e. Includes Dh 28 million extended to Malta.
f. May not total to 100 per cent due to rounding.

Table 7.6: Regional Allocation of Abu Dhabi Fund, 1976–9 (per cent)

	1976	1977	1978	1979
Asia	25.2	16.1	8.1	–
Other Arab countries	38.2	45.2	84.5	–
Arab–Africa	33.6	30.2	6.5	95.3
Non-Arab Africa	3.0	8.4	7.1[a]	4.8

Source: Abu Dhabi Fund for Arab Economic Development (ADFAED), *Annual Report, 1978 and 1979*; computed from Table 7.5.
a. Includes Malta.

Table 7.7: ADFAED Allocation to Projects, 1974–9 (per cent)[a]

	1974	1975	1976	1977	1978	1979
Agriculture (fisheries, rural development)	9.9	21.9	18.9	–	1.1	7.9
Transportation, communications, storage	6.2	2.7	9.0	35.8	4.6	8.7
Electricity and water	43.8	71.0	36.1	29.7	11.9	3.8
Housing	–	–	6.0	–	–	–
Tourism (including hotels)	19.1	4.4	–	–	–	–
Manufacturing and extractive industries	21.1	–	41.1	34.5	82.4	80.0

Source: ADFAED, *Annual Report, 1978 and 1979*; see Table A.2 in appendices for breakdown of amounts.
a. Columns may not total to 100 per cent due to rounding.

in 1967. As a member of AFESD, the UAE participated in the Fund's operations which anticipated major expansion in 1976 when cumulative loan commitments were projected to rise to 177 million Kuwaiti dinars (KD) ($610.7 million) from KD 93.2 million ($321.5 million) in 1975. The paid-up capital of the Fund reached KD 164.9 million ($596.7 million) in 1978; none the less, this was but slightly over half the subscribed capital of KD 370.4 million. In April 1979 the Board of Governors of AFESD announced that full payment of subscribed capital would be due in 1982. Moreover, it was agreed that extra funds would be subscribed to bridge the difference between the Fund's subscribed and authorized (KD 400 million) capital.[19] (See Table 7.8.)

Table 7.8: Shareholders of the Arab Fund for Economic and Social Development (AFESD)

	Shares	Per cent
Kuwait	7,500	20.25
Saudi Arabia	7,400	19.98
Libya	4,776	12.89
Egypt	4,050	10.93
Algeria	3,000	8.10
Iraq	2,941	7.97
United Arab Emirates	2,000	5.40
Syria	1,200	3.20
Jordan	800	2.16
Morocco	800	2.16
Oman	800	2.16
Sudan	588	1.59
Qatar	400	1.08
Lebanon	200	0.54
Tunisia	200	0.54
North Yemen	200	0.54
Bahrain	100	0.27
Mauritania	40	0.11
Palestine Liberation Organization	25	0.07
Somalia	20	0.05
South Yemen	4	0.01
Total	37,044	100.00

Source: John Law, *Arab Aid: Who Gets It, for What and How?* (New York: Chase World Information Corporation, May 1978).

As of 1 January 1979, the AFESD had approved loans to 14 countries totalling KD 295.3 million. Of that amount, just over 34 per cent of the total loan commitments was for transportation, almost 14 per cent for water and drainage projects, 21 per cent for electricity, close to 15 per cent earmarked for intermediate industries, agricultural projects accounted for almost 9.5 per cent, oil and gas storage schemes received just over 4 per cent, and some 2.7 per cent for telecommunications.[20]

The purpose of the Fund is to participate in the economic and social development projects in the Arab states through: (1) financing economic projects of an investment character by means of loans granted on easy terms to governments and to public or private organizations and institutions, giving preference to economic projects vital to overall Arab development and to joint Arab projects; (2) encouraging directly or indirectly the investment of public and private capital in such a manner as to ensure the development and growth of the Arab economy; and (3) providing technical expertise and assistance in the various fields of economic development. Participation in the Fund is given in Table 7.8.

The Fund is giving more attention to infrastructural investment in order to boost the absorptive capacity of the recipient countries. In selecting projects, priority is given to projects in which the AFESD's role goes beyond financing, and includes assistance in attempting to solve some of the basic problems of the recipient nations. In all its activities the Fund seeks to increase its professional capabilities through joint programmes with Arab and internationally specialized agencies, and by using Arab consultants with special emphasis on attracting Arab talent from abroad.[21]

An important recent move which will aid the UAE's development as a financial centre as well as the other Arab League members, came with establishment of the Arab Monetary Fund (AMF), having an initial capitalization of nearly $900 million under the terms of the April 1976 convention signed during a meeting of all 21 Arab League Finance Ministers in Rabat. The headquarters for the institution is Abu Dhabi. Saudi Arabia and Algeria were the largest initial contributors to the AMF with $136,800,000 each, followed by Kuwait, Iraq, and Egypt ($90 million each), and the UAE ($54 million). Five of the large Arab oil exporters have, since then, pledged over half of the total capital, but all 21 Arab League members have pledged part of their reserves to the AMF. The Fund is to complement the International Monetary Fund in seeking to redress member states' balance-of-payments deficits, stabilize Arab currency-exchange rates, and work towards the

The Financial Sector

establishment of a unified Arab currency. Members will be allowed to draw up to twice their capital contribution in any one year; the maximum debt allowed will be three times the contribution, but may be increased to four times in exceptional circumstances. Credit will be available for a maximum of 7 years. The Arab Monetary Fund is operated by a Council of Governors and a Board of Directors led by a President.

Table 7.9: Abu Dhabi Capital Payments, 1970–8[a] (in millions of Dh)

Year	Capital payments	As % of total expenditures	Total expenditures	Total revenues
1970	2.3	0.3	720.1	856.1
1971	22.4	2.0	1,103.7	1,651.3
1972	90.0	5.2	1,735.6	1,180.8
1973	353.5	10.4	3,390.7	3,221.8
1974	1,236.3	17.8	6,923.5	14,131.1
1975	2,701.2	23.6	11,456.9	15,015.3
1976	7,361.7	37.0	19,896.6	19,663.3
1977	6,110.5	28.6	21,368.0	21,655.5
1978	1,960.6	9.9	19,824.1	20,280.9

Sources: UAE, Currency Board, *Bulletin*, June 1979, p. 151, and June 1980, p. 147.
a. Capital payments are defined as capital contributions in the form of participation, loans to foreign governments and other lending (net). Also includes the 1976 appropriation for investment fund transferred to the Abu Dhabi Investment Authority. Does not include grants proper to foreign countries which are counted in the current expenditures category.

Thus the AMF is responsible for concerted inter-Arab efforts to ease economic and monetary problems and for consultations on financing development projects. Other contributors to the AMF are: Sudan, Qatar, and Morocco – $36 million each; Libya – $33,480,000; Tunisia, Lebanon, and North Yemen – $18 million each; Jordan, Bahrain, Somalia, Syria, Oman, Mauritania, and South Yemen – $14,400,000 each.

By early 1979 the AMF's total financial resources reached Arab Accounting Dinars (AAD) 63.9 million ($249.2 million), about one-

Table 7.10: UAE Participation in Regional and International Organizations, 1978–80 (in Dh)

	1978	1979	1980
International Finance Corporation	3,148,000	3,148,000	7,000,000
World Bank	41,100,000	8,000,000	22,000,000
International Monetary Fund	125,000,000	30,000,000	50,000,000
International Development Agency	20,000,000	20,490,000	28,000,000
UAE Currency Board	–	90,000,000	90,000,000
Settlement of real estate loans	–	–	1,000,000,000
Arab Monetary Fund	–	53,550,000	–
Inter-Arab Investment Guarantee Corporation	4,200,000	3,447,600	3,500,000
Arab Bank for Investment and Trade	–	10,000,000	–
Arab Fund for Economic and Social Development	25,986,000	26,173,200	51,217,000
Arab Bank for Economic Development in Africa	26,667,000	66,667,000	26,700,000
Islamic Development Bank	100,000,000	107,121,500	–
Arab Insurance Group	–	–	150,000,000
Organization for Agricultural Development in Sudan	37,260,000	38,329,200	37,800,000
Arab Shipbuilding and Repair Yard Company	64,500,000	14,000,000	20,670,000
Arab Mining Company	27,780,000	41,844,100	42,000,000
Arab Maritime Petroleum Transport Company	37,020,000	10,000,000	6,949,000
Arab Petroleum Services Company	14,700,000	14,700,000	7,350,000
Arab Company for Livestock Resources	28,000,000	34,525,100	49,000,000
Real estate for embassies abroad	50,000,000	75,000,000	–

Table 7.10: Continued

	1978	1979	1980
Joint Productions and Programs Organization	–	6,981,300	–
Arab Company for Pharmaceutical Industries	22,167,000	17,416,300	17,500,000
UAE-Tunisia Engineering Studies Company	–	607,000	–
Emirtel	25,000,000	55,000,000	5,000,000
United Arab Shipping Company	724,000	735,000	140,000,000
Arab Satellite Corporation	5,280,000	7,920,000	5,280,000
International Telecommunications Satellite Organization	16,000,000	8,000,000	9,000,000
Arab Armaments Organization	284,000,000	–	–
Gulf Organization for Development in Egypt	330,000,000	–	–
Al-Khalij Commercial Bank	6,000,000	–	–
OPEC Special Fund	2,058,000	–	–
Residential buildings for UAE students in Cairo	4,000,000	–	–
Total	1,300,590,000	743,685,300	1,768,966,000

Source: *Middle East Economic Survey*, 26 November 1979, p. IV, and 28 July 1980, p. III.

Table 7.11: Regional Bodies with Initial UAE Participation (in millions of Dh)

	Country of incorporation	Total paid-up capital[a]	UAE share
Arab Petroleum Investments Co. (APIC)	Saudi Arabia	1,347.6	229.1
Arab International Co. for Hotels & Tourism	Egypt	79.4	11.9
Arab Investment Co. (AIC)	Saudi Arabia	1,147.8	178.7
UAE-Sudanese Investment Co.	Sudan	79.4	39.7
Arab-Joint Investment Co.	Egypt	198.6	99.3
Gulf International Bank	Bahrain	280.8	40.1
Arab Fund for Technical Assistance to African and Arab States	Egypt	–	–[b]
Arab-African Oil Assistance Fund	Egypt	–	–[c]
United Arab Maritime Co.	Kuwait	2,474.1	468.8
Arab International Bank	Egypt	–	–[d]
Compagnie Arabe et Internationale d'Investissement (CAII)	France	–	–[e]

Source: *Middle East Economic Survey*, 9 May 1977, p. II.
a. Capital figures here are the dirham equivalent of capitalizations in Saudi riyals, dollars and Kuwaiti dinars.
b. UAE payments to mid-December 1976, Dh 11.9 million.
c. UAE payments to mid-December 1976, Dh 158.4 million.
d. UAE payments to mid-December 1976, Dh 234.4 million.
e. UAE payments to mid-December 1976, Dh 132.6 million.
f. UAE payments to mid-December 1976, Dh 7.3 million.

The Financial Sector

Table 7.12: UAE Contributions to the OPEC Fund as of 31 December 1979 (in US $)

	Amount
Pledged contributions	
International Fund for Agricultural Development (IFAD)	16,500,000
Net	49,500,000
Total	66,000,000
IMF gold sales profits	1,393,226
Total pledged contributions	67,393,226
Paid contributions	
IMF Trust Fund	1,393,226
IFAD	11,000,000
Investment account and 1976 budget	445,250
Loans and technical assistance	18,763,701
Total paid contributions	31,602,177

Source: The OPEC Fund, *Annual Report 1979* (Vienna: The OPEC Fund, 1980), p. 57.

quarter of its authorized capital of AAD 250 million ($975 million).[22] Between August 1978 and April 1979 the AMF disbursed automatic loans to Egypt, Sudan, Mauritania, Morocco, and Syria totalling AAD 10.1 million. The loans represented 75 per cent of the members' individual paid-up Fund subscriptions.

The Finance Ministers also set up a five-state committee to study ways to develop economic co-operation among Arab nations and to make recommendations. The committee, composed of ministers from Egypt, Sudan, Saudi Arabia, Morocco, and Iraq was to evaluate the role and effectiveness of existing Arab economic institutions and to make proposals for strengthening or reforming them.

Finally, it should be noted that Abu Dhabi allotted 10 per cent of its 5-Year Development Plan's total budget to support development projects in other nations. It is believed that many more grants-in-aid and loans will follow as the UAE continues in its capital-surplus stature and in the role of a major international donor.

For example, in early 1980 Abu Dhabi extended a $50-million loan for balance-of-payments support to Sudan, carrying a very reasonable rate and terms: 4 per cent, a 10-year duration including a 3-year grace period. Abu Dhabi's lending and grant tradition is well established. In the half decade from 1971 to 1976, foreign grants consistently and overwhelmingly exceeded domestic grants: in 1971 Dh 142.5 million foreign grants only; in 1972, also foreign grants only of Dh 180.1 million; Dh 1,121.9 million (foreign) and Dh 2.7 million (domestic) for 1973; during 1974 some Dh 2,154.1 million (foreign) and Dh 37.2 million (domestic); Dh 2,400 million (foreign) and Dh 100 million (domestic) during 1976.[23] A number of credits have been extended as outright aid from Abu Dhabi over the years, e.g. to Syria for defence support, the World Food Programme, to Egypt for housing projects and to Pakistan for reconstruction after flooding. Table 7.9 offers some indication of the high proportion of capital expenditure in Abu Dhabi's total expenditures.

Tables 7.10, 7.11 and 7.12 offer a recent listing of UAE participation in regional and international organizations. There are a number of other entities in which the UAE has participated or participates, including the Arab Petroleum Investments Company. These are briefly outlined in Table 7.11.

Expressed as a percentage of GNP, during the 1970s the UAE contributed more than 10 per cent per annum in grants and loans to developing countries. This ranks the Emirates second in the world only to Qatar, which provided nearly 12 per cent of its GNP for economic and financial assistance to the Third World during most of the 1970s. Kuwait, the third largest extender of aid, has averaged 5.3 per cent of its GNP for development assistance, or nearly $2.5 billion. In absolute terms, the UAE is *the second largest* contributor to the Third World among the oil producers, giving nearly $2.9 billion through most of the decade of the seventies.[24]

To put UAE aid in perspective, one need only scan Table 7.13 to note the declining trend in the proportion of aid in the GNP of the traditional industrialized assistance-extending bloc. Even before the quadrupling of oil prices in late 1973 and 1974, United States aid was falling in terms of its share in the GNP; a few members of the OECD have increased their level of assistance. None the less, no Development Assistance Committee member has given even 1 per cent of its GNP in aid as compared with the approximate 10 per cent of the UAE.

Table 7.13: Flow of Official Assistance from Development Assistance Committee (DAC) Members of OECD to Developing Countries and Multilateral Institutions, 1965, 1970, 1975–80 (as per cent of GNP)

Country	1965	1970	1975	1976	1977	1978	1979	1980[a]
Australia	0.53	0.59	0.59	0.41	0.42	0.54	0.52	0.51
Austria	0.11	0.07	0.17	0.12	0.24	0.29	0.19	0.23
Belgium	0.60	0.46	0.59	0.51	0.46	0.55	0.56	0.59
Canada	0.19	0.41	0.52	0.39	0.48	0.52	0.47	0.46
Denmark	0.13	0.38	0.58	0.56	0.60	0.75	0.75	0.67
Finland[b]	0.02	0.06	0.18	0.17	0.16	0.17	0.22	0.22
France	0.76	0.66	0.62	0.62	0.60	0.57	0.59	0.59
Germany	0.40	0.32	0.40	0.36	0.33	0.37	0.44	0.44
Italy	0.10	0.16	0.11	0.13	0.10	0.14	0.09	0.09
Japan	0.27	0.23	0.23	0.20	0.21	0.23	0.26	0.27
Netherlands	0.36	0.61	0.75	0.83	0.86	0.82	0.93	0.94
New Zealand[c]		0.23	0.52	0.41	0.39	0.34	0.30	0.30
Norway	0.16	0.32	0.66	0.70	0.83	0.90	0.93	0.95
Sweden	0.19	0.38	0.82	0.82	0.99	0.90	0.94	0.95
Switzerland	0.09	0.15	0.19	0.19	0.19	0.20	0.21	0.22
United Kingdom	0.47	0.41	0.39	0.40	0.46	0.48	0.52	0.52
United States[d]	0.58	0.32	0.27	0.26	0.25	0.27	0.19	0.18

Source: Address by President Robert McNamara, President of the World Bank, delivered to the annual joint meeting of the World Bank and International Monetary Fund, Washington, DC, 30 September 1980.

a. Estimate.
b. Became a DAC member in 1975.
c. Became a DAC member in 1973.
d. In 1949, at the beginning of the Marshall Plan, US official development assistance amounted to 2.79 per cent of the GNP.

158 *The Financial Sector*

Notes

1. For a detailed discussion of the evolution of the currency system in the UAE, see United Arab Emirates (UAE), Currency Board, *Bulletin*, November 1974, pp. 1-4.

2. The Chairman of the Currency Board has been Sheikh Hamdan Ibn Rashid al-Maktoum, Minister of Finance and Industry, and the Deputy Chairman, until his resignation as Minister of Foreign Affairs, was Ahmed Khalifa al-Suweidi. The Currency Board rendered four types of services to the government: It (1) served as a banker, fiscal agent and depository of the government; (2) administered the public debt, and bought, sold, and dealt in various government securities; (3) advised the government on financial and money matters, and was usually expected to gather, analyze, and publish statistics on money and banking; and (4) acted as an agent for the administration of exchange control regulations.

3. UAE, Currency Board, *Bulletin*, May 1976 and November 1977. In February 1978, the Currency Board lowered the reserve requirement from 7.5 to 7 per cent, perhaps indicating that the financial crisis had subsided and an effort made to stimulate the economy, *Middle East Economic Digest*, 24 February 1978. (Hereafter *Middle East Economic Digest* will be cited as *MEED*.)

4. *MEED*, 29 June 1973, p. 8.

5. Restricted licence banks (RLBs), although conducting operations both inside and outside the UAE, cannot accept dirham deposits from either residents or institutions, only from non-residents. None the less, RLBs can extend loans in dirhams either domestically or externally; additionally, they are exempt from the 20 per cent profits tax imposed on commercial banks by each emirate. Representative offices of international banks, by comparison, have been authorized by the Currency Board to carry out general operations but conventional banking business must be booked outside the UAE.

Still another aspect of banking in the UAE is the venture into international financing through subsidiaries abroad. The National Bank of Abu Dhabi (NBAD), for example, incorporated a new wholly owned subsidiary – the Abu Dhabi International Bank (ADIB) – headquartered in Curaçao, Netherland Antilles. The $1 million initial capital has been 20 per cent paid up as of late summer 1980; all ADIB obligations are guaranteed by NBAD. The ADIB is charged with developing business of the NBAD group in both North and South America. The new international bank began operations in global capital markets by comanaging a $20-million loan guaranteed by the Brazilian government, with European-Brazilian Bank for the Brazilian state of Mato Grosso Do Sul. *Middle East Economic Survey*, 25 August 1980, p. I. (Hereafter *Middle East Economic Survey* will be cited as *MEES*.)

6. *MEED*, 25 June 1976, p. 8.

7. UAE, Currency Board, *Annual Report* (Abu Dhabi, 21 December 1979), p. 37.

8. *Arab Report*, 1 May 1976, p. 3.

9. N.A. Shilling, *Doing Business in Saudi Arabia and the Arab Gulf States* (New York: Intercrescent Publishing and Information Corp., 1975), p. 416.

10. *MEES*, 24 January 1977, p. 8.

11. Shilling, *Doing Business*, p. 416.

12. *MEES*, 20 October 1980, p. I.

13. *MEED*, Special report, October 1980, p. 16.

The Financial Sector

14. *MEES*, 18 August 1980, p. III.
15. Ibid., 17 November 1980, p. II.
16. Both Abu Dhabi and Dubai participate in the Egyptian International Bank, which is a development entity established by Egyptian President Sadat for Egypt and other Arab countries.
17. Abu Dhabi Fund for Arab Economic Development (ADFAED), *Annual Report, 1978 and 1979*. Two major factors which contributed to the move to raise ADFAED's capital were the relatively high utilized commitments ratio achieved (i.e. Fund commitments divided by its authorized capital which during the first year of the Fund's operation reached 42.45 per cent and the desire to extend economic aid to developing nations in Asia and Africa).
18. *MEES*, 18 August 1980, p. III.
19. *MEES*, 8 October 1979, P. II. Fund income in 1978 was KD 11.3 million while accumulated reserves rose to KD 21.3 million ($77.1 million).
20. *MEED*, 30 April 1976, p. 31 and *UAE News*, May 1976, p. 1.
21. Ibid. Cumulative distribution of AFESD loans by country as of 1 January 1979, were (in millions of KD):

Algeria	18.3	Somalia	14.4
Bahrain	5.0	Sudan	33.2
Egypt	67.9	Syria	25.4
Jordan	16.9	Tunisia	13.0
Lebanon	11.0	North Yemen	27.8
Mauritania	12.2	South Yemen	16.2
Morocco	28.0		
Oman	6.0	Total	295.3

22. 1 AAD = 3 SDR (Standard Drawing Right of the International Monetary Fund) = approximately $3.90. *MEES*, 17 September 1979), pp. II-III.
23. *MEES*, 9 May 1977, p. I.
24. John Law, *Arab Aid: Who Gets It, For What, and How?* (New York: Chase World Information Corporation, May 1978), p. xiv.

8 BUSINESS AND INVESTMENT: PATTERNS AND OPPORTUNITIES

The Indigenous Market

Establishing business relations in the United Arab Emirates follows much the same pattern that would be considered acceptable in other Gulf states. A strong interest in attracting foreign business enterprises is demonstrated with the most important commercial requirements being common sense and sound business practices. The availability of market opportunities at present is open, and trade publications frequently suggest fast action in commencing business as competition increases daily. One will find in the Emirates a market bent toward modernization in which keen competition has evolved — a mixture of traditional mercantilism and rapid adjustment to vastly widened business horizons. The development projects planned proffer markets for staggering quantities of equipment for schools and colleges, hospitals and clinics, residential and business construction, new towns or communities; infrastructural goods — such as all forms of transportation, power and communication systems, industrial estates, mills, factories and processing plants, model farms, fishing facilities, and water supply and purification systems. Businessmen from a wide range of occupational areas, therefore, may be certain to find a potentially profitable venture in the UAE. A broad spectrum of consumer-oriented products also may find lucrative markets; yet the Emirates' small population could act as an ultimate constraint.

To take the example of the food and beverage industry in the UAE, a number of factors exist which clearly outline the parameters for development of this industry. Most of the raw material inputs in the manufacturing of foodstuffs and beverages were imported (70 per cent for flour and 40 per cent for soft drinks-beverages). In 1973 just over 5 per cent of the total foodstuff and beverage consumption in the UAE was met by domestic production; however, its share had risen to over 13 per cent by 1977 (falling a little in the following year to close to 9.5 per cent).[1] Specifically, domestic output of mineral water and other beverages rose substantially as witnessed by a drastic reduction — 47 per cent — in the imports of these items. This turn of events reflects the import substitution nature of these domestic enterprises and the gradual slowing of the population growth rate compared to the early and mid-1970s. None the less, *per capita* expenditure on foodstuffs and beverages rose from Dh 5,133 to Dh 5,616 between 1977 and 1978. A last element is the labour-intensive nature of these specific industries in the UAE at present, as determined by the estimated capital/output and the marginal capital/output ratios (1.9/1 and 1.66 in 1978, respectively).[2] Although all these aspects may seem academic, sufficient data along these lines exist to indicate economic trends and realities to assist foreign and domestic investors in determining promising areas of business concentration.

Some problem areas do exist in the Emirates which should be carefully reviewed by foreign companies considering the UAE for business purposes. Until recently there has been little effective administration to handle business proposals and problems as the existing business laws and long-range policy objectives for the commercial sector have been inadequately defined. It is thus imperative for most foreign entrepreneurs to operate through a middleman although such an intermediary extracts high percentage fees from the negotiations. A further problem for companies which collaborate with local partners is that the foreign enterprise must usually provide the technical and management skills, marketing expertise, and other inputs as well as a percentage of the equity capital. In addition, the lack of sufficient office space, storage facilities, private housing for personnel, and until recently, an uncertainty in the supply of electricity and water, skilled and trainable labour, and other infrastructural requirements, not to mention the high cost of living, can make small-scale business ventures costly or risky.

Considering these drawbacks, weighing the possible net benefits of a foreign venture in the UAE becomes a rather complex task. Most proposed ventures must be approved by emirate rulers; often the use of an agent middleman of local reputable status is needed to further facilitate negotiations. While it is not a requirement in some emirates to choose an agent, it is highly suggested especially in cases where it is desired to keep foreign exposure to the market to a minimum. A local agent becomes an exclusive representative for the firm and can provide services such as: bringing complaints against competitors who try to sell any of the lines his company represents; informing the customs department to prevent the importation by competitors of products which he sponsors; and providing all services connected with the marketing and distribution of the product or service that he represents. To choose a responsible and financially sound agent, a review of information from objective sources, such as local commercial officials of the company's embassy, the Chamber of Commerce, bankers, local consultants or professionals, is strongly suggested.[3]

Another important preliminary step to be taken before initiating a business activity should be a personal trip to the Emirates. This is a good insurance policy for any undertaking of this nature as the visit should provide exposure to the market, a feeling for the business community, knowledge of service accessibility, the advantage of uncovering trade leads, assistance in locating an agent or distributor, as well as the opportunity to conduct a market research study. Most helpful at this initial stage can be emirate Chambers of Commerce. The main services offered at present by the Chambers to foreign entrepreneurs and correspondents are the following: (1) circulation of foreign offers among the concerned member firms; (2) publication of such offers in the official Chamber bulletins and invitations to interested firms to scan the related literature (brochures, leaflets, and illustrated catalogues) in the Chambers' offices; (3) supplying upon request the names and addresses of dealers in specified items for direct contacts; (4) supplying the latest but sometimes limited available statistics and other information about the Emirates; (5) offering facilities for the proper display of samples and catalogues in its office; (6) providing help to visitors by way of supplying necessary information, as well as by helping them in making their contacts; and (7) to some extent, offering extensive indoor exhibition space.

Embassies in the UAE might be of assistance in terms of providing preliminary readings on marketable products and trade leads.

If market penetration for a product is sought, a firm should proceed to conduct a survey of the market for the commodity and research the sectors of the economy which will be affected by its introduction. The profit potential should then be studied in terms of new or expanded sales. A company which provides its own market analysis gains a proficiency for conducting the sales of its product that may be sacrificed when a firm hires a Middle East market research company to carry out investigations for their product. Some useful research tools are available for starting businesses and are worthy of attention. These include emirates' development programmes or plans, budget documents, and lists of planned projects. Development plans may furnish the most valuable data as they often include the most accurate assessment of social and economic needs. The plans also may give clear indications of the direction of industrial, agricultural, and service activities; for example, important clues may be gained for anticipated purchases of industrial machinery and equipment needs. Proposals should be formulated in advance and the necessary documents required for setting up a business may then be made available. It is advantageous for a businessman to review the availability of financial sources and of local representation and collaboration. Sample plans and specifications for use of the business may be presented to government administrators as a means for introducing a business. At present the UAE is planning a few years in advance, and it is usually wise for a firm wishing to establish business there for more than a cursory period to do the same.

The insurance of prompt, effective after-sales service to vehicles and industrial projects, local representation, a high degree of personalization, and media-advertising all serve to generate marketing gains. Some of the most promising opportunities to exporters are capital equipment, technology, and services involving the participation of foreign companies in local industrial ventures. Chiefly, these projects are linked to the petroleum, petrochemical and natural gas industries which rank high on the list of most successful enterprises; however, the fishing, aluminium, finance and hotel sectors should not be overlooked. Recent trade publications indicate that local companies are expanding their interest in securing expertise, not profit alone.[4]

Joint ventures generally require a major portion of a company's equity to be provided locally, although a substantial degree of equity participation is required from the foreign partner to ensure continuing interest in the efficient operation of the enterprise and ongoing access to new technological advance. (Appendix V lists some of the governmental and private projects in the individual emirates, especially in those other than Abu Dhabi which were given more coverage earlier in the text.)

In Abu Dhabi it has become increasingly difficult to incorporate companies with limited liability by emiri decree, although in 1980 it was not only possible but relatively easy to do so in Dubai. The joint-venture company has evolved as the principal business format in Abu Dhabi for the eighties. This arrangement, where partners have unlimited liability, is of growing importance in the UAE as Abu Dhabi, due to its heavily oil-related commercial base, is the leading business centre in the federation. Dubai continues to hold sway in its traditional areas of specialization as import–export, but none of the other emirates can challenge the relative geographical and resource diversity of Abu Dhabi.

Some limiting factors an investor must face in the UAE are, as noted previously, the small area and population shortages of appropriately trained labour, and a limited variety of known or developed natural resources. Opportunities for foreign investors are most attractive in the following areas: civil aircraft, vehicles, construction machinery, building systems and materials, air conditioning and refrigeration equipment, oil field equipment and supplies, agricultural machinery and food-processing equipment, textile and related machinery, general industrial machinery and infrastructural capital goods, such as biomedical equipment, education equipment materials, and power-generating machinery. Exceptionally attractive ventures are open for design engineering companies and consulting firms for contractors and heavy-equipment producers. The boom in the construction industry has been caused by the sharp rise in oil revenues and offers a promising source for further income. Large sums of money are likely to be spent in the 1980s in the areas of petroleum refining and liquefied natural gas, petrochemicals, and such downstream products as fertilizers, as well as steel mills, aluminium and copper smelters, cement plants, textile plants, sugar and paper refining.

In all business endeavours special attention should be given to planning a sales approach, investigation of avenues for vertical and horizontal expansion, complete packaging of the products, and/or provision for parts, repairs and maintenance as well as promotion, careful pricing and production of the good or service. Sales plans arranged to accommodate market fluctuations add to a firm's ability to gain a competitive market edge, not only in the UAE itself but also throughout the Gulf region.

Legal Environment for Business in the UAE

The legal environment for business opportunities requires examination and should be considered in the initial stage of a firm's market analysis. Existing regulations with regard to commercial law involve registration of the company, payment of the appropriate corporate tax, and the requirement of the minimum percentage of local equity participation in the company's capital. As of March 1978, the government was in the process of revising the partnership laws of Abu Dhabi which require that nationals must own a minimum of 51 per cent of controlling share of commercial ventures in order to extend it to the rest of the federation.[5] Also, the updated Law on Commercial Agencies of 1973 provides that, with the exception of persons exempted by the Ruler, no person shall perform any trade unless he obtains a trade permit from the municipal authority concerned and pays the appropriate fee. All persons engaged in trade or business enterprises must obtain the required licence from the affected municipality, which must be renewed annually for a fee. To obtain these licences foreigners must fulfil certain prerequisites. For example, in Dubai foreigners have been required to obtain a leading Dubai citizen as a guarantor; this guarantor must hold real estate valued at Dh 100,000 or a financial guarantee of Dh 100,000 must be secured from any local bank. Although certain professions may be exempted from an emirate's particular requirement, evidence of professional qualifications is necessary before the permit will be issued. Foreigners obtaining the licence must also sign an agreement that they will not attempt to take over any agency or sub-agency from local merchants. The law provides that the duration of the trade permit be one calendar year, renewable by the end of each year on payment of the required fee.[6] Further, foreign contracts with government organizations in Abu Dhabi must be cleared through the Minister of State for Cabinet Affairs or the Secretary-General of the Executive Council.

Law No. 1 of 1973 concerning the organization of industry established the rules and conditions for beginning national industries with foreign capital participation. This law defines the term 'commercial agencies' as the undertaking for an agreed commission by a person or a commercial business on behalf of another person, in his name and on his own account, whether for a limited or an unspecified period of time. Article 1 of this law prohibits the performance of commercial agency business in Abu Dhabi except by a person whose name has been registered in the appropriate register provided by the Ministry of Commerce. Article 2 restricts the right of registration in the register only to those persons and companies which are wholly owned by a national of Abu Dhabi.

The law provides for the formation of a committee called the 'Committee for Developing National Industries', with the object of evaluating industrial projects, in addition to offering advice to the government on matters related to the protection of national industries.

The law states that the Ruler may use his authority to offer the industrial establishment certain exemptions and facilities which include the following: (1) exemption of its profits from income tax for five years commencing from the year the project starts yielding profits; (2) customs-duty exemptions on all imported raw materials, spare parts, equipment and experimental materials needed by the establishment for the execution of its work; (3) exemption of the industrial establishment from all taxes and other fees for a period of five years from the date of obtaining its licence; and (4) granting the establishment a plot of land for a period of five years, after the expiry of which it may be rented to the company for a nominal rental.

The facilities and exemptions offered to the industrial establishment, in accordance with the above provisions, apply only to an establishment satisfying the following conditions: (1) that all of its employees and workmen are nationals of Abu Dhabi or Arab countries. (This is with the exception of those non-Arab technicians and experts whose services are essential.) (2) The percentage of participation by nationals of Abu Dhabi and other emirates, with the exception of Sharjah, in the capital of the industrial establishment should not be less than 51 per cent. Sharjah expects the foreign partner to bring technical, management, and marketing skills and to provide local equity participation in the 25–33 per cent range with the rest provided locally by the private sector or by government, depending upon the nature of the project.

The Federal Ministry of Finance and Industry has drafted a bill to provide federal industrial incentives to the private sector especially outside Abu Dhabi and Dubai cities. The bill should provide the basis for extending long-term credits at low interest rates to develop industries proposed by the Ministry and for offering information and guidance. It is foreseen that top priority will be exhibited for projects designed to produce consumer goods for local markets and those using local raw materials. In addition, the bill would, among other things, give a five-year tax holiday, exemption from export tax and import duties on raw materials, and allow the government to provide free infrastructure for industries which are supportive of the federation's development plans.[7] Abu Dhabi is now trying to rationalize and harmonize industrial incentives available in the public and private sectors to establish an administrative apparatus to handle both types of incentives and to decide the extent to which these incentives will be federal or local in form and application.[8] (See Appendix VI for summaries of steps which should be taken to establish a business in Abu Dhabi, Dubai and Sharjah.)

The payment of corporate taxes varies according to different industries. Except for corporation taxes on oil, there is no income tax on profits of companies or individuals in the Emirates. Similarly, there are no present restrictions on the repatriation of capital or profits in the Emirates.

With regard to taxes applied to oil companies, the Income Tax Law of 1969 for Dubai, and the Abu Dhabi Income Tax Decree of 1965 are in effect and contain specific requirements as to liability for taxes after deductions for overheads, depreciation, losses, bad debts and other usual deductible expenses. In Abu Dhabi, the first Dh 1 million is tax exempt; thereafter, a rising scale of 10 to 40 per cent on profits from Dh 1 to 4 million and 50 per cent of all profits over Dh 5 million is applied. Locally it is held that the tax scale for oil companies will not apply to either local or foreign non-oil companies, except possibly as a restrictive action against a particular company if a serious dispute should arise with the government over fulfilment of a contract. For some major industries and construction enterprises, companies pay a 10 to 20 percentage tax on profits to the Ruler as part of its Charter of Incorporation. Most foreign banks pay up to 20 per cent of net annual profit through individual agreements with the Ruler.[9] Dubai collects a 10 per cent municipal tax on rentals of commercial property and 5 per cent tax on residential property to pay for municipal services.[10]

So that business activities and economic development in the territories of the UAE are enhanced, there are no restrictions against foreign companies opening branches, except that in 1978 there was a moratorium on the establishment of new banks.

The ownership of land for foreign companies is governed differently by each Emirate. In Sharjah ownership is permitted, while in both Abu Dhabi and Dubai foreigners are allowed to build and to rent land with the stipulation that upon termination of the agreed lease the property and any improvements made upon it revert to the owner, irrespective of any contract to the contrary existing between partners. In Abu Dhabi the present term of land leases is 8 years for small-scale projects with the lease either negotiated privately or obtained from the municipality; for larger industrial projects, a longer lease may be granted. In Dubai land leases may be issued for a maximum of 10 years. Again, the rental agreement must be registered with the municipality and also with the Engineering Department of the Ruler's office.

Labour relations in Abu Dhabi have been governed by the Labour Law of 1966 and its amendments up to 1969. That law defined labour contracts and described the relations between employers and workmen regarding such matters as wage, work licence, work conditions, leaves, indemnities, service awards, termination of service, and the like. According to Article 13 of the 1966 law, employers may dismiss workmen without notice in cases which include the following: (1) if the employee has deliberately committed any act or negligence with intent to cause material loss to the employer; (2) if the employee fails to fulfil the essential obligations arising from the labour contract; and (3) if the employee is proved to have adopted bad conduct or have committed an act affecting honesty. With respect to the employment of foreign nationals, the law is open in all cases for which local labour is not available.

Legislation, enacted in January 1980 and put into effect in June of that year, was geared toward controlling the influx of illegal aliens into the UAE. The immediate impact of this new law was to reduce the mobility of expatriate labour in every category: technicians, managers, and skilled workers as well as the semi- and unskilled labourers coming largely from the Indian subcontinent. If the typical foreign worker wishes to change jobs, the law as applied in 1980 would require him to leave the UAE for one year. The exceptions to this stipulation are those in a partnership arrangement with Emirates' citizens or whose employers go out of business.

Presently, all expatriates must be properly sponsored; their UAE employers are liable for their repatriation, and when their authorized stay has expired, they must leave the country at once. Moreover, the

1980 labour law delineates the rights of employees which steadies the legal position of foreign workers in seeking redress of grievance in UAE courts against UAE employers.

Each emirate, of course, has somewhat differing regulations on foreign participation in companies located in their individual territories. It is now possible, for example, for a national of any part of the UAE to sponsor a business enterprise in Abu Dhabi — a marked change from the past policy of that emirate.

In Abu Dhabi, new regulations for tenders and contracts have been promulgated. They specify that government contracts may be concluded by public tenders, limited tenders, local tenders, and negotiated contracts as well as service fees. Further specified is that the minimum preliminary guarantee for bids must be within 2 per cent and 5 per cent of the value of the bid, and that the guarantee for contract awards must be within 5 per cent and 15 per cent of the value of contract.[11]

The United Arab Emirates with its high income *per capita* is certainly an attractive market for foreign goods and services. The limited economic base coupled with increased oil revenue will continue to make the Emirates a profitable market for consumer goods. On the other hand, as the absorptive capacity of the economy expands, the market for capital goods, and technological, managerial, financial and other services will continue to grow. In summary therefore, the UAE will continue to constitute a vital component of the expanding Middle East market, a market which has been nourished and will continue to be nourished in the future by spiralling oil revenue.

Notes

1. United Arab Emirates (UAE), Currency Board, *Bulletin*, June 1980, pp. 60 and 62.
2. Ibid., pp. 67 and 69.
3. 'The Legal Environment for Doing Business in Bahrain, Qatar and the UAE', an address by Dr Husain M. Al-Baharna, Minister of State for Legal Affairs, Government of Bahrain, delivered in New York, 30 May 1974.
4. E.g. *Middle East Economic Digest*, Special report, October 1980, p. 44. (Hereafter *Middle East Economic Digest* will be cited as *MEED*.)
5. *MEED*, 24 March 1978, p. 38.
6. Husain M. Al-Baharna, 'Doing Business in Bahrain, Qatar and UAE'.
7. *MEED*, 23 September 1977, p. 35.

8. As noted previously in Chapter 2, the trend has been toward legislation to require new industrial projects in the UAE to have a federal licence. The goal of such a law would be to attempt to reduce duplication of plans and to co-ordinate industrial development throughout the Emirates. At various times free water and electricity have been offered as inducements to businessmen setting up in the UAE along with other tax and customs incentives.

9. N.A. Shilling, *Doing Business in Saudi Arabia and the Arab Gulf States* (New York: Intercrescent Publishing and Information Corporation, 1975), p. 425.

10. S. Dickson Tenneys, Commercial Action Group for the Near East, Bureau of International Commerce, US Department of Commerce, 'Marketing in the UAE', *Overseas Business Reports* (Washington, DC: Government Printing Office, 1979), p. 28.

11. *Middle East Economic Survey*, 30 May 1977, p. 12.

APPENDIX I: GOVERNMENT OF THE UAE

Head of State:

President Sheikh Zayed Ibn-Sultan al-Nahayyan

Supreme Council of Rulers:

President Sheikh Zayed Ibn-Sultan al-Nahayyan, ruler of Abu Dhabi
Vice President Sheikh Rashid Ibn-Said al-Maktoum, ruler of Dubai
Members include:
Sheikh Sultan Ibn-Mohammad al-Qasimi, ruler of Sharjah
Sheikh Saqr Ibn-Mohammad al-Qasimi, ruler of Ras Al-Khaimah
Sheikh Ahmad Ibn-Rashid al-Mualla, ruler of Umm Al-Quwain
Sheikh Hammad Ibn-Mohammad al-Sharqi, ruler of Fujairah
Sheikh Rashid Ibn-Humaid al-Nuaimi, ruler of Ajman

Council of Ministers:

Prime Minister, Sheikh Rashid Ibn-Said al-Maktoum
Deputy Prime Minister, Sheikh Maktoum Ibn-Rashid al-Maktoum
Deputy Prime Minister, Sheikh Hamdan Ibn-Mohammad al-Nahayyan
Finance and Industry Minister, Sheikh Hamdan Ibn-Rashid
    al-Maktoum
Interior Minister, Sheikh Mubarak Ibn-Mohammad al-Nahayyan
Defence Minister, Sheikh Mohammad Ibn-Rashid al-Maktoum
Foreign Affairs Minister, Sheikh Rashid Ibn-Abdullah al-Nuaimi
Economy and Trade Minister, Sheikh Sultan Ibn-Ahmad al-Mualla
Information Minister, Sheikh Ahmad Ibn-Hamed
Communications Minister, Mohammad Said al-Mualla
Public Works and Housing Minister, Mohammad Khalifah al-Kindi

Education, Youth and Sports Minister, Said Salman
Petroleum and Mineral Resources Minister, Dr Mana Saeed al-Obtaiba
Electricity and Water Resources Minister, Humaid Nasser al-Owais
Justice, Islamic Affairs and Awqaf Minister, Mohammad Abdel-Rahman al-Bakr
Health Minister, Hamad Abdel-Rahman al-Madfa
Agriculture and Fisheries Minister, Said al-Raqbani
Planning Minister, Said al-Ghobash
Labour and Social Affairs Minister, Said al-Jarwan

Ministers of State:

Cabinet Affairs, Said al-Ghaith
Supreme Council Affairs, Sheikh Abdel-Aziz al-Qasimi
Foreign Affairs, Sheikh Ahmad Ibn-Sultan al-Qasimi
Interior Affairs, Hamuda Ibn-Ali Dhariri

APPENDIX II: SPECIAL EDUCATION PROGRAMMES IN THE UAE

Commercial Education

A commercial course of 3 years duration was introduced in the Dubai Trade School in 1966. The first-year class of students was required to have completed a minimum of 8 years education. This commercial course was reorganized in 1970, with classes taught both in Arabic and English. The offerings include: bookkeeping, commercial geography, commercial arithmetic, office practice, and typing. Upon completion of the programme, the graduate is awarded a Diploma in Commercial Studies and may also sit, then, for a number of external examinations at the elementary and intermediate level. The programme is open to males only.

Also in Dubai is a programme of part-time evening courses in accountancy and secretarial studies. The 2-year undertaking is open to applicants with a reasonable elementary education; instruction time is on the level of 3 hours daily. In addition to bookkeeping and commercial and finance practice (in the accountancy course) and to commercial office work, public relations, and Arabic typing (in the secretarial segment), both programmes offer training in the Arabic language.

Agricultural Training School

Founded in 1955 and situated in Ras Al-Khaimah, entry originally began at the fifth grade level. In 1964 the school was upgraded to a 3-year secondary institution with admission dependent upon completion of 8 years of primary and preparatory schooling. The curriculum includes: Arabic, religion, English language, maths, chemistry, physics, biology, zoology, plant protection, economics, agri-business, animal husbandry, among other offerings. As with so many of the special education programmes in the UAE, only males are accepted into this school.

English Language Training

Established by the Ministry of Education during the 1972/3 academic year, the English Language Institute is located in Abu Dhabi. The programme envisages meeting four needs: (1) holding short courses for government officials to provide them with a foundation in the English language; (2) providing in-service teacher training in English as a foreign language; (3) training English-Arabic interpreters; and (4) experimenting with preparatory school students in language laboratory approaches to language instruction. The Institute has also provided a special course for Nursing School students.

Nurse Training

Nursing training programmes at three levels are conducted in the UAE by the Ministry of Health. The Army Medical Corps also operates a nurse training course. (1) The Abu Dhabi Nursing School, run at the Abu Dhabi Hospital, was established in 1971. The 3-year programme includes 11 months in each academic year. Arabic and English language training is offered along with the standard nursing courses. (2) The assistant or practical nurse training programmes in Dubai and Ras Al-Khaimah require 2 years study. In Dubai, some 576 hours of theoretical instruction is involved along with more than 2,500 hours of practical, on-the-job training. Among the courses are community health, child care, first aid, nursing principles, and general medicine. (3) The nurse aid (auxiliary nurse) training course is of 3 months duration, composed of 163 hours theoretical instruction and almost 300 hours of practical training.

Both males and females are accepted at the Abu Dhabi Nursing School; classes are mixed. Preparatory school completion is a requirement for admission, although in the past some exceptions were made for UAE nationals. The age range of applicants should be between 18 and 21. As all training is free, applicants agree to work for 3 years in

Appendix II: Special Education Programmes in the UAE 175

the UAE Ministry of Health upon graduation. Only nationals of the UAE and other Gulf states are eligible for admission. Applicants for the programme in Dubai in practical nursing are required to have completed preparatory school, while the nurse aid training course requires a minimum of 6 years of education. Most programmes include a stipend for those accepted, this in addition to covering all costs of the training.

Teacher Training

Teacher training institutes were established in Dubai (for males) and Sharjah (for females) in 1966/7. The purpose of the two bodies is to prepare elementary school teachers. The institutes offer a 4-year, secondary school level programme of instruction comprised of religious studies, Arabic and English languages, general science, mathematics, history, geography, social studies, principles and psychology of education, school hygiene, fine arts, technical orientation, physical training, music, and, for females, domestic science (home economics). Admission is dependent upon having completed 8 years of education or through the first year of general secondary education and success in an entrance examination. Here also, students receive stipends during their 4-year training period. All other costs are covered by the government.

Technical Education

Three technical schools exist in the UAE, one each in Sharjah (established in 1958), Dubai (set up in 1964), and Ras Al-Khaimah (begun in 1969). The Sharjah Trade School was created with the primary purpose of servicing the vehicles of the desert locust survey. The first class had no previous education; consequently, literacy training preceded skills training. By 1962 a primary education certificate was required for entry to the school and the period of the programme extended to 3 years.

Beginning with the 1974/5 academic year, all schools in the UAE went on a 6–3–3 system of primary, preparatory, and secondary education. As a consequence, the technical education stream begins at the intermediate stage and extends through the secondary cycle. Curricula were geared to allow students to sit for the London City and Guilds examinations. Along with carpentry, general engineering has been the other major area of emphasis. Within the engineering classification, however, a number of specializations could be undertaken: electrical engineering, mechanical engineering, automotive or fabrication engineering. Only males were accepted into the technical institutions.

Vocational training has been centred in Abu Dhabi at the Vocational Training Institute, begun in 1968 and originally under the administration of the Ministry of Labour. In 1973, the Centre was transferred to the jurisdiction of the Ministry of Education. Now offering a 2-year programme, 75 per cent of the time is devoted to practical-technical skills training and the remainder to theoretical studies and English language. Seven specializations are offered: secretarial; carpentry; refrigeration and air conditioning; welding; electrical; forging; automechanics. Between the first and second years, all trainees are placed with an employer, something of an apprenticeship arrangement, for on-the-job training. All trainees must continue with the standard academic education as well, i.e. for those not having completed elementary school, evening classes on the appropriate level, while for those having completed the elementary classes, enrolment is required in the preparatory school course. As in the other technical education institutions, only males are accepted. Again, stipends are paid to the trainees during their periods of instruction.

APPENDIX III: OIL COMPANIES AND AFFILIATES OPERATING IN THE UAE

Abu Dhabi

As the largest and oldest oil-producing emirate within the UAE, Abu Dhabi has the most numerous oil-related companies, a large number of which are affiliates of the Abu Dhabi National Oil Company (ADNOC). The following is a listing of major firms in the oil sector in Abu Dhabi.

(1) Abu Dhabi National Oil Company (ADNOC)
    PO Box 898
    Abu Dhabi, UAE

Founded in 1971, ADNOC has full legal capacity to act in all matters concerning oil and natural gas exploration, production, refining, transportation and storage of their derivatives, marketing and industrialization of their by-products. With such broad powers, the company in the past 2 or 3 years has assumed a dominant role in petroleum affairs of the emirate. As a state-owned petroleum company, its role has been similar to that of other national firms in other producing countries. In accordance with Abu Dhabi oil policy, ADNOC, however, has not acquired 100 per cent ownership of the oil industry but continues to have the participation of foreign companies in many undertakings. In late 1979 the company took over majority ownership of the principal onshore and marine producing firms. It additionally has responsibility for development of the Upper Zakum field and the Ruwais industry projects and gas-gathering facilities. In assuming a pre-eminent role in the oil sector, ADNOC has established a number of subsidiary companies.

(2) Abu Dhabi Company for Onshore Oil Operation (ADCO)
    PO Box 270
    Abu Dhabi, UAE

A subsidiary of ADNOC, this company is the successor of the Iraq

Petroleum Company established in the Emirate since 1939 with a long and successful history of oil exploration and export. Present shareholders in ADCO include: ADNOC, 60 per cent; BP, 9.5 per cent; CFP, 9.5 per cent; Shell, 9.5 per cent; Exxon, 4.75 per cent; Mobil, 4.75 per cent; and Partex, 2 per cent. Current production, all from onshore fields, has averaged about 850,000 b/d in recent months although capacity has been estimated to be about 300,000 b/d or more. ADCO was established in October 1978, taking over the activities of the company formerly known as Abu Dhabi Petroleum Company (ADPC).

(3) Abu Dhabi Drilling Chemicals and Products Ltd. (ADDCAP)
PO Box 6121
Abu Dhabi, UAE

Created in 1975, ADDCAP is a joint venture of ADNOC and N.L. Industries (an American company) to produce drilling chemical products such as barite and pentonite. ADNOC holds an 80 per cent interest in the company with its principal facilities located on Saadiyat Island.

(4) Abu Dhabi Gas Industries Company (GASCO and ADGIL)
PO Box 665
Abu Dhabi, UAE

GASCO is one of the largest subsidiaries of ADNOC. Established in 1977, GASCO is charged with the exploitation of natural gas liquids produced from onshore fields. The project to tap the gas, now being flared, is estimated to cost over $1 billion. Its facilities will include: extraction and collection facilities, pipeline, storage tanks and loading berths at Ruwais. GASCO's shareholders are ADNOC, 68 per cent; CFP, 15 per cent; Shell, 15 per cent; and Partex, 2 per cent.

(5) Abu Dhabi Gas Liquefaction Company (ADGLC)
PO Box 3500
Abu Dhabi, UAE

Established in 1972, then reincorporated in 1977, ADGLC's main activity is the liquefaction and export of associated gas. The company's present LNG plant, located on Das Island, has been operating below capacity for some time because of leaks. This plant uses gas from the offshore fields of Umm Shaif, Zakum, and Bunduq. Shareholders

Appendix III: Oil Companies and Affiliates Operating in the UAE

are ADNOC, 51 per cent; Mitsui, 22.05 per cent; BP, 16.33 per cent; CFP, 8.166 per cent; and Bridgestone, 2.45 per cent.

(6) Abu Dhabi Marine Operations Company (ADMA-OPCO)
    PO Box 303
    Abu Dhabi, UAE

Another subsidiary of ADNOC, this company is the principal producer of petroleum offshore Abu Dhabi. Founded in 1978, ADMA-OPCO is the successor of the old marine-areas concession. Present shareholders include: ADNOC, 60 per cent; BP, 14.666 per cent; CFP, 13.333 per cent; and Japan Oil Development Company, 12 per cent. Current production averages 450,000 b/d, with estimated capacity at a somewhat higher level.

(7) ADNOC Dredging
    PO Box 3649
    Abu Dhabi, UAE

Founded in 1976, ADNOC Dredging was formed by its parent company to carry out dredging and land reclamation along the coast. The firm was, in part, established to free the Emirate of Abu Dhabi of dependence upon foreign dredging companies. ADNOC has 100 per cent ownership of this firm.

(8) Abu Dhabi Petroleum Ports Operations Company (ADPPOC)
    PO Box 61
    Abu Dhabi, UAE

This relatively new company, a joint venture between ADNOC (60 per cent) and Lamnalco (40 per cent) is charged with operating the petroleum port of Jabel Dhanna, Ruwais port, and other petroleum ports to be agreed upon in the future. Its activities are to include the maintenance of ports, water passages, berths, port equipment, and water pollution control. The Alireza group of Saudi Arabia participates in Lamnalco.

(9) Abu Dhabi Pipeline Construction Company (APCC)
    PO Box 2608
    Abu Dhabi, UAE

This recently founded company (October 1978) is a joint venture of

ADNOC (60 per cent) and the French construction company Entrepose (40 per cent). The firm seeks to bid on ADNOC contracts for pipeline construction. Creation of the company is part of Abu Dhabi's efforts to establish a locally owned petroleum service industry.

(10) Abu Dhabi National Oil Company for Distribution (ADNOC FOD)
PO Box 4188
Abu Dhabi, UAE

This company was formed in 1973 to take over the marketing of petroleum products in the Emirate of Abu Dhabi. It assumed the assets of Gulf, Caltex, Shell, and BP and is a wholly owned subsidiary of ADNOC. At present, it markets the products from Umm Al-Nar refinery (15,000 b/d) and imports and markets products under contract with the Kuwait National Oil Company. Upon completion of the Ruwais refinery in 1980 (estimated throughput capacity of 110,000–120,000 b/d), the company plans to become an exporter of petroleum products.

(11) Abu Dhabi National Plastic Pipe Fabricating Company (NPP)
PO Box 2915
Abu Dhabi, UAE

This small company is owned by ADNOC (51 per cent) and C. Itoh (49 per cent). C. Itoh is a Japanese firm which manufactures and markets PVC pipe and fittings. Although founded in 1974, its Abu Dhabi facility did not go into production until 2 years later.

(12) Abu Dhabi National Tankers Company (ADNATCO)
PO Box 2977
Abu Dhabi, UAE

In order to further the UAE policy favouring increased integration of its oil industry and more downstream activity, Abu Dhabi National Tankers Company was created in 1975 to own ADNOC's tanker fleet. At present the company has three vessels which it reportedly manages without outside technical assistance. ADNOC holds 100 per cent of the company's shares.

(13) Arab Petroleum Pipeline Company (SUMED)
PO Box 2056
Alexandria, Egypt

Appendix III: Oil Companies and Affiliates Operating in the UAE 181

ADNOC has a 14.9 per cent interest in the Egyptian pipeline which links the Red Sea with the Mediterranean. The holding is basically a financial participation as ADNOC does not have management control over SUMED.

(14) National Drilling Company (NDC)
   PO Box 4017
   Abu Dhabi, UAE

This fully owned subsidiary of ADNOC was established in 1972 and charged with carrying out drilling of exploratory wells and participating in development of the national petroleum wealth in onshore and offshore areas. In the last 4 years, NDC has conducted a drilling programme for water reinjection and for oil exploration in the Emirate. One of the goals of the company is to make the Abu Dhabi oil industry self-sufficient in drilling services.

(15) National Marine Services (NMS)
   PO Box 7202
   Abu Dhabi, UAE

Established in 1978, this company carries out all work relating to acquisition, lease, and charter of specialized boats used in offshore areas. ADNOC holds a 60 per cent interest while the remainder is owned by Jackson-Marine (a subsidiary of Halliburton).

(16) National Petroleum Construction Company (NPCC)
   PO Box 2058
   Abu Dhabi, UAE

As a joint venture between ADNOC (60 per cent) and the Consolidated Contractors Company (40 per cent), a large Lebanese construction firm, the NPCC was established in 1973 to build marine scaffolds and to supply barges and small tugs. Headquartered on Saadiyat Island, the company possesses modern warehouses and industrial facilities.

(17) Pak-Arab Fertilizers Ltd
   PO Box 1713
   Lahore, Pakistan

A joint venture founded in 1973 between ADNOC (48 per cent) and the Government of Pakistan (52 per cent), this company owns and operates a nitrogenous fertilizer plant in Multan, Pakistan. The products include ammonia, urea, nitric acid, ammonium nitrate, among others.

(18) Pak-Arab Refinery Ltd
PO Box 8925
Karachi, Pakistan

The Pak-Arab Refinery is the second joint venture between ADNOC (40 per cent) and the Government of Pakistan (60 per cent). The main activity of the company is the operation of a refinery at Multan, Pakistan, with a throughput capacity of 40,000 b/d. When fully operational the refinery will produce jet fuel and a range of other refined products.

(19) Umm Al-Dalkh Development Company (UDECO)
PO Box 6866
Abu Dhabi, UAE

Created in 1978, UDECO is a joint venture of ADNOC (50 per cent) and the Japan Oil Development Company (50 per cent). The purpose of the company is to provide services for the development of the offshore Umm Al-Dalkh field which is owned by ADNOC (88 per cent) and Japan Oil Development Company (12 per cent).

(20) Zakum Development Company (ZADCO)
PO Box 6808
Abu Dhabi, UAE

Founded in 1977, this joint venture of ADNOC (87.5 per cent) and Japanese oil companies (12.5 per cent) has assumed a large role in the development of the offshore oil industry. The company is charged with carrying out oil exploration and development in the Upper Zakum Zone offshore, believed to contain large, low-pressure reserves. CFP plays an important role in the management of the project and provides technical expertise to ZADCO. CFP had an initial part in the creation of the company.

Other oil companies in Abu Dhabi include:

(21) Total-Abu Al Bukhoosh
PO Box 4058
Abu Dhabi, UAE

Appendix III: Oil Companies and Affiliates Operating in the UAE 183

This subsidiary of CFP is involved in oil production.

(22) BP Projects Group (BPPG)
 PO Box 3566
 Abu Dhabi, UAE

BPPG was formed in 1976 as management consultants for further development of ADMA-OPCO's Umm Shaif and Zakum oil fields. The organization is to provide the petroleum industry with engineering and project services for offshore production facilities and onshore treatment handling systems. Coverage is offered from feasibility studies through to supervision of construction.

(23) Amerada Hess Oil Corporation of Abu Dhabi
 PO Box 2046
 Abu Dhabi, UAE

The company is involved in exploration, drilling, production and tanker loading.

(24) Abu Dhabi Oil Company Ltd (Japan)
 PO Box 630
 Abu Dhabi, UAE

Companies in the other emirates include:

(25) Dubai Petroleum Company (DUPETCO)
 PO Box 2222
 Dubai, UAE

This is the major oil company of Dubai involved in exploration and production of crude oil. Its ownership breakdown is: Continental Oil Company, 60 per cent; Texaco, 20 per cent; Sun Oil, 10 per cent; and Wintershall, 10 per cent. DUPETCO holds half of the exploration and production concession offshore Dubai. The other half is held by Dubai Marine Areas, the shareholders of which are CFP (50 per cent) and Hispanoil (50 per cent).

(26) Amoco Sharjah Oil Company
 PO Box 1191
 Sharjah, UAE

Appendix III: Oil Companies and Affiliates Operating in the UAE

This subsidiary of Standard Oil Company of Indiana is involved in exploration in Sharjah.

(27) Crescent Petroleum Company
 PO Box 211
 Sharjah, UAE

An affiliate of Buttes Gas and Oil Company, Crescent Petroleum carries out exploration and production.

Additionally, there are a number of drilling, tool, equipment, construction, and services companies directly related to the oil industry working in the various emirates.

(28) Emirates General Petroleum Corporation (EGPC)

Established by a federal law on 3 November 1980, is EGPC a 100 per cent state-owned company for the marketing and distribution of petroleum products within the UAE. Capitalized at Dh 800 million ($216.8 million), EGPC will eventually function throughout the UAE although initially its activities will be concentrated in all the emirates except Abu Dhabi. Chairman of the Board is H.E. Mana Saeed al-Otaiba, Minister of Petroleum and Mineral Resources. As of 1 January 1981, EGPC will take over all the assets and installations of the existing marketing companies which operate in the six northern emirates — Caltex, Shell, and BP — in return for payment of compensation calculated on the basis of net book value or market value, whichever is lower. Installations include product tanker vessels and overland tanker trucks, pipelines, gas stations, and other equipment.

APPENDIX IV: TEXT OF LAW CONCERNING ABU DHABI OWNERSHIP OF GAS RESOURCES

The law was promulgated by Sheikh Zayed Ibn Sultan, the Ruler of Abu Dhabi, concerning state ownership of all gas resources in Abu Dhabi.

Article 1

All gas that has been discovered or may be discovered in the territory of the Abu Dhabi Emirate and gas which is being extracted or produced from oil and gas wells therein shall be the exclusive property of the Emirate. The territory of the Abu Dhabi Emirate includes its onshore areas, territorial waters and Continental Shelf.

Article 2

In the implementation of the provisions of the preceding Article, the word gas shall be understood to mean the following: gas associated with crude oil; gas caps of crude oil reservoirs; natural gas not associated with crude oil; and all components of the associated gases stipulated above which include methane, ethane, propane, butane, natural gasoline and condensates composed of pentanes and heavier hydrocarbons.

Article 3

The Emirate of Abu Dhabi shall have the exclusive right to handle the total quantities of gas referred to in the preceding Article and it shall exercise its ownership rights as follows:
(i) As regards gas associated with crude oil, at the gas exit points of the gas/oil separator plants in all phases of the gas separation

operation.
(ii) As regards unassociated natural gas and gas caps of crude oil reservoirs, at the well-head.

Article 4

The Abu Dhabi National Oil Company (ADNOC) shall have the right to exploit and utilize all the quantities of gas referred to in Article 1 of this Law, and to handle all other matters related to such gas. In addition, all the rights derived from the petroleum agreements concluded by the Government of the Emirate of Abu Dhabi relating to discovered or produced gas or to gas extraction and production facilities shall revert to ADNOC.

Article 5

All oil companies operating in the Emirate of Abu Dhabi shall deliver the gas produced from the oil and gas fields to ADNOC in accordance with the conditions and technical arrangements determined by ADNOC after consultations with the aforementioned companies.

Article 6

ADNOC shall have the right to develop the gas referred to in Article 1 of this Law either alone or jointly within the framework of agreements or joint ventures concluded with other parties. In the latter case, ADNOC's participation shall be not less than 51 per cent of the capital of the venture concerned.

Article 7

ADNOC shall place, free of charge, at the disposal of the companies operating in the Emirate of Abu Dhabi all the quantities of gas required for their operations in respect of the production of crude oil from oilfields covered by the agreements concluded between the Government and these companies, as well as the quantities of gas required for gas-lift crude oil production operations, maintenance of reservoir pressures and implementation of secondary recovery methods.

Article 8

Any provision which conflicts with the provisions of this Law shall be cancelled.

Article 9

This Law shall be published in the *Official Gazette* and shall come into effect as from the date of its publication.

APPENDIX V: ABU DHABI FUND FOR ARAB ECONOMIC DEVELOPMENT

Board of Directors

Chairman: H.H. Sheikh Khalifa Ibn-Zayed al-Nahayyan
Vice Chairman: Sheikh Surour Ibn-Mohammad al-Nahayyan
Members of the Board:
Sheikh Tahnoun Ibn-Mohammad al-Nahayyan
Mr Mohammed Habroush al-Suweidi
Mr Rashid Abdullah al-Nuaimi
Mr Adnan Pachachi
Dr Hassan Abbas Zaki
Mr Nasser al-Nowais (Director General of the Fund)

Basic Information about the Fund

(1) Founded: July 1971
(2) Original authorized capital: Dh 2,000 million (U.S. $500 million)
(3) Paid-up capital as of 1 January 1980: Dh 1,565.78 million
(4) Objectives: To assist Arab, African and Asian countries in economic development by extending loans, participation in capital investment development projects, and provision of technical assistance for exploratory studies and other technical investment endeavours.
(5) Activities up to January 1980:
    (a) Loans granted – 61 loans totalling Dh 2,947.5 million
    (b) Equity participation – Dh 128.1 million
    (c) Technical assistance and cost of field studies – Dh 19.78 million
    (d) Loans and grants administered by the Fund on behalf of the Abu Dhabi Finance Department – Dh 1,477.2 million
    (e) Fund's authorized capital increased to Dh 4,000 million per Board of Directors' decision of 25 September 1979 (see Table A.1 for details of the ADFAEC's financial status)

Table A.1: Fund Financial Status, 1974–9 (in millions of Dh)

	1974	1975	1976	1977	1978	1979
Paid-up capital	580.00	—	37.50	100.00	155.61	692.67
Cumulative	580.00	580.00	617.50	717.50	873.11	1,565.78
Reserves	18.72	45.21	36.90	30.99	40.87	56.36
Cumulative	22.25	67.46	104.40	135.35	176.22	232.58
Capital and reserves	602.33	647.46	721.86	852.85	1,049.33	1,798.36
Loans signed by the Fund	199.20	191.00	661.00	539.00	840.00	402.80
Cumulative	199.20	390.30	1,051.80	1,590.80	2,430.80	2,833.60
Equity participation	11.00	8.40	—	—	5.60	103.10
Cumulative	11.00	19.40	19.40	19.40	25.00	128.10
Grand total of loans and equity participation	210.20	417.55	1,071.20	1,610.20	2,455.80	2,961.70
Drawings on loans	1.96	9.03	140.21	392.48	296.13	573.17
Cumulative	1.96	10.99	151.20	543.68	839.81	1,412.98
Equity participation disbursed	4.57	8.24	6.53	1.22	8.23	104.23
Cumulative	4.57	12.81	19.34	20.56	28.79	133.02
Total drawings on loans and on equity participation	6.53	23.80	170.54	564.24	868.60	1,546.00
	%	%	%	%	%	%
Percentage loans to paid-up capital	34.4	67.3	170.3	221.7	278.4	181.0
Percentage of drawings to total loans	1.0	2.8	14.4	34.2	34.5	49.9
Percentage of loan drawings to paid-up capital	0.3	1.9	24.5	75.8	96.2	90.2
Percentage of loan drawings and drawn equity participation to paid-up capital	1.13	4.1	27.6	78.6	99.5	98.7

Source: Abu Dhabi Fund for Arab Economic Development, *Annual Reports*, various issues.

(6) H.E. Said Ghobash Building
Tourist Club Area
PO Box 814
Abu Dhabi, UAE
Cable: FUND
Telex: 22287 FUND EM
Telephone: 822865

Fund's Lending Policies

(1) Non-discrimination among nations requesting loans in regard to terms applied to the various projects.
(2) Non-prejudicial treatment of various sectors or projects over others (except for priorities assigned in the development programmes or plans of the nation concerned), in order to achieve the best standard of economic development.
(3) Facilitation of lending in regard to interest rates and liberal repayment periods, plus establishment of a reasonable grace period for loan repayments.
(4) Participation in capital improvement projects offering suitable trade benefits, especially inasmuch as such participation results in considerable encouragement and incentive for involvement of individuals and institutions.
(5) The vital importance and value of projects to the economies and commercial sectors of nations benefiting.
(6) A special emphasis on co-ordination of and participation in financing of relatively large-scale projects (particularly in co-operation with international financial institutions) in order to guarantee such projects' success.
(7) In July 1974 the Fund ceased to be exclusively Arab, with the authorization under provisions of Law No. (7) 1974 to offer aid in addition to African, Asian, and other Islamic nations; its original authorized capital was increased from Dh 500 million to Dh 2,000 million.

Table A.2: Classification of Fund Loans According to Sectors, 1974–9 (percentages[a] given in ( ); value in millions of Dh)

Sector	1974 No.	1974 Value	1975 No.	1975 Value	1976 No.	1976 Value	1977 No.	1977 Value	1978 No.	1978 Value	1979 No.	1979 Value	Total No.	Total Value
Agricultural, rural development and fishery resources	1	21.5 (9.9)	1	40.0 (21.9)	8	126.6 (18.9)	—	—	2	9.0 (1.1)	1	40.0 (7.9)	13	237.1 (8.0)
Transportation, communications and warehouses	1	13.5 (6.2)	1	5.0 (2.7)	1	60.0 (9.0)	5	192.9 (35.8)	3	39.0 (4.6)	2	44.0 (8.7)	13	354.4 (12.0)
Electricity and water	3	95.5 (43.8)	1	130.0 (71.0)	2	168.0 (25.1)	4	160.1 (29.7)	2	100.0 (11.9)	2	19.2 (3.8)	14	672.8 (22.8)
Housing	—	—	—	—	1	40.0 (6.0)	—	—	—	—	—	—	1	40.0 (1.4)
Tourism and hotels	2	41.7[b] (19.1)	1	8.0 (4.4)	—	—	—	—	—	—	—	—	3	49.7 (1.7)
Manufacturing and extractive industries	2	46.0 (21.1)	—	—	5	275.0 (41.1)	5	186.0 (34.5)	3	692.0 (82.4)	3	402.0[c] (80.0)	18	1,601.5 (54.2)
Total	9	218.2 (100.0)	4	183.0 (100.0)	17	669.6 (100.1)	10	539.0 (100.0)	10	840.0 (100.0)	8	505.7 (100.4)	62	2,955.5 (100.1)

Sources: Abu Dhabi Fund for Arab Economic Development, *Annual Reports, 1977, 1978* and *1979* and mimeographed data; *Middle East Economic Survey*, 13 October 1980. p. II.

a. May not total to 100 per cent due to rounding.
b. Includes Dh 11 million equity participation in a Tunisian project.
c. Includes Dh 102.8 million in equity participation in a Tunisian project.

Lending Activities

ADFAED credits are characterized by their 'softness', that is, the low interest rates, relatively long maturity, and generous grace periods negotiated with each loan. Every project supported is evaluated on the basis of its place in the recipient's overall development programme, the nature of the enterprise (whether commercial or infrastructural), and the time lag before the project can become profitable. Agricultural development projects tend to have longer repayment periods than those in the area of tourism and hotels. The emphasis on infrastructure schemes and on the industrial sector becomes clear in Table A.2.

Table A.3: Fund Technical Assistance and Financing of Studies, 1975–9 (in thousands of Dh)

Country	1975	1976	1977	1978	1979	Total
Bahrain	340[a]	—	—	—	—	340
Arab Republic of Yemen (North)	300	—	—	5,000	—	5,300
Democratic Republic of Yemen (South)	—	6,580[b]	—	—	—	6,580
Arab League's Industrial Development Centre	—	—	560[a]	—	—	560
Senegal	—	—	—	—	4,000	4,000
Lesotho	—	—	—	—	3,000	3,000
Total	640	6,580	560	5,000	7,000	19,780

Source: ADFAED, *Annual Report, 1978 and 1979*.
a. Grant.
b. Included in Table A.4 by geographical distribution.

More and more, the Fund is moving toward co-financing of some of the larger projects along with such institutions as the Arab Bank for the Economic Development of Africa, the Saudi Development Fund, the United States Agency for International Development, the OPEC Fund, the Japanese Co-operation Fund, the Kuwait Fund for Arab Economic Development, the African Development Bank, the

Appendix V: Abu Dhabi Fund for Arab Economic Development

Canadian International Development Agency, the Arab Fund for Economic and Social Development, and the World Bank.

In addition to the loans listed in Table A.4, the ADFAED has financed a number of studies as a form of technical assistance (Table A.3).

The willingness of the Fund to lend for technical and other studies is critical in financing feasibility and specialized evaluations of proposed schemes. Financing for this type of project, rather in the planning than in the implementation stage, can be difficult for many developing nations to secure. Yet adequate evaluation of projects is a prerequisite to structuring successful programmes and schemes. As seen in Table A.3, some ADFAED support has taken the form of outright grants.

As discernible from Table A.4, the average Fund loan has very favourable terms: 3.75 per cent interest, a 16-year maturity, and a 4-year grace period. This indicates a relatively high grant element in such lending when compared with financing available in the commercial markets or through some agencies.

Finally, as noted in Chapter 7, the Fund administers projects which have financial support from the government of Abu Dhabi. The following listing suffices to round-out the direct functions of the ADFAED in the lending and financial sector, although the Fund participates in a number of informational and data-gathering activities as well.

North Yemen: Sana' a-Marib road (Dh 200 million) and Marib dam (Dh 201 million)

Somalia: Juba sugar scheme (Dh 304.2 million) and the Berbera-Burao Road (Dh 187 million)

Syria: sugar plants at Riqa, Masqanna, Tel-Salhab (Dh 332 million); Deir az Zor paper mill (Dh 440 million); Damascus International Airport (Dh 50 million)

Egypt: Suez Canal development (Dh 147 million)

Comoro Islands: health and education sectors (Dh 8 million)

Uganda: Packwache-Arua road (Dh 40 million)

Zaire: special studies for provision of appropriate medical equipment for hospitals (Dh 19 million)

Maldives: communications satellite earth station (Dh 4 million)

Table A.4: Fund Loans by Geographical Distribution, Countries, Terms and Purpose, 1974—9

Region/Country	Amount (Dh million)	Interest (%)	Maturity (years)	Grace (years)	Project
Arab countries					
Jordan (1974)	21.5	3	18	3.5	King Talal dam
(1975)	5.0	3	18	3.5	Al Azraq-to-borders road
(1977)	100.0	5	12	2	Al-Hasa phosphate mining, Phase I
Bahrain (1974)	40.0	3.5	16	1.5	Sitra power and water station, Stage I
(1976)	100.0	3.5	19.5	4	Sitra power and water station, Stage II
(1976)	60.0	4.5	14	4	Small-scale industries
(1977)	20.0	3.5	20	5	Power generation
Tunisia (1974)	13.5	3.5	14.5	3	Railway cars
(1974)	6.0	5	12.5	3	Can-manufacturing plant
(1974)	20.7	5	15	5.5	North Sousa tourism
(1974)	11.0	Equity Participation			North Sousa tourism
(1977)	47.0	4	14	2	Modernization of transport
(1979)	218.8	5	11	4	Phosphate fertilizer factory
Sudan (1976)	80.0	5	12.25	3	Cotton spinning mill
(1978)	4.0	4.5	12	5	(Supplemental) Cotton spinning mill
(1976)	16.5	3.5	20.25	6	South Darfur rural development
(1977)	40.0	3.5	20	4	Railroad development
Syria (1974)	51.5	4	19	4.5	Electric power distribution
(1976)	56.0	3.5	20	5	Power project

Table A.4: Continued

Region/Country	Amount (Dh million)	Interest (%)	Maturity (years)	Grace (years)	Project
Oman (1976)	60.0	4	20	3.5	Gas utilization project
(1978)	663.0	4	7	2	Development of southern oilfields
Lebanon (1977)	41.0	4.5	20	5	Beirut port reconstruction
(1977)	27.0	4.5	15	5	Electricity supply expansion
Egypt (1974)	40.0	4	18	5	Talkha I fertilizer complex
(1974)	10.0	4	19	4.75	Omar Al-Khayam hotel
(1975)	8.0	4	19	4.75	(Supplemental) Omar Al-Khayam hotel
(1975)	130.0	3.5	20.5	6	Abu Qir power station
(1977)	60.0	3.5	20	4	Suez Canal development
Morocco (1976)	40.0	3	17	2.5	Business centre
(1976)	70.0	5.5	11	1.75	Cotton spinning mills
(1979)	40.0	4.5	19	5	Gharb agricultural scheme
Mauritania (1977)	16.0	4.5	12	2	Steel bar factory
(1979)	40.0	3.5	19.5	5	Kifa-Al Nimat road
(1979)	80.0	4.5	16.25	5	Al Guelb iron mines
Yemen Arab Republic (1974)	4.0	3.5	12	3.75	Sana'a water supply
(North Yemen) (1975)	40.0	3	22.5	8	Southern Uplands rural development
(1978)	40.0	3.5	19.5	5	Ta'iz water and drainage system
(1978)	5.0	1.5	19.5	5	Studies of the Wadi Siham

Table A.4: Continued

Region/Country	Amount (Dh million)	Interest (%)	Maturity (years)	Grace (years)	Project
Peoples Democratic Republic of Yemen (South Yemen) (1976)	29.1	3.5	13	4	Fishing trawlers
	6.58	2.5	13	4	Geological survey, Stage I
Total of Arab countries	2,361.18	3.8[a]	16[a]	4[a]	
African countries					
Burundi (1976)	4.0	2.5	21	6.5	Fisheries development
Mali (1976)	16.0	3.5	20	5	Selingue dam construction
Gambia (1977)	5.2	3.5	15	3	Yandum airport
Tanzania (1977)	24.0	4.5	15	5	Sugar factory
Guinea (1977)	16.0	5	14	4	Clinker factory
Malagasy/Madagascar (1979)	16.0	3.4	14.5	5	Rogee electric power scheme
Comoro Islands (1979)	4.0	2	18.25	4	Reconstruction of Anjouan airport
Seychelles (1979)	0.8	4.5	11.5	2	Ice plant in Mahe
(1979)	3.2	4.5	11.5	2	Electric power on the Island of Bralin
Uganda (1978)	25.0	4.5	13	3.5	Rehabilitation of African textile mill
Senegal (1978)	4.0	3.5	20	5	Studies for the Kamobeule and Bila dams
Lesotho (1978)	3.0	2	14.5	5	Engineering studies for Maseru airport
Total of African countries	121.2	3.6[a]	16[a]	4[a]	

Table A.4: Continued

Region/Country	Amount (Dh million)	Interest (%)	Maturity (years)	Grace (years)	Project
Asian countries					
Bangladesh (1976)	40.0	4.5	13.25	3.75	Reconstruction and expansion of machine tools plant
(1978)	60.0	3.5	19.5	5	Toungi-Ishodri power line
India (1976)	68.0	3.5	19.5	5	Hydroelectric power
Maldives (1976)	8.0	3.5	12	1.5	Refrigeration and storage ships
(1978)	8.0	3	13	3.5	Expansion of Hululi airport
Malaysia (1976)	16.0	4	14.5	5	Sabah flour and feed mills
(1976)	17.0	4	14.5	5	Suai palm oil processing
Sri Lanka (1976)	20.0	5	13.5	4	Fisheries development
Indonesia (1977)	57.0	4	20	5	Bandung electricity distribution
Afghanistan (1977)	30.0	4	20	5	Baglan sugar mill
Total of Asian countries	324.0	4[a]	16[a]	4[a]	
Other					
Malta (1978)	28.0	2.5	15.5	3	Development of port of Marsaxlokk

Sources: ADFAED, *Annual Reports, 1974 to 1978 and 1979*.
a. Average.

APPENDIX VI: ESTABLISHING BUSINESS IN THE UAE

Establishing a Business in Abu Dhabi

There is no minimum capital requirement for starting a business in Abu Dhabi. However, a sponsorship agreement with a native-born sponsor must be signed at the Abu Dhabi Civil Court. There is a nominal once-only fee charged by the court.

A copy of the sponsorship agreement, a copy of the office rental agreement, and four photographs of each partner in the business must be sent to the office of the Abu Dhabi Municipality to obtain approval of the location selected for the business. If it considers the location suitable, the Municipality will issue a provisional trade licence. Care must therefore be taken to obtain an appropriate location for the business venture. Licences are issued in five categories: trading, contracting, transport, industrial and service. A foreign firm is allowed to obtain a licence in only one category at a time.

A copy of the partnership agreement, a copy of the provisional trade licence from the municipality, and one photograph of each partner must then be personally submitted to the Abu Dhabi Chamber of Commerce for membership, which is mandatory for all firms except those offering only professional services, for which membership is optional. The Chamber of Commerce calls a firm with minority local participation a foreign firm. Chamber fees for external firms which are branches of foreign corporations are a Dh 1,000 ($256) initiation fee and Dh 1,050 ($270) annual dues. Fees for external firms where the foreign owner is an individual are Dh 300 ($77) initiation and Dh 550 ($141) annual dues. When the membership committee approves the application, the Chamber issues a certificate of approved membership.

In order to obtain the final licence, the certificate of approved membership should be taken back to the municipality. The licence fee depends on the amount of initial capital invested in the business, and is usually Dh 400–800 ($102–205) a year. Without the municipality

Appendix VI: Establishing Business in the UAE

trade licence it is impossible to clear goods through customs, to obtain telephone or telex facilities, or to open letters of credit. The trade licence will specify by broad category the type of product which the firm is permitted to import. An established firm wishing to expand into other product lines must have its trade licence amended. Generally, the municipality will allow up to three amendments and will permit a firm to market product lines related to those in the original licence.

The Abu Dhabi trade licence is valid only for the city of Abu Dhabi, and does not permit the holder to do business in other UAE cities, without first meeting their individual requirements. Conversely, the holder of an Al-Ain or Sharjah or Dubai trade licence may not do business within the city of Abu Dhabi without first obtaining an Abu Dhabi trade licence.

Special requirements for certain businesses are the following:

(1) An additional requirement for contractors is Dh 100,000 ($25,600) guarantee, in the form of a stand-by letter of credit payable to the Abu Dhabi Chamber of Commerce and valid for 1 calendar year, must be obtained from a local bank at the time of applying for Chamber membership. This guarantee must be renewed annually and maintained as long as the contracting firm is in Abu Dhabi.

(2) In 1975, the Abu Dhabi Department of Planning initiated a registration system for consulting firms wanting to do business in the Emirate. Although some government departments do not require their consultants to be registered with the Planning Department, more and more of them are now requiring this registration. The filled-out application for registration is sent (in triplicate) to Public Projects Committee, Department of Planning, PO Box 12, Abu Dhabi, UAE, with any other brochures or material which the consultant believes would enhance his presentation.

Establishing a Business in Dubai

Dubai is one of the seven member states of the United Arab Emirates. It is located on the southern coast of the Gulf between the Emirate of Sharjah and the Emirate of Abu Dhabi.

A foreign businessman wishing to establish an office in Dubai would be well advised to obtain a 1-year, multiple-entry visa for the United

Arab Emirates from one of its consulates in his country of residence. This visa, under ordinary circumstances, allows a foreign national to reside in the Emirates for 30 days per entry. Those 30 days will be very busy ones if the businessman is to accomplish everything required by law to open an office in Dubai.

The necessary forms to enrol on the register of commerce can be obtained from the offices of the Dubai Municipalities. Contractors and consultants have one extra form to submit called a 'Technical Data Questionnaire.' The Technical Data Questionnaire for Consultants and the Technical Data Questionnaire for Contractors both require the signature of the 'principal officials or members of the firm.' Consultants and contractors are advised to obtain the Technical Data Questionnaire, fill it out, and have it notarized before going to Dubai. Copies of the Technical Data Questionnaire forms as well as the Commercial Registry form are available on request from the commercial offices of embassies in Dubai.

The officer of the firm who will be in charge of its activities in the UAE should also bring with him a notarized general power of attorney to act for the firm. In addition, he should have a letter appointing him to direct the firm's office and activities here. If the parent company is a corporation he should also bring a notarized copy of the corporate minutes authorizing him to act for the firm and specifying what he may or may not do on the firm's behalf. The Municipality prefers that these documents be on corporate letterhead. If the firm had not been sponsored by a Dubai national or by a corporation licensed to do business in Dubai, the firm will have to deposit Dh 100,000 ($25,654) in a Dubai bank as a guarantee. The bank's manager must certify that the deposit has been made, and his certificate must be submitted to the Municipality.

The Municipality also requires the submission of legalized copies of the certificate of incorporation of the parent company or its articles of partnership (or the equivalent). The Municipality requires that these be certified by an appropriate official of the parent company and that a notarized statement be affixed to these documents certifying them to be true copies. In addition, the corporation may find it useful to have certifications that the documents are true copies made by the nearest consulate of the UAE, or failing that, by any Arab consulate.

Copies of the leases for an office and residences leased by the firm must also be submitted to the Municipality before the firm can be

Appendix VI: Establishing Business in the UAE

enrolled on the Register of Commerce. The Municipality verifies through an inspector that the leases are genuine and that the buildings are complete and ready to occupy. Other requirements include the submission of three photo-copies of the relevant pages of the passport of the resident manager (those containing details of the holder, dates of issue and expiration, place of issue, and UAE visa allowing at least 30 days residence) and three photographs of the resident manager. The licence to do business in Dubai, along with the supporting documents needed to obtain it, allow the resident manager to live permanently in the UAE. All other employees must obtain individual residence permits and labour certificates. These may be obtained after the company is enrolled on the Register of Commerce.

Normally, a fee of approximately Dh 1,000 ($256) will be charged for enrolment on the Register of Commerce. Other taxes are a charge of 10 per cent of the annual rental of the office and 5 per cent of the annual rental of any residential premises used by employees of the firm. If one apartment or house serves as both office and residence – this is the common practice – the rate is 15 per cent of the annual rental of the premises. Finally, a fee of approximately Dh 300 ($77) per year must be paid to the Palestine Relief Fund, and another Dh 300 ($77) fee is for the licence document itself.

There are a number of ministries that are concerned with work relating to architecture and engineering. Several of these ministries have separate registration requirements for architects and engineers as follows:

(1) *Ministry of Public Works* Send a cover letter introducing the firm along with a brochure and a copy of one's membership in the appropriate Chamber of Commerce and Industry. No charges are made.

(2) *Ministry of Housing and Town Planning* A cover letter introducing the firm and brochures are all that are needed. No charges are made.

(3) *Ministry of Planning, Permanent Projects Committee* This requires the completion of a 'Questionnaire for Consultants' along with brochures. No charges are made. Completion of the above only puts the firm's name on a list.

Doing Business in Sharjah

Although Sharjah and Dubai can be considered part of the same economic area, there are a few special features of Sharjah that make doing business there slightly different. First, the native merchant class in Sharjah is much smaller and much newer than that of Dubai. There are perhaps only three or four Sharjah businessmen with the experience, resources, and the broad range of interests of their Dubaian counterparts. Thus much more of the commercial activity in Sharjah is in the hands of the local government, the members of the ruling family, or foreigners.

The Sharjah government has made a special effort to encourage foreign banks and companies to locate in the Emirate by offering attractive incentives of taxation and land. Many Lebanese have found it easiest to relocate their businesses in Sharjah after facing strong opposition from established merchants in Dubai.

The development plans in Sharjah are not as ambitious as those of Dubai, but the Emirate is planning sizable and expensive projects for port expansion, airport development, hotel construction, town planning and power capacity expansion. Competition in these fields in Sharjah is more open than in Dubai and firms will find the procedures less labyrinthine and more straightforward. The local government prefers foreign firms bidding on government contracts *not* to have a local agent but to quote directly to the government agency concerned.

BIBLIOGRAPHY

Abu Dhabi Fund for Arab Economic Development (ADFAED) *Annual Reports* Abu Dhabi, United Arab Emirates: ADFAED, 1974–5 to 1978–9

Al-Baharna, Husain, M. 'The Legal Environment for Doing Business in Bahrain, Qatar, and the UAE.' Address delivered in New York, 30 May 1974

Al-Otaiba, Mana Saeed. *The Economy of Abu Dhabi, Ancient and Modern* (Beirut: Commercial and Industrial Press, 1971)

Arab Economic Review

Arab Report

Dubai Municipality, Department of Information *Dubai: Pearl of the Gulf.* (France: Editions Del Roisse)

El Mallakh, Ragaei. *Economic Development and Regional Cooperation: Kuwait* (Chicago: University of Chicago Press, 1968)

_____ 'Challenge of Affluence: Abu Dhabi.' *The Middle East Journal*, spring 1979

Fenelon, K.G. *The Trucial States* (London: Longman Publishers, 1973)

_____ *The United Arab Emirates: An Economic and Social Survey* (London: Longmans, 1973)

Hawley, Donald *The Trucial States* (London: George Allen and Unwin Ltd, 1971)

Henley Centre for Forecasting *Middle East Prospects: Forecasts to 1985* (London, 1975)

Irani, M. *The United Arab Emirates: An Educational and Socio-Economic Study* Expert UNESCO Mission to Kuwait and Lower Gulf Arab States, March 1974

Law, John. *Arab Aid: Who Gets It, For What and How?* (New York: Chase World Information Corporation, May 1978)

Little, Arthur D. *Industrial Development Opportunities for Abu Dhabi: Final Report* (Cambridge: Arthur D. Little)

The Times, London

McDermott, Anthony. 'United Arab Emirates.' *Financial Times*, 23 June 1980

McLachlan, Keith and Ghorban, Narsi. *Oil Production, Revenues and Economic Development* (London: The Economist Intelligence Unit Ltd, 1974)

Mertz, Robert A. *Education and Manpower in the Arabian Gulf* (Washington DC: American Friends of the Middle East, September 1972)

Middle East Annual Review

Middle East Economic Digest

Middle East Economic Survey

Middle East Journal

Oil and Gas Journal

Omor, O.I.H. *Assignment Report: Health Manpower Development in the Gulf States, 17 February–10 April 1973*, May 1973

The OPEC Fund *Annual Reports*. (Vienna: The OPEC Fund, 1977, 1978–1979)

Organization of Petroleum Exporting Countries (OPEC). *Annual Statistical Bulletin, 1978*. (Vienna: OPEC, September 1979)

Petroleum Intelligence Weekly

Quarterly Economic Review

Ras Al-Khaimah. (Beirut: Middle East Media, 1971)

Shell International Petroleum Company Limited *Information Handbook*. (London: Shell International Petroleum Company Ltd, 1972–80)

Shilling, N.A. *Doing Business in Saudi Arabia and the Arab Gulf States* (New York: Intercrescent Publishing and Information Corporation, (1975)

Socknat, James A. *An Inventory and Assessment of Employment-Oriented Human Resources Development Programs in the Gulf Area* (Manama, Bahrain: The Ford Foundation, February 1975)

State of Abu Dhabi *Official Gazette*

Tenneys, S. Dickson. 'Marketing in the UAE.' *Overseas Business Reports* Bureau of International Commerce, US Department of Commerce. (Washington, DC: Government Printing Office, 1979)

United Arab Emirates News

United Arab Emirates *Education Statistics Yearbooks*. 1972/73. (Arabic)

———— 'Industry and Plans of Industrial Development in UAE', Ministry

of Finance. Paper presented to Third Arab Industrial Development Conference held in Tripoli, Libya in April 1974. (Arabic)
_____ *Second Anniversary*
_____ *Statistical Abstract, 1973/74.* UAE Ministry of Education, Statistical Division, February 1974 and October 1974
_____ Currency Board, *Annual Reports*
_____ *Bulletin*
_____ *Statistical Supplements*
United Nations *Demographic and Related Socio-Economic Data Sheets for Countries of ECWA*. (Beirut: Economic Commission for Western Asia (ECWA), January 1978)
United States Embassy, Abu Dhabi *Doing Business in Abu Dhabi – A Guide for Businessmen*, June 1977

INDEX

absorptive capacity 3, 26-7, 29, 71, 72, 82, 87, 107, 115, 119, 169
Abu Bukhoosh field 101, 103, 104
Abu Dhabi Chamber of Commerce 145, 198
Abu Dhabi Cold Storage Company 143
Abu Dhabi Company for Onshore Oil Operations (ADCO): production ceiling 102; production cut 114n22, 177-8; responsibilities of 95; shareholders 90, 95; sulphur premium 91
Abu Dhabi Development Finance Corporation 136, 141, 144
Abu Dhabi economy: agriculture 25, 38; airport 75; budget 17; business ventures in 198-9; cement industry 55; development expenditures 60n15; fishing industry 42; government contracts 169; government structures 16; health services 68, 69; imports 119; industrial projects 49-51; industrial survey of 143; investment abroad 141; labour 25, 29; Labour Law of 1966 168; Law No.10 46; Law on Ownership of Gas Resources 185-7; petrochemicals 24; ports 80; private investment 29; revenues 95; sulphur plant 47; tourism 128
Abu Dhabi Fertilizer Industries Company 84, 100, 110
Abu Dhabi First 5-Year Plan 23-4, 25, 46, 66, 68, 155, 174, 176
Abu Dhabi Fund for Arab Economic Development (ADFAED) 145-50, 188-94; Board of Directors 188; capital 145; financial status 189; interest rates 192, 193; lending policies 190; loans 147, 148, 191, 192, 194; operations of 146; purpose 150; rules of 146;

technical assistance 194
Abu Dhabi Gas Industries Company (GASCO) 178; government participation 47; natural gas rights 110; products 110; shareholders 110
Abu Dhabi Gas Liquefaction Company (ADGLC): production 107, 178-9; shareholders 47
Abu Dhabi Investment Authority 136
Abu Dhabi Investment Board 141
Abu Dhabi Marine Areas Ltd (ADMA): natural gas, production 108, utilization 108; oil, agreement 90, concessions 89, production ceiling 102, shareholders 89, state participation 94, *see also* Abu Dhabi Marine Operating Company (ADMA-OPCO)
Abu Dhabi Marine Operating Company (ADMA-OPCO), natural gas: allocations of 111; discovery 91; offshore operations 89, 107, 179; production 114n22, 183; *see also* Abu Dhabi Marine Areas Limited (ADMA)
Abu Dhabi National Insurance Company 136
Abu Dhabi National Oil Company (ADNOC): authority 99-100, 111; government participation 47; joint-ventures 111, 180, 181, 182; natural gas, discovery 91, gas line 92, LNG tank farm 86; objectives 99; participation rights 186-7; petroleum, buy-back arrangements 100, 113n2, concessions 92, offshore well 92, sales cutbacks 113n21, 113n22; subsidiaries 177, 178, 179, 180; tankers 54
Abu Dhabi National Tankers Company (ADNATCO) 180

206

Index

Abu Dhabi Natural Gas, law on ownership of 185-7
Abu Dhabi Nursing School 174
Abu Dhabi oil: exports 5, importance of 5; production 7; share of UAE output 7
Abu Dhabi Oil Company (ADCO): natural gas, production 108, 114n22, utilization 108; oil, entitlements 92; exploration 91-2
Abu Dhabi Petroleum Company (ADPC): concessions 88, 89, 95; exports 91; offshore dispute 89; participation agreement 90; production 90-1; shareholders 112n3; state ownership of 94, 178
Abu Dhabi Petroleum Ports Operations Company (ADPPOC) 179
Abu Dhabi Pipeline Construction Company (APCC) 179-80
Abu Dhabi Real Estate Fund 144
Abu Dhabi 3-Year Socio-economic Plan 29, 30, 31
Abu Musa 97
African Development Bank 192
Agip 91
agricultural research: Arid Land Research Centre 38-9; irrigation 38; trials station 21, 37
agriculture: crops 36; employment 40, 42; *falaj* systems 36; loans 21, 137, 139, 141, 142, 143; mechanization of 36-7; natural gas utilization 112; obstacles 37; prices 112
airports 75-6
Ajman: characteristics of 9; income 9; industrial projects 52, 58, 143; petroleum exploration 98-9
Ajman Arab Bank 133, 134
Al Ahli Bank Limited (CSC) 134
Al-Ain: airport 75; excavation of 10-1, 127; tourism 129, 143
al-Maktoum, Sheikh Maktoum Ibn-Rashid 13
al-Maktoum, Sheikh Rashid Ibn-Said 7, 13
al-Mualla, Sheikh Ahmad Ibn-Rashid 9
al-Mualla, Sheikh Rashid Ibn-Ahmad 9
al-Nahayyan, Sheikh Khalifa Ibn-Zayed 188
al-Nahayyan, Sheikh Surour Ibn-Mohammad 133, 188
al-Nahayyan, Sheikh Tahnoun Ibn-Mohammad 188
al-Nahayyan, Sheikh Zayed Ibn-Sultan 7, 13
al-Nowais, Nasser 188
al-Nuaimi, Rashid Abdullah 188
al-Nuaimi, Sheikh Rashid Ibn-Humaid 9
al-Otaiba, Mana Saeed 184
al-Qasimi, Sheikh Saqr Ibn-Mohammad 8
al-Qasimi, Sheikh Sultan Ibn-Mohammad 8
al-Sharqi, Sheikh Hammad Ibn-Mohammad 7
al-Suweidi, Mohammed Habroush 188
Algemene Bank Nederland NV 134
Alpha Oil of London 93
aluminium industry 52, 54, 57, 111; ancilliary industries 54; marketing 54; projects 52, 54; recycling 57
Amerada-Hess 93, 104, 108
American Express International Banking Corporation 135
Aminoil 91
ammonia plants 47, 49, 56
Amsterdam Rotterdam Bank (AMRO Bank) 135
Arab African International Bank 134
Arab Bank for Investment & Foreign Trade 134, 152
Arab Bank for the Economic Development of Africa 152, 192
Arab Bank Limited 134
Arab Company for Shipbuilding and Repair 55
Arab Emirates Investment Limited 137
Arab Fund for Economic and Social Development (AFESD): decision to establish AFESD 39, 152; loan commitments 149-50; members 149, 152, 193; purpose 150; UAE participation 146
Arab Industrial Investment Company (AIIC) 59
Arab Institute for Investment in

208 Index

Agricultural Development (AIIAD) 39
Arab League 15, 22, 150, 192
Arab Monetary Fund (AMF) 152, 155; capitalization 150, 151; purpose 150, 151
Arab Petroleum Investment Company 156
Arab Republic of Yemen (North) or Yemen Arab Republic 124, 192, 193
Arabian Gulf 42
Arabian Gulf Organization for Industrial Consultancy 59
archaeological sites 126, 127
Arid Land Research Centre 38, 39
Arthur D. Little, Inc.: fishing survey of Abu Dhabi 42; industrial survey 46, 47; recommendations 47; study on UAE economic future 43
Asab field 93, 104, 110, 114n22
Atlantic Richfield 96

Bab field 93, 104, 110, 114n22
Bahrain 12, 13, 22, 23, 42, 59, 79, 81, 120, 124, 151, 192, 194
Banca Commerciale Italiana 135
Banco Urquijo SA 135
Bank of America 135
Bank of Baroda 134
Bank of Credit and Commerce International (overseas) 135
Bank of Credit and Commerce International SA 134
Bank of Nova Scotia 135
Bank of Oman Limited 134
Bank of the Arab Coast 134
banking: assets of commercial banks 137; demand deposits 137; lending abroad 139; lending ratios 137, 138; money supply 137; reserve requirements 132-3; total bank credits 137
Banque de l'Indochine et de Suez 135, 141
Banque du Caire 134
Banque du Liban et d'Outre Mer SAL 135
Banque Libanaise pour le Commerce SA 135

Barclays Bank International Limited 134
Belgium 54
Bernard Sunley (UK) 128
Bint Saud 124; *see also* archaeological sites
Britain *see* United Kingdom
British Bank of the Middle East 134
British Bank of the Middle East (BBME) 133
British Petroleum 89, 90, 107, 178, 179, 180, 184
British Smelter Construction 54
Bu Hasa field 93, 104, 110, 114n22
Bu Tinah 92
Bunduq Company 92
Bunduq field 92, 103, 178
business opportunities: attractive features 164, 167, 169; embassy assistance 162; food and beverage industry 160; legal environment 165; limiting factors 164; local agents for 161, 162; prospective markets 160
Buttes Gas and Oil Company 97

Canadian International Development Agency 193
capital-intensive industries 45, 59
capital-surplus economies 3, 25, 31, 43, 53, 115, 130n1, 145, 155
cement industry 24, 26, 45, 47, 50, 52, 54, 57
Central Bank 43, 133
Chartered Bank, The 133, 134; *see also* Eastern Bank
charters of incorporation 167
Chase Manhattan Bank 136
Chemical Bank 135
Citibank NA 134
Cleveland Bridge and Engineering Factory 85
climate 5, 37, 127
Commercial Bank of Dubai Limited, The 134
Committee for Developing National Industries 166
Comoro Islands 193
Compadec 53
Compagnie Francaise des Petroles (CFP) 89, 90, 95, 107, 178, 179,

Index

182, 183
comparative advantage 43, 55, 142
conservation 57, 102
construction 47, 55, 57, 58, 86, 87, 137, 141, 143, 164, 183
corporate taxes 167
Council of Ministers 143
Crédit Lyonnais 136
Crédit Suisse 136
currency 132
Currency Board 132, 133, 139, 152, 158n2

Dalma Island field 92
Darky Oil 91
Das Island 89, 90, 107, 109, 178
desalination plants 50, 51, 52, 54, 56, 82, 83, 90; agricultural need 36, 38, 44
Desert Development Station 39
development Assistance Committee of the Organization for Economic Cooperation and Development 156
development planning: Abu Dhabi 23-6, 29-31; Britain 21-2; Federal 23, 26-9, 31
development strategy: capital as solution to problems 35; diversification of economy 35; need for 35-6
development theory: agriculture 36, 43; capital investment 35; choice of industry 45; comparative advantage 43; human capital 64-5
Diversification 24, 48, 136, 142, 144, 145, 180, 181; agriculture 25; fishing 42, 43; industry 45-7
Dubai Aluminium Company (Dubal) 54, 85
Dubai Bank Limited 134
Dubai Creek 7, 22
Dubai: economy, agriculture 39, airport 75, aluminium smelter 52, 54, 92, business ventures in 199-201, cement industry 55, 57, exports 77, 79, 119, 126, imports 119, industrial projects 52, 56, population 65, 128, ports 21, 56; natural gas, development of 111, government participation 47, LPG facility 54, production 106, reserves 106, 107; oil, concessions 88, 95, exploration 96, government participation 47, history 95-6, production 103, 106, refining capacity 106, reserves 96, 106, secondary recovery needs 32-3, share of UAE output 7
Dubai International Trade and Exhibition Centre 80
Dubai Islamic Bank 134
Dubai Marine Areas Ltd 95, 183
Dubai Natural Gas Company (Dugas) 47, 111
Dubai Petroleum Company (DUPETCO) 95, 113n11, 183
Dubai Trade School 173

Eastern Bank 133; *see also* Chartered Bank, The
economic base activity 62
economic development 22, 23, 43-5, 59-61
economic integration 59
education: adult education 66; agricultural 37, 173; to alleviate labour shortage 45, 60; budget allocations for 64-7; commercial 173; elementary 21; emphasis on 114; English language 174; enrolment 66; facilities 64, 66, 67; foreign aid for 21, 22; illiteracy rate 64; nursing 174; secretarial 173; teacher 64, 66, 67, 175; university 67; vocational 21, 22, 66, 67, 173, 175
Egypt 22, 54, 67, 68, 121, 124, 149, 150, 155
Emirates Commercial Bank 134
Emirates General Petroleum Corporation (EGPC) 184
Emirates National Bank 134
English Language Institute 174
Environmental Research Laboratory 38
expatriate labour 46, 58, 168
exports 115, 119, 160; composition of 126, 127; destination of 122, 124; determination of 43, 45; non-oil 127; oil, 127; re-exports 127; taxes 167

Exxon Corporation 90, 178

factors of production 43
Fateh field 96
Federal Council of Ministers 16
Federal Ministry of Finance and Industry 166
Federal National Council 15-16
Federal Republic of Germany 54, 120, 127
fertilizers 56, 115, 116
financial institutions 132-45; insurance companies 136, 145; investment companies 139-41; public sector 141-5
First Gulf Bank 134; see also Ajman Arab Bank
fishing industry: annual catch 42; employment 40, 41, 42; fleets 41; loans for 142; potential of 41; types of fish 62n29
foreign equity 94, 95
forestation 40
France 120, 127
free-trade zone 57-8
Fujairah economy: cement industry 55; characteristics of 7; crops 8; fishing potential 41; health services 69; industrial projects 52; petroleum concessions 99, 143; water resources 7
Fujairah Oil Exploration and Development Company 99

gas bottling industry 63n42
gas liquefaction plant 53
Germany see Federal Republic of Germany
gold trade 21, 77-8, 119, 127
Grindlays Bank Limited 135
Gulf Citicorp 136
Gulf Finance Company 133
Gulf International Company 144
Gulf of Oman 41, 42, 62n29

Habib Bank AG Zurich 135
Habib Bank Limited 135
health services: British aid for 21; comprehensive health care 68; emphasis on 19; facilities 68, 69, 70; mental 70; nurse training 174-5; percentage of budget 69; services 69
Hili 127; see also archaeological sites
Hispanoil 95, 183
hotels 71, 128, 142-3
housing: allocations for 71, 86; construction of 71; loans for 71, 137, 142, 143, 144; prefabricated 85; prices 71
human resources 45, 64-5, 68

immediate-value industries 47
immigration 60
imports: classification of 117; composition of 77, 116, 126; determination of 43, 46; duties on 167; income elasticity of 119; pattern of 119; projections to 1985 116; requirements 119, 160
import substitution 25-6, 35, 161, 164, 179, 180, 181
Income Tax Decree of 1965 167
Income Tax Law of 1969 167
India 20-1, 55-6, 100, 119, 126, 131n2
industrial base 119
industrial complexes 85-6
industrial co-ordination 58-9
Industrial Investment Company 58
industrial policy: comparative advantage 46; emphasis on petroleum-based industries 47; foreign participation 47; Law No. 10 46
industrial projects 49-59; loans for 142, 144
industrial surveys: Arthur D. Little, Inc. 46, 47; World Bank 48
industrial zones 84
industry: capital-intensive 45, 59; categorization of 47; choice of 45; contribution to GNP 45; custom exemptions for 46; domestic needs 47; labour-intensive 161; priority in planning 46; private investment 46
infant industry protection 44, 45
inflation 25, 143
infrastructure: bottlenecks 60-1; economic 74-87; social 64-72
insurance companies 136

Index

Intergulf Cold Storage Services 60
International Marine Oil Company (IMOC) 89
International Monetary Fund 15, 132, 150, 152
Investment Bank for Trade and Finance 134
investment opportunities 160-1, 164
Iran 119, 127, 130n1, 131n2
Iran crisis 3
Iran-Iraq conflict 102, 126-7
Iraq 59, 81, 121, 124, 130n1, 149, 150
Iraq Petroleum Company 88

Japan 2, 54, 91, 109, 120, 126, 127
Japan Line 97, 113n21
Japan Oil Development Company (JODCO) 92, 113n21, 179, 182
Japan Petroleum Development Company 90
Japanese Co-operation Fund 192
Japanese Institute for Desert Development 39
Jebel Ali 79, 80, 85; aluminium smelter 54; free trade zone 58, 85; gas line 92; industrial city 57; projects 58
John Harris and Associates (UK) 128
Jordan 120, 125, 149, 151, 194

Kellog International Corporation 90
Kenya 54
Khalij Commercial Bank 134
Khartoum Conference 146
Khor Fakkan 42, 128
Kuwait 3, 59, 64, 120, 124, 144, 149, 150, 156; aid to UAE 22, 64; current account 130n1; land purchase scheme 25; oil exports 88; production ceiling 102
Kuwait Fund for Arab Economic Development 127, 146, 192
Kuwait National Petroleum Company 180

labour 46, 58, 66, 68, 115; and oil policy 100; scarcity of 59, 164; training 60
Labour Law of 1966 (Abu Dhabi) 168

labour relations 168-9
land ownership 167, 168
Law No. 1 165
Law No. 10 46
Law on Commercial Agencies 165
Law on Ownership of Abu Dhabi Gas Resources 185-7
Lebanon 120, 124, 149, 151
Lesotho 192
Libya 102, 130n1, 149, 151
liquefied natural gas: capital-intensive nature 53-4; exports 53, 115; production 109; utilization 111, 114n24
liquefied petroleum gas: Das Island production 109; exports 109; utilization of 111, 114n24
livestock 40
Lloyds Bank International Limited 135
loan activity 137, 138, 139, 142, 143
locational resources 44

Maldives 193
manufacturing 57
market size 61, 115
marketing 180, 184
marketing centres 143
Maruzen Oil 91
Merrill Lynch 136
Mexico 102
Middle East Bank Limited 134
Middle East Finance Corporation 136
Middle East Oil Company Limited 90, 91
Mileiha 127; see also archaeological sites
minerals 63n37
Mitsubishi 91, 99
Mitsui and Company 107, 179
Mobil Oil 90, 178
motor vehicle industry 59
Mubarak field 8, 97, 101, 104
Mubarraz field 91, 92, 101, 104, 114n22
Murban field 88, 90, 101
museums 128, 131n2

National Bank of Abu Dhabi 133, 134
National Bank of Bahrain 133, 135
National Bank of Dubai Limited 133,

134
National Bank of Oman 135
National Bank of Ras Al-Khaimah 134
National Bank of Sharjah 134
National Drilling Company (NDC) 181
National Housing Council 143
National Industrial Corporation 58
National Marine Services (NMS) 181
National Visitors Centre 129; *see also* tourism
Near East Development Corporation 90
Nippon Mining 91
Nissho-Iwai 54
Norway: oil imports 127; production ceiling 102

Occidental Petroleum 93
oceans, economic importance of 41
offshore oil production 89, 92, 95, 96, 97, 182
oil industry: companies, 92, 94, 177-84; development of 88-105; foreign equity 94, 113n21; government participation 47, 92, 94; participation agreements 90, 92, 94, 100; royalties 94; taxes 94; vertical integration of 54
oil refining: ADNOC refinery 50, 53; capital-intensive nature of 53; encouragement of 47; Umm Al-Nar refinery 90, 93, 113n6
Oman 13, 59, 81, 120, 124, 131n2, 149, 151
Oman Finance Company 136
OPEC Fund, UAE contribution to 155, 192
Organization of the Arab Petroleum Exporting Countries (OAPEC) 1, 2, 79
Organization of the Petroleum Exporting Countries (OPEC) 1, 2, 130; participation agreements 94; pricing 102; UAE moderate stance in 3, 106
Oryx Merchant Bank Limited 136
Overseas Petroleum Corporation 90

Pachachi, Adnan 188

Pak-Arab Fertilizers Ltd 181
Pakistan 54, 119, 181, 182
Participation & Explorations Corporation 90, 178
partnership laws 165
pearling industry 20, 24
People's Democratic Republic of Yemen (South) 152, 192
petrochemicals: as feedstock 112; exports 115
petrochemical industry: capital-intensive nature of 53; economic characteristics of 53; encouragement of 47; population needs of 61
Petroleum Concessions Ltd 88
Petroleum Development (Trucial States) Ltd (PDTC) 88; *see also* Abu Dhabi Petroleum Company (ADPC)
Phillips Petroleum 91
physical resources: hydrocarbons 44; minerals 44, 63n37; soil 43-4, salinity of 44
port facilities 77-82, 85, 89, 179; Abu Dhabi 24; Dalma Island 92; Dubai 80; growth of 78; Mubarraz field 91; Sharjah 80
Port Rashid 45, 78, 79, 80
power plants 82-3
Property Development Bank 141, 144
public utilities: demand for 82-3; loans for 137, 139

Qatar 12, 13, 59, 120, 127, 130n1, 149, 151; aid to UAE 22, 23; fishing 42; foreign aid 156; oil exports 88; oil production ceiling 102; oil revenue 92
Qatar National Bank 133, 135

Rafidain Bank 135
Ras Al-Khaimah economy: agricultural training 21, 37, 173; airports 75; amount of cultivated land 37; cement industry 55; characteristics of 8; crops 37; early oil concessions 88; government participation in oil industry 47, 143; incentives for farming 38; industrial projects 52,

Index

58; intensive cultivation 37; land use policies 38; livestock 40; membership in UAE 13, 18n3; natural gas 97; offshore oil 95; ports 81; surplus agricultural production 37
raw materials 48, 142
real estate, loans for 142, 143
Real Estate Bank 143; *see also* UAE Development Bank
Real Estate Finance Corporation, The 136
refrigeration warehouses 47, 60, 143
regionalism 145, 150, 151
repair machine shops 55
resource base 43-5
restricted licence banks 133, 158n5
roads 22, 23, 42, 60-1, 74, 76-7
Royal Bank of Canada 135
Ruwais complex 84, 85, 93-4, 110, 177, 178, 179, 180

Sahil Investment Company 145
Saudi Arabia 59, 81, 120, 124, 130n1, 150; aid to UAE 22, 23; and OPEC 106, 107; oil participation agreements 94; oil production ceiling 102; trade 127
self sufficiency 55
Senegal 192
Sharjah: economy, airport 75, cement industry 55, financial institutions 144, fishing potential 41, health services 69, industrial projects 53, 58, ports 8, 80-1, tariff 80-1, tourism 128; natural gas, discovery 97, utilization 111; oil, concessions 88, 97, 98, participation agreements 97, production 33, 97, 103
Sharjah Group 144
Sharjah Insurance Company 136
Sharjah Trade School 175
Shell International 90, 178, 180, 184
shrimp industry 42, 62n31
single-commodity exporter 31, 35
Somalia 120, 124, 193
Southwire Company 54
sponge-iron plant 50
Standard Oil Company of Indiana (AMOCO) 93, 97, 184
Strait of Hormuz 41
Sudan 125, 194
sulphur plant 47
Sunningdale Oils of Canada 54
Superior Oil Company 95
Syria 121, 125, 193, 194

tankers 54, 109, 180
taxes: corporate 167; income 167; oil company 167
teacher training 21, 64, 66, 67, 175
telecommunications: development of 83, 84; direct exchange lines 83; domestic circuits 83; expansion of 61; expenditures on 74, 86; satellite system 84; telex industry 83
Tokyo Electric Power Company Inc. 53
tourism 71, 127, 128, 129, 130, 142, 143
trade: loans for 137, 139; permits 165; wholesale and retail 137, 139
transportation 60, 74; airports 75; internal (road) 76, 77; port facilities 77, 78, 79, 80, 81; shipping surcharges 81; systems 76
Trucial States 4
Trucial States Council Capital Works Progam 74, 76
Trucial States Council Development Fund 22-3
Trucial States Development Fund 66, 76
Tunisia 149, 151, 194

Uganda 193
Umm Al-Dalkh Development Company (UDECO) 92, 182
Umm Al-Nar Island 82, 90, 93, 113n6, 127
Umm Al-Quwain: characteristics of 8-9; exports 9; industrial projects 52, 143; natural gas reserves 97; oil exploration 98
Umm Shaif 101, 104, 114n22, 178, 183; gas discovery 91; oil discovery 89

214   *Index*

Union Bank of the Middle East 134
Union Bank of Switzerland 136
Union Defence Force (UDF) 15
Union Oil Company 97
United Arab Bank 134
United Arab Emirates (UAE):
background, European interest in 11, lack of American interest 11, location of 3, 4, 5, Perpetual Maritime Truce of 1853 11, population 9, 10, 164, Portuguese influence 11, strategic position of 3, 4, Trucial Oman Council 12, United Kingdom withdrawal 12; Central Bank 48, 133; Chamber of Commerce 162; Currency Board 132, 133, 139, 152, 158n2; Development Bank, lending 142, 143, loan policy 141, purpose 142, *see also* Real Estate Bank; economy, as financial centre 145, 146, as recipient of aid 21, 22, balance of payments 31, 32, banks 134, 135, 167, budget 17, business enterprises 161, 163, 164, 169, comparative advantage 43, 55, 142, contribution of oil to GDP 95, current account 130n1, deficit in non-oil trade 33, development allocations 17, expenditures 26-7, 28, 115-16, 119, exports 32, 43, 45, 115, 119, 122, 126, 127, 160, 167, foreign aid 3, 145, 156, 157, foreign capital in 46, foreign investment of 27, 28, 29, 145, imports 32, 33, 35, 46, 77, 116, 117, 119, 126-7, 160, membership in international organizations 152-4, per capita income 31, 33, petroleum product consumption 93-4; government, finance ministers 155, provisional constitution 13, 14, 15, structure of 15, Supreme Council 13; natural gas, competitiveness of 112, development of 11, 111, discovery 91, exports of 32, 109, feasibility studies 54, flaring of 53, government participation 47, ownership of 47, 111, production of 106, 108, 114n22, 183, reserves 106, 107, utilization of 107, 108, 111, *see also* liquefied natural gas and liquefied petroleum gas; oil, affect of price on current accounts 130n1, Article 23 14, buy-back arrangements 100, 113n21, concessions 33, 39, 88, 89, 90, 91, 95, conservation of 102, consumption 93-4, contribution to GDP 95, discovery of 89, 90, 91, 92, economic life of 35, exploration for 88, 96, exports 32, 126-7, limits to production 32, offshore production 89, 92, 95, 96, 97, 182, policy 99-100, 102, prices 91, 101, 102, production 2, 7, 18n1, 100, 103, 105, 106, production ceiling 32, 102, refining capacity 106, reserves 4, 96, 106, revenues 26, 46, sales cuts 113n21, 113n22, secondary recovery 32-3, 92, sulphur premium 91
United Bank Limited 137
United Fisheries Company 114
United Kingdom 126, 144; aid to UAE 21, 22-3; five-year development plan for 21-2; hegemony 11-12; oil imports 2; trade 120
United Nations, UAE membership in 15
United Nations Food and Agricultural Organization (FAO) survey of fishing industry 41-2
United Nations Industrial Development Organization (UNIDO) minerals study 63n27
United Petroleum Development 92
United Realty Company 144
United States: Agency for International Development (AID) 192; trade with UAE 2, 120, 127; Upper Zakum field 95, 101, 104, 114n22, 177, 178, 182, 183

veterinary clinic 40

vocational training 21, 22, 46, 60, 66, 67, 175-6
Vocational Training Institute 176

Wardley Middle East Limited 136
water supplies: Qatar aid for UAE 22; supply schemes 23; surveys 21
World Bank: categorization of projects 48; fishing industry study 42; industrial survey 48; UAE participation in 193

Zaire 193
Zaki, Hassan Abbas 188
Zakum Development Company (ZADCO) 182